International Political Economy Series

General Editor: **Timothy M. Shaw**, Professor of Political Science and International Development Studies, and Director of the Centre for Foreign Policy Studies, Dalhousie University, Halifax, Nova Scotia

Titles include:

Francis Adams, Satya Dev Gupta and Kidane Mengisteab (*editors*)
GLOBALIZATION AND THE DILEMMAS OF THE STATE IN THE SOUTH

Leslie Elliott Armijo (*editor*)
FINANCIAL GLOBALIZATION AND DEMOCRACY IN EMERGING MARKETS

Preet S. Aulakh and Michael G. Schechter (*editors*)
RETHINKING GLOBALIZATION(S)
From Corporate Transnationalism to Local Interventions

Elizabeth De Boer-Ashworth
THE GLOBAL POLITICAL ECONOMY AND POST-1989 CHANGE
The Place of the Central European Transition

Edward A. Comor (*editor*)
THE GLOBAL POLITICAL ECONOMY OF COMMUNICATION

Helen A. Garten
US FINANCIAL REGULATION AND THE LEVEL PLAYING FIELD

Randall D. Germain (*editor*)
GLOBALIZATION AND ITS CRITICS
Perspectives from Political Economy

Barry K. Gills (*editor*)
GLOBALIZATION AND THE POLITICS OF RESISTANCE

Takashi Inoguchi
GLOBAL CHANGE
A Japanese Perspective

Stephen D. McDowell
GLOBALIZATION, LIBERALIZATION AND POLICY CHANGE
A Political Economy of India's Communications Sector

Ronaldo Munck and Peter Waterman (*editors*)
LABOUR WORLDWIDE IN THE ERA OF GLOBALIZATION
Alternative Union Models in the New World Order

Michael Niemann
A SPATIAL APPROACH TO REGIONALISM IN THE GLOBAL ECONOMY

Ted Schrecker (*editor*)
SURVIVING GLOBALISM
The Social and Environmental Challenges

Kendall Stiles (*editor*)
GLOBAL INSTITUTIONS AND LOCAL EMPOWERMENT
Competing Theoretical Perspectives

Caroline Thomas and Peter Wilkin (*editors*)
GLOBALIZATION AND THE SOUTH

Kenneth P. Thomas
CAPITAL BEYOND BORDERS
States and Firms in the Auto Industry, 1960–94

Geoffrey R. D. Underhill (*editor*)
THE NEW WORLD ORDER IN INTERNATIONAL FINANCE

Amy Verdun
EUROPEAN RESPONSES TO GLOBALIZATION AND FINANCIAL MARKET
INTEGRATION
Perceptions of Economic and Monetary Union in Britain, France and Germany

Robert Wolfe
FARM WARS
The Political Economy of Agriculture and the International Trade Regime

International Political Economy Series
Series Standing Order ISBN 0–333–71708–2
(*outside North America only*)

You can receive future titles in this series as they are published by placing a standing order.
Please contact your bookseller or, in case of difficulty, write to us at the address below with
your name and address, the title of the series and the ISBN quoted above.

Customer Services Department, Macmillan Distribution Ltd, Houndmills, Basingstoke,
Hampshire RG21 6XS, England

US Financial Regulation and the Level Playing Field

Helen A. Garten
Professor of Law
Rutgers University School of Law
Newark
New Jersey

First published 2001 by
PALGRAVE
Houndmills, Basingstoke, Hampshire RG21 6XS and
175 Fifth Avenue, New York, N.Y. 10010
Companies and representatives throughout the world

PALGRAVE is the new global academic imprint of
St. Martin's Press LLC Scholarly and Reference Division and
Palgrave Publishers Ltd (formerly Macmillan Press Ltd).

ISBN 0–333–77086–2

This book is printed on paper suitable for recycling and
made from fully managed and sustained forest sources.

A catalogue record for this book is available
from the British Library.

Library of Congress Cataloging-in-Publication Data
Garten, Helen A.
    US financial regulation and the level playing field / Helen A. Garten.
        p. cm.
    Includes bibliographical references and index.
    ISBN 0–333–77086–2 (cloth)
    1. Financial institutions—Deregulation—United States. 2. Financial
institutions—Law and legislation—United States. 3. International
finance. 4. Competition—United States. I. Title: United States financial
regulation and the level playing field. II. Title.
    KF974 .G369 2000
    346.73'082—dc21
                                                    00–055691

10   9   8   7   6   5   4   3   2   1
10 09 08 07 06 05 04 03 02 01

Printed and bound in Great Britain by
Antony Rowe Ltd, Chippenham, Wiltshire

Contents

Preface   vii

List of Abbreviations   x

Glossary of Key US Financial Statutes   xi

Introduction: Regulation and the Level Playing Field   1
The need for a better explanation   4
The 'level playing field' as metaphor   6
The four elements of fairness   7
Three caveats and three responses   13

1 How to Think About Financial Regulation   16
Three theories of regulation   17
The normative power of regulatory explanation   39
Finding common ground   41

2 Is Regulation Beneficial?   45
Regulation and the theory of equal starts   46
Regulatory handicapping in financial markets   48
Regulatory subsidy and global competitiveness   53
Regulatory subsidy and market integration   60
Regulatory subsidy and US markets   62
Subsidy to burden – a reprise   67

3 Deposit Insurance and the Politics of Regulatory Subsidy 69
Deposit insurance as subsidy   70
The case against the bank subsidy   78
The politics of subsidy   85
Yes, there is a regulatory subsidy (at least for credit unions) 88
The future of regulatory handicapping   90

4 Results Matter   91
Regulatory competition in theory   96
Interagency competition   100
The roles of Congress and the courts   104
Regulatory competition in action   106
The Travelers decision   112
Regulatory competition and congressional reform   115
Conclusion   117

5 **Regulatory Conflict and Competitive Equality** 119
Competition and entity regulation 122
Entity regulation from Carter Glass to Rule 3b–9 126
Competitive equality and entity regulation 131
Competitive equality and functional regulation 132
The superregulator model 135
Globalization and regulatory competition 138

6 **The Level Playing Field and Rules of Fair Play** 142
Fair play and market bifurcation 147
The rules of fair play 148
Are retail markets overregulated? 152
The price of overregulation 155
Market bifurcation and underregulation 159
Globalization and rules of fair play 160

7 **Failure on a Level Playing Field** 163
Deposit insurance and failure policy 165
Penn Square and the problem of resolution cost 171
Continental Illinois and failure prevention 173
Long-Term Capital Management and market disruption 179
The lessons 182
The failure of collective action 185
Legal and market constraints on collective action 188
The globalization of failure policy 191

8 **Let the Market Pick the Winners** 194
Let the consumer decide 200
Failure of collective action 203
Failure of government strategic planning 205
Lessons from the level playing field 210

Notes and References 214

Index 234

Preface

Does regulation matter? That question is being asked more and more frequently by students of US financial markets, especially now that US policymakers, after many false starts, have signaled their willingness to overhaul US financial regulatory structure by dismantling legal barriers to financial industry diversification and consolidation. Now that banks, securities firms and insurance companies at long last may enter each others' businesses in US markets, will there be anything left for financial regulatory scholars to talk or write about? Will deregulation finally bring about the convergence of US financial law with other financial regulatory schemes, ending America's distinction of having the most heavily regulated financial markets in the world?

The answer is probably no, for several reasons. First, despite deregulation, US financial institutions will not be treated from a regulatory standpoint just like any other business enterprise. Although in late 1999 Congress finally amended national banking laws to permit combinations of banks with other financial firms, there was surprisingly little political will to complete the deregulatory process by dismantling all legal barriers between banking and commerce. This lack of interest may have reflected the fact that US financial regulation continues to impose tight restrictions on interaffiliate funds transfers from banks to their non-bank operations, removing a key incentive for commercial firms to combine with banks. In any event, for now, US financial regulation continues to resist transition to the full universal banking model.

This suggests a second reason why regulation still matters. Despite considerable deregulation, much of the US financial regulatory framework endures, and it continues to influence both the ways in which US financial markets operate and the US government's attitude toward issues of cross-border financial regulation. Financial experts in the US need not worry that deregulation will render them obsolete. Regulatory critics will still complain of overregulation. And regulatory supporters will still advance the US approach as a model for regulation of international financial markets.

Finally, in the US, financial regulatory reform tends to increase rather than decrease regulatory complexity. The Banking Act of 1933 (commonly known as Glass-Steagall), the source of much of classic US bank regulation, including the federal deposit insurance program and the separation of commercial and investment banking, contained just thirty-four sections. The Gramm-Leach-Bliley Act, that repealed key portions of Glass-Steagall in 1999, ran to over one hundred sections. The legislation permitted affiliations among bank, securities and insurance firms, but financial institutions remain closely regulated. A financial firm's choice of organizational form continues to determine permissible powers and responsible regulatory authority. To outside observers, this may sound suspiciously like the state of affairs that prevailed under the old regulatory regime. Financial firms seeking to do business in the US in the future must be concerned with many of the same legal questions that they asked in the past: Who regulates? What activities may be conducted within a bank, or an affiliate, or a subsidiary? And why, in the US, does financial modernization never really mean regulatory simplification?

This book seeks to answer the last question by offering a perspective on the forces that drive the US financial regulatory process. Understanding why the US regulates its financial markets may help to explain how US financial regulation gains and retains legitimacy. This, in turn, may offer some insight into the recent deregulatory process that, although producing changes in the specifics of financial law, has ensured that regulation will continue to matter very much in US financial markets of the future.

This book does not claim to offer a complete account of the current state of US financial regulation. Financial regulation is extraordinarily complex, deriving from multiple legal sources, both national and state, legislative and administrative. Moreover, regulation is in the process of transition, frustrating efforts to predict what the law will be years, or even months, from now. (For example, throughout 1999, prospects for enactment of long awaited financial modernization legislation appeared uncertain up until the very moment that final agreement was reached between Congress and the White House.) Therefore, any comprehensive description of where the law stands today runs the danger of sudden obsolescence as well as demanding a level of detail that is beyond the scope of this book.

Instead, this book will focus on certain fundamental norms, easily described and relatively constant, that influence the process by which financial regulation (and deregulation) are legitimized and delegitimized in the US. In so doing, it will attempt to account for the anomaly, long apparent to outside observers but often overlooked by US financial market players, that despite the US's professed commitment to promoting freer and more open financial markets, particularly abroad, its own financial markets do not always appear to be so free. The explanation may be found in the peculiar role that US financial market players assign to regulation. Regulation is legitimized to the extent that it furthers the particular requirements of competitive fairness that US financial players demand from their financial markets. The purpose of financial regulation, simply put, is to create a more level playing field, a perspective that has colored the evolution of modern financial regulation in the US and is largely responsible for the positions taken by US financial players, including policymakers, on questions of international supervision of financial markets.

This book will illustrate this point by looking at several examples of how regulation has been employed in US financial markets to promote the ideals of competitive fairness. In telling these stories, it will assume that most readers have at least a passing familiarity with the basic building blocks of US financial law, such as the separation of banking and commerce, as well as with its leading statutes, which will be referenced by common name in text and notes. (For those readers to whom US financial regulation is entirely unfamiliar, a glossary is provided giving current descriptions of statutory sources.) The aim is not to distract the reader with too many specifics of US financial law, but to tell the story of financial regulation in a way that demonstrates how regulation has shaped the growth of US financial markets and, perhaps even more important, the attitudes of US financial players toward their markets.

HELEN A. GARTEN

List of Abbreviations

FDIC   Federal Deposit Insurance Corporation
LTCM   Long-Term Capital Management
NASDAQ   National Association of Securities Dealers Automated Quotations
RFC   Reconstruction Finance Corporation
US   United States of America

Glossary of Key US Financial Statutes

This glossary is designed to provide a working acquaintance with the principal national laws that have shaped modern US financial markets. It does not even attempt to reference the many state statutes that affect the business of financial firms in the US. In the last few decades, some key statutes have been amended or repealed but, to the extent that they have influenced financial market evolution and are discussed in this book, they are noted here. Although specific citations are not provided, banking law is found in volume 12 of the United States Code and securities regulation in volume 15.

The Bank Holding Company Act of 1956 prohibited commercial firms from owning or controlling banks and limited the permissible activities of bank holding companies and their non-bank affiliates to those so 'closely related' to banking as to be a proper incident thereto. In the 1980s and 1990s, the Federal Reserve, chief regulator of bank holding companies, construed this language to allow banks some flexibility to diversify their financial activities through the use of non-bank affiliates, including the securities affiliates that revolutionized US financial markets. By the late 1990s, most major banking organizations in the US had adopted the holding company form of organization. In 1999, Congress amended the Bank Holding Company Act to permit the formation of financial holding companies composed of banks, securities firms, insurance companies and other financial firms subject to Federal Reserve umbrella regulatory oversight. Although bank/commercial combinations continued to be prohibited, financial holding companies were authorized to engage in merchant banking.

The Bank Holding Company Act is significant for two additional reasons. Until interstate banking was legalized in 1994, the Douglas Amendment allowed each state to opt to permit out-of-state bank holding companies to acquire banks within its jurisdiction, providing an avenue for geographical diversification by bank holding companies. And the *Bank Holding Company Act Amendments of 1970* created the special antitying rules that prohibit banking organizations from directly or indirectly conditioning the sale of one financial product on the buyer's purchase of a second product from the bank.

The Banking Act of 1933 created much of the modern 'special' regulation of the banking industry, including (1) the separation of commercial and investment banking (Glass-Steagall), (2) the creation of the federal deposit insurance program, (3) the prohibition on deposit-taking by unlicensed financial or non-financial businesses, and (4) the ceilings on interest rates payable on bank deposit accounts. Although interest rate ceilings disappeared in the 1980s and Glass-Steagall's prohibitions on bank/securities affiliations and management interlocks were repealed in 1999, key parts of the statute remain law, and all of its regulations profoundly influenced the structure of the modern US banking industry and financial markets.

The Community Reinvestment Act of 1977 requires insured depository institutions (banks and thrifts) to help to meet the credit needs of the local communities in which they are located, especially low and moderate income neighborhoods. Although the statute does not contain any specific lending targets, federal bank and thrift regulators consider an institution's community lending record when deciding applications for mergers, acquisitions, branch openings or relocations and assign a community lending rating to all institutions that they supervise, which ratings are made public.

The Depository Institutions Deregulation and Monetary Control Act of 1980 increased federal deposit insurance coverage to $100 000 per insured account and began the deregulation of interest rates payable on time deposits, with the aim of making bank deposits more competitive with higher yielding non-bank investments such as money market mutual funds offered by securities firms.

The Federal Deposit Insurance Act now contains all regulation pertaining to the federal deposit insurance fund and the Federal Deposit Insurance Corporation, the agency that administers the insurance system and acts as chief federal regulator of state-chartered insured banks that are not members of the Federal Reserve system.

The Federal Deposit Insurance Corporation Improvement Act of 1991 made several important changes to bank failure policy, notably, limiting the discretion of the federal banking agencies to arrange dispositions of troubled banks that result in the protection of uninsured depositors. The statute also mandated the prompt closing and liquidation of undercapitalized banks and limited the Federal Reserve's ability to keep ailing banks afloat by making long-term liquidity loans. The statute was a rare modern instance of congressional reregulation, adopted in response to the costly failures that had weakened the bank and thrift industries in the 1980s. It took aim at the business of deposit brokerage, imposing new interest rate ceilings on deposits solicited through professional brokers, and temporarily halted state bank diversification into insurance and other new markets by limiting the non-banking powers of insured state-chartered banks to those available to national banks.

The Federal Reserve Act, which established the Federal Reserve system consisting of the centralized Federal Reserve Board and regional Federal Reserve banks and made the Federal Reserve chief federal regulator of member state-chartered banks, also contains Sections 23A and 23B that limit funds transfers and other financial transactions between insured banks and their non-bank affiliates.

The Foreign Bank Supervision Enhancement Act of 1991 strengthened US regulatory oversight of non-US banks doing business in the US, giving the Federal Reserve supervisory authority and requiring all US offices of non-US banks to meet uniform financial, management and operational standards equivalent to those imposed on US banks. It also prohibited the US branches of non-US banks from accepting retail insured deposits.

The Garn-St Germain Depository Institutions Act of 1982, although continuing the deregulation of bank deposit markets begun in 1980, also removed the Federal Reserve's discretion under the Bank Holding Company Act to decide that general insurance activities were closely related to banking and therefore permissible for bank holding company affiliates. This change in the law restricted the ability of the Federal Reserve to expand the insurance powers of banking organizations until 1999, when Congress permitted affiliations between banks and insurers.

The Glass-Steagall Act is the common name for those provisions of the Banking Act of 1933 that separated commercial (deposit) banking from investment (merchant) banking. Best known was Section 20, barring affiliations between banks and firms engaged principally in corporate securities underwriting and dealing, which was interpreted by the Federal Reserve in the 1980s to permit bank holding companies to establish securities affiliates to engage in limited amounts of corporate securities underwriting. Section 20 was repealed in 1999 along with Section 32's ban on management interlocks between banks and securities firms. Section 16 continues to prevent banks from directly underwriting securities, with exceptions for US government and municipal securities. (Banks may engage in broader securities activities through subsidiaries.) Section 21 continues to limit deposit-taking to licensed banks.

The Gramm-Leach-Bliley Act in 1999 repealed Glass-Steagall's ban on affiliations and management interlocks between banks and securities firms and also permitted affiliations between banks, insurance companies and other financial firms. The preferred organizational structure for conglomeration was the financial holding company, whose separate affiliates are subject to functional regulation by their respective bank, securities and state insurance supervisors, with the Federal Reserve acting as consolidated home country regulator. Diversified securities firms that do not own bank affiliates may opt for the Securities and Exchange Commission as their consolidated supervisor. National banks may diversify through financial subsidiaries into most financial businesses open to financial holding companies, except insurance underwriting, real estate and, temporarily, merchant banking.

To the extent that the Act ratified past regulatory and market innovations, such as the 1998 Travelers/Citicorp merger, it was not expected to transform US markets. Nevertheless, by removing remaining regulatory restrictions on financial combinations, the Act made diversification easier, which was likely to accelerate the pace of financial conglomeration and encourage entry into US markets by non-US financial firms. At the same time, however, some significant regulatory barriers remain, including restrictions on inter-affiliate funds transfers and transactions between bank and non-bank financial operations. Moreover, the Act strengthens enforcement of the Community Reinvestment Act against diversified banks and requires financial regulators to develop new privacy rules to prevent misuse or disclosure of personal financial information about retail bank consumers.

The International Banking Act of 1978 was designed to eliminate perceived regulatory advantages enjoyed by non-US banks operating in the US by subjecting those operations to US bank regulation. In the name of competitive equality, non-US banks doing business in the US were made subject to the same restrictions on diversification, including Glass-Steagall, and on geographical expansion that were applicable to US banks.

The McCarran-Ferguson Act of 1945 confirmed state autonomy over regulation of the insurance business by providing that no national law would preempt conflicting state insurance regulation unless the national legislation specifically related to the business of insurance. The reach of the statute became an issue in the 1990s when the Comptroller of the Currency, chief regulator of national banks, began to interpret national banking laws to permit national banks to act as insurance agents in contravention of state insurance regulation. The Supreme Court resolved this conflict in favor of the Comptroller, finding that the relevant provision of the national banking law did specifically relate to the business of insurance and therefore did not invoke the anti-preemption doctrine of McCarran-Ferguson. Today, McCarran-Ferguson still permits states to license and regulate insurance companies, including those affiliated with banks, so long as state regulation does not discriminate against banks or prevent them from conducting an insurance business.

The National Bank Act provides a national chartering option for banks. National banks are regulated by the Comptroller of the Currency, an official of the US Treasury Department, and may exercise the banking powers enumerated in the statute together with additional incidental powers authorized by the Comptroller of the Currency. In 1999, Congress authorized national banks to establish financial subsidiaries to engage in a broad array of financial activities, with the important exceptions of insurance underwriting, real estate and, for five years, merchant banking.

The Riegle-Neal Interstate Banking and Branching Efficiency Act of 1994 effectively ended most legal restrictions on interstate bank acquisitions and interstate branching. Previously, national law had deferred to state banking law, which, until the 1980s, had been hostile to interstate banking.

The Securities Act of 1933 provides for registration with the Securities and Exchange Commission of new public issues of securities by most corporations and the dissemination of information about the issuer to prospective investors. Banks, although not bank holding companies, were exempted from this scheme.

The Securities Exchange Act of 1934 provides for the registration and regulation of securities brokers and dealers and of national securities exchanges (like the New York Stock Exchange). In addition, companies with corporate securities traded on a national securities exchange or in the NASDAQ market are required to disseminate periodic public disclosure concerning their operations and financial position. By virtue of registration, securities brokers and dealers become subject to regulation by the Securities and Exchange Commission (although, as a practical matter, day-to-day supervision is the responsibility of the securities exchanges and the National Association of Securities Dealers, an industry group that functions as a self-regulatory organization). Originally, all banks were exempt from broker–dealer registration and regulation, but this exemption was significantly narrowed in 1999. Bank affiliates engaged in most securities activities must also register as broker–dealers.

Introduction: Regulation and the Level Playing Field

To non-US observers of the US financial scene, Americans must seem to be preoccupied with regulation. Despite the often-repeated promise of deregulation, US financial markets remain the most heavily regulated in the world, and US scholars, legislators and even bankers continue to spend an enormous amount of time studying, analyzing and debating the efficiency and legitimacy of their own regulatory process. Yet despite the considerable amount of time and ink that has been devoted to explaining US financial regulatory structure, its contradictions remain as apparent, and as puzzling to outside observers, as ever. For example, for at least the last two decades, virtually every scholarly work on US financial regulation has begun with the assertion that US financial markets are undergoing a transition to deregulation. Yet, as anyone who has tried to navigate the waters of the US financial regulatory system is painfully aware, significant legal obstacles remain and may be ignored only at one's peril. Although pundits predict that the passage of comprehensive financial reform legislation will rationalize the regulatory process, even a cursory examination of recent legislative action suggests that US financial reform may be leaving the regulatory waters as dangerous and as difficult to navigate as ever.

At the same time, however, it is becoming increasingly apparent that, despite their crushing regulatory burden, many US financial institutions are able to do exactly what they please. One example was the announcement in 1998 of the merger of Travelers Group, a holding company for insurance, securities and other non-bank financial businesses, and Citicorp, the huge banking concern, to form Citigroup. In 1998, combinations of banks, insurance companies and securities firms were still forbidden, although pending congressional

1

legislation[1] proposed to relax barriers to affiliation; interestingly, prior to the announcement of its merger with Travelers, Citicorp was a vocal opponent of this reform.[2] Nevertheless, the merger of Travelers and Citicorp was approved by the Federal Reserve Board *before* Congress adopted legislation in 1999 to legalize cross-industry acquisitions.[3] This raises a fundamental question about the American regulatory system: if Citicorp and Travelers could combine despite regulation, then why does regulation, or, in this case, deregulation, matter?

One answer is that US financial regulation does not always treat similarly situated financial firms equally. Citicorp and Travelers may have merged, and their merger may have persuaded the US Congress to act to legitimize their combination post hoc. But this precedent does not mean that, in the future, all regulation is vulnerable. Other financial players may find regulatory barriers insurmountable, and the regulators less helpful.

This contradiction may be explained in part by the degree of discretion that the US regulatory system traditionally has afforded its financial regulators. Judicial deference to regulatory agency expertise is an established principle of American law.[4] In the financial arena, it has facilitated a process of 'deregulation by regulatory application', as regulators have embraced creative interpretations of restrictive statutes in order to approve applications by regulated firms (their constituents) to expand and diversify. A dramatic example was the so-called 'Section 20' revolution that, in the 1980s and 1990s, challenged the long-standing legal divide between banking and securities markets created by the Glass-Steagall Act in 1933.[5] Section 20 was the paragraph of Glass-Steagall that barred affiliations between banks and firms 'engaged principally' in securities underwriting and dealing. For fifty years, Section 20 was presumed to prevent banks from acquiring securities companies. In the 1980s, however, the Federal Reserve Board began reading the phrase 'engaged principally' to mean any 'substantial' activity as defined by the Board. This reading allowed the Federal Reserve to approve applications by bank holding companies to establish securities affiliates that could underwrite and deal in corporate securities subject to quantitative revenue limits set from time to time by the Board.[6] Reviewing courts for the most part were willing to defer to the Board's interpretation,[7] and the Section 20 revolution began.

The Section 20 revolution made affiliations between banks and securities firms possible for the first time since Glass-Steagall was adopted in 1933, but the Federal Reserve emerged as gatekeeper to deregulation. Individual banking organizations seeking to take advantage of the new Section 20 powers were required to go through a regulatory application process and to receive the blessing of the Federal Reserve. As a result, the Federal Reserve had considerable discretion to decide which banking firms were the first to re-enter the securities markets, at least through the Section 20 door.

The Federal Reserve has not been the only regulatory agency with a say over who in the financial industry may diversify. The regulatory process is complicated by the existence of multiple financial regulatory agencies that are independently staffed and funded but that share jurisdiction over financial markets and institutions. This division of regulatory authority has engendered a curious competition among regulators that has allowed for multiple and occasionally inconsistent regulatory outcomes. For example, lest it be assumed that in 1998 the only way for an insurance company to enter the banking business was to follow the lead of Travelers and Citicorp and apply for permission from the Federal Reserve, consider the example of State Farm Mutual Automobile Insurance Company. In 1998, State Farm received permission from the Office of Thrift Supervision to charter a federally regulated thrift in order to market consumer banking and insurance products through its 16 000 insurance sales offices.[8] To the average customer, State Farm's offices looked a lot like a typical bank branch, but, to lawyers and regulators, they were quite different. As a legal matter, thrift institutions were not banks, but were regulated under a separate and competing regulatory regime by separate and competing regulators. As a result, thrifts (and firms like State Farm seeking to own them) were subject to different regulatory limitations from those applicable to banking organizations like Citigroup. These differences have always been very important to financial firms seeking to maximize their regulatory advantage. For example, had State Farm followed Travelers' lead and filed an application with the Federal Reserve to acquire a bank, it might not have fared so well in the regulatory process.

Regulatory competition is a fact of life in US financial markets, but at times it may seem fundamentally unfair, producing outcomes that are at odds with the US legal system's professed adherence to the goal of equal treatment under the law. Nevertheless, this is just one of many instances when US financial regulation appears to go against the grain of US political and cultural values. For example, in a society that claims to reject most elements of the welfare state and to champion the free market over government subsidy, financial regulation, with its customary reliance on asset controls and consumer guarantees, seems an anachronism, a lone remaining example of the paternalistic regulation last associated with the US in the 1930s. Financial regulation even survived the 1970s and 1980s, an era in the US that one regulatory historian has dubbed the 'economist's hour',[9] when most other aging federal regulatory programs affecting business, including airlines, trucking and telecommunications, were dismantled in the name of efficiency and restoration of competitive markets.

So why did financial regulation emerge relatively unscathed? Some observers may point to the American public's well-known distrust of banks, a standard theme of literature and popular culture, as the source of political support for maintaining tight governmental controls on the financial markets. Nevertheless, public antipathy toward Wall Street, if real, has produced a regulatory regime that, on balance, has been quite friendly to the financial industry. Far from seeking to destroy Wall Street, US financial regulators have always actively promoted its interests, first in domestic markets and now in the emerging global competition.

The need for a better explanation

These contradictions certainly account for Americans' fascination with deconstructing their own financial regulation, but should US regulation matter to non-US observers? The answer is yes, for several reasons. First, as a practical matter, non-US financial institutions must still operate in US markets, which appear to be retaining their dominant position in the global capital-raising process even as rival financial markets improve their own liquidity and transparency. Even if the significance of US markets does eventually decline, most major non-US financial institutions already have a presence in the US, and that presence will require them to take US regulation into account. This may ensure future employment for US financial lawyers who specialize in helping non-US clients to comply with the intricacies of US regulation, but it is still essential for non-US financial experts, whether they choose to participate in, compete with or simply observe US markets, to understand the principles that inform the US regulatory process.

Second, as globalization and technological innovation promise to weaken barriers between national financial markets, there is a natural desire to harmonize regulatory strategies. Here, however, US financial regulation creates several difficulties. The US model is sufficiently different from other national models to complicate attempts to develop a uniform cross-border regulatory framework for financial services. In fact, given its tradition of encouraging competition among rival supervisory agencies, the US model may not even consider uniformity to be an essential regulatory goal. Understanding the role of regulatory competition in US financial markets, as well as the other values that inform the US regulatory process, will help policymakers to identify both common ground and points of difference between US and their own regulatory regimes.

Finally, despite their complaints about their regulatory burden, US financial market participants are wedded to their model and will to try to export it to non-US markets. US financial regulation has influenced the organization of the US financial industry, and US financial institutions are taking their unique structure and competitive style with them as they enter non-US markets. US financial regulators are likely to champion their own regulatory strategies when questions of international supervision arise. The US model's impact on global financial supervision is already becoming apparent in areas such as bank capital standards, disclosure and rules prohibiting insider trading. Whether because the US was first to regulate or because US regulators have been particularly effective advocates, the US position has proved influential.[10] Therefore, a better understanding of the forces that drive US financial regulation may assist efforts to develop a workable supervisory framework for global financial markets.

Although the need for regulatory explanation may be apparent, the task of explaining US financial regulation, with all of its complexities and inherent contradictions, has never been easy. As Chapter 1 describes, financial scholarship too often has tried to identify a definitive cause for regulatory phenomena, explaining US financial regulation as all politics or all ideology or all economics. As a result, traditional scholarship, although helping to illuminate one aspect of the regulatory process, is too narrow to provide a common understanding of US financial regulation.

Moreover, most scholarship that purports to explain US financial regulation has implicit normative content, reflecting an unarticulated political agenda that may be more revealing about the values that inform US financial regulation than the explanation itself. For example, it is no accident that today's scholarship on financial regulation rarely, if ever, pays tribute to the classic public interest model of regulation that views regulation as a rational government response to market failure. Instead, scholarship on financial regulation tends to begin with the premise that it is regulation, not the market, that has failed, and then looks for an explanation of the origins of financial regulation that may account for this failure.

This modern scholarly approach reflects a fundamental shift in paradigm that has greatly influenced academic scholarship on regulation generally, particularly the literature of law and economics, and may even have fueled the successful deregulatory movement that has so influenced American politics since the 1980s. One prominent law and economics scholar has called this paradigm shift the 'greatest intellectual triumph in US public policy in modern times'.[11] It is certainly not surprising that this scholarship, with its basic skepticism about the wisdom of the regulatory process, should have influenced public debate over the legitimacy of US financial regulation. It is also not surprising that recent generations of academics, particularly those trained in economics, should have become critics of regulation.

Nevertheless, what is somewhat surprising is that the normative power of this regulatory critique has been only partly successful in delegitimizing financial regulation. Despite the assault, financial regulation apparently still enjoys support, not just among policymakers, who in the case of financial law seem loathe to experiment with the kinds of radical changes that have been made to other regulatory programs, but even among some of regulation's most persuasive critics, who readily admit that deregulation of financial markets must stop short of the point of 'firing the police force'.[12] Thus, financial regulation apparently still matters, and the reasons why it matters are not completely captured by scholarly explanations that begin with the premise that regulation is suspect. A more complete explanation of US financial regulation is needed to identify its sources of support as well as its vulnerabilities.

The 'level playing field' as metaphor

If traditional explanations of financial regulation suffer from narrowness or normative parochialism, is there a better way to explain why regulation matters? This book's theme is that understanding US financial regulation requires reference to the shared values that inform the regulatory process as those values are articulated by its players, who include financial firms and other market participants (such as consumers of financial products), regulators, policymakers and scholars. Especially recently, these values most frequently find expression through the metaphor of the *'level playing field'*. Of course, reference to the level playing field as a political ideal is not new, nor is it confined to discussion of US financial regulation. Nevertheless, the phrase is employed so frequently in the debate over the legitimacy of US financial regulation (and deregulation) that it is worthwhile to stop and think about why the players in the financial regulatory process are wedded to the notion of a level playing field and what they mean when they invoke the level playing field as a guiding principle for financial regulation.

In practice, of course, different participants in financial markets would design the level playing field in very different ways. For that reason alone, playing fields are hardly ever level, nor are they likely to become so in the future regardless of who constructs them. Nevertheless, when players in US financial markets talk about a level playing field, they are referencing a particular conception of fairness that is widely shared in US financial markets and that accounts for many of the strengths, and many of the weaknesses, of US financial regulation. This conception of fairness has four basic elements that define the perimeters of the level playing field. Financial regulation, to the extent that it retains its claim to legitimacy, attempts to ensure that these four elements of fairness are present in financial markets.

The four elements of fairness

First, on the level playing field, all players must start equally. At the risk of mixing metaphors, this means that some players must be handicapped through regulatory burdens and others assisted by subsidies to ensure a fair start. A useful way of understanding US financial regulation is to view it as creating a complex balance of burden and subsidy that prevents one participant in financial markets, whether a bank, broker or insurance company, from enjoying competitive or bargaining advantages over other participants, whether a rival financial firm, supplier or consumer of financial products.

A good example of the handicapping function of financial regulation is provided by the legitimization and ultimate delegitimization of the Glass-Steagall Act, which was finally repealed in 1999. Glass-Steagall had been almost universally condemned for imposing an unfair regulatory burden on banks by keeping them out of the securities business. Moreover, the statute had spawned an enormous body of scholarly work that sought to solve such conundrums as why Congress had unfairly burdened the banking industry in the first place (was it rent-seeking by securities firms or populist fear of banks?) and why Glass-Steagall reform was proving so difficult to achieve (again, was it rent-seeking by securities firms or populist fear of banks?).

It was often forgotten that Glass-Steagall imposed a separate, but roughly equal, burden on the securities industry, keeping securities firms out of the deposit-taking business. As Chapter 1 describes, when Glass-Steagall was enacted by Congress in 1933, the handicap that it placed on securities firms was at least as significant as the burden that it created for the banking industry. Moreover, this dual regulatory handicapping explains why, at least until modern times, Glass-Steagall retained considerable legitimacy. In fact, Glass-Steagall was both burden and subsidy: excluding securities firms from the deposit-taking business proved as beneficial for banks as excluding banks from the securities business proved for securities firms. Glass-Steagall succeeded because it achieved a regulatory equilibrium, creating a level balance of burdens and subsidies that permitted each industry to operate successfully in its own protected financial market. That this handicapping was viewed as fair by financial market players is suggested by the fact that Glass-Steagall did not provoke significant challenge from either industry for many decades after its enactment. So long as banks and securities firms were able to prosper in their respective markets, neither player had cause to complain of an unlevel playing field and neither did.

By the 1970s, however, the balance had shifted as market changes, such as rising interest rates and changing patterns of investment, made the core banking business appear less lucrative than the core securities business. Banks longingly looked over the fence at securities markets and began to complain of the regulatory burden created by Glass-Steagall. And bank regulators such as the Federal Reserve responded by reinterpreting Glass-Steagall creatively to allow banks to re-enter securities markets, culminating in the Section 20 revolution that has already been described. Inevitably, the banking industry's attempt to lighten its regulatory burden provoked a response from the securities industry, which, still barred from deposit-taking by Glass-Steagall, perceived the unfairness of its own regulatory handicap. Securities firms unveiled the money market mutual fund, a liquid investment account designed to compete directly with bank deposits.[13] By the late 1990s, neither industry was satisfied that the playing field was level, and an unlikely coalition of banks and securities firms emerged to support Glass-Steagall reform.

Thus, the process of Glass-Steagall reform began as a effort to restore competitive balance by readjusting regulatory handicaps. Nevertheless, arriving at a rehandicapping that would be viewed as guaranteeing an equal starting position for all players proved difficult, particularly for policymakers in Congress. Decades of informal burden-shifting by both industries and their regulators, such as the Section 20 revolution, had put different financial firms in very different starting positions. Should the gains already made by some firms through the regulatory process be codified, or should they be rolled back to ensure competitive equality? Would all financial market players, including the consumer of financial services, be guaranteed equal starts in deregulated financial markets, or would some new handicapping be required?

These questions were important, because convincing all players that financial modernization would create a level playing field (or one that was substantially more level than before) was essential to ensure that any congressional reform would gain and retain legitimacy. This explains why financial modernization legislation was so slow in coming, and why the final product was so complex. The statute had to do far more than simply repeal Glass-Steagall. It had to create a new system of regulatory handicaps to equalize the starting positions of multiple competing players in US financial markets.

The regulatory rehandicapping process is further complicated by the necessity that policymakers answer the often thorny question of when regulatory subsidy actually becomes regulatory burden. As Chapter 2 describes, although US banks began to complain in the 1970s that Glass-Steagall imposed an unfair regulatory burden on their industry, the painfully slow process of regulatory reform may actually have benefited US financial firms facing competitive challenge from non-US universal banks. In US markets, for example, Glass-Steagall may have discouraged entry by universal banks, which faced higher transactions costs than US firms both when complying with US regulation and when seeking to exploit regulatory loopholes such as the Section 20 route. As a result, from the perspective of non-US banks, the playing field was anything but level.

US banks were hardly likely to admit this, since fairness would have required that regulatory handicaps be reallocated. Once rehandicapping begins through the regulatory reform process, it is in the interest of individual players to make the case that their own regulatory burdens outweigh their regulatory subsidies. As Chapter 3 explains, a looming battle in US financial regulation concerns the extent of the regulatory subsidy enjoyed by the banking industry in the form of federal insurance of bank deposits. The existence of this subsidy traditionally has justified the imposition of special regulatory burdens on banks, including, for example, a legal requirement that banks (but not rival financial firms) must provide for the credit needs of their local communities. This and other special regulatory burdens traditionally have been viewed as legitimate because they level the playing field by ensuring that subsidized banks and their unsubsidized rival firms enjoy equal starting positions. If federal deposit insurance no longer provides a net subsidy to the banking industry, however, it may no longer provide a legitimate basis for special regulatory handicapping of banks.

This argument has both economic and political components, and, if successful, would undercut the legitimacy of large portions of US bank regulation. Ironically, however, although the banking industry has denied that it enjoys any special regulatory subsidy, it has been quick to cite regulatory subsidy as a reason to impose special regulatory burdens on its competitors, such as the credit union industry. Thus, the ideal of a level playing field, with its requirement that all players start equally, may be used at different times and by different players either to legitimize or to delegitimize a particular regulatory equilibrium. Put another way, whether the playing field is level or not is often in the eyes of the beholder.

Second, on the level playing field, results count.   Once the players are handicapped, fairness demands that the competition proceeds unfettered. This helps to explain why the US financial regulatory regime typically tolerates high entry barriers but seldom if ever interferes with the progress of the game. It also accounts for the apparent anomaly that, despite cartelization and high regulatory costs, US financial markets are highly competitive and reward innovation. The value accorded to competition and innovation is reflected even in the financial regulatory structure. As Chapter 4 describes, the legitimacy of US financial regulation is derived in part from a theory of regulatory competition that assumes that rivalry among regulatory agencies will encourage innovation and lead ultimately to the choice of the most efficient regulatory strategy. From this perspective, the Travelers/Citicorp merger was the logical outcome of regulatory competition.

Regulatory competition has a dark side, potentially increasing transactions costs both for firms operating in US financial markets and for US regulators charged with supervising those firms. Moreover, although, in theory, regulatory competition should result in the survival of the most efficient regulation, in practice, competition has been imperfect, producing unequal regulatory outcomes that are unequally enforced. This anomaly, which seems at odds with the ideal of a level playing field, is addressed in Chapter 5 in the context of the debate over the relative merits of 'functional' or 'entity' regulation of financial firms. The outcome of this debate will not only determine the future of regulatory competition in US markets but will also have implications for efforts to harmonize international supervision of cross-border financial firms.

Third, on the level playing field, fair play is demanded.   Despite the value attached to free competition, the level playing field requires a commitment to fair process. The need to ensure procedural fairness results from inequality of bargaining power, which prevents some participants in financial markets from negotiating for the degree of protection from risk that they require. Regulation seeks to equalize that bargaining power and, in so doing, to convince the least powerful and least sophisticated participants in financial markets that the playing field is truly level. Thus, financial regulation performs a psychological as well as an economic function, reassuring players that the game is fair and thereby encouraging broad participation.

Since retail customers tend to be the most vulnerable, many (although not all) procedural rules are designed specifically for their benefit. These rules, which continue to proliferate in spite of, and perhaps in response to, the financial regulatory reform process, occasionally seem to impede rather than enhance competitive efficiency. For example, rules prohibiting product tying (formal or informal arrangements that require the joint purchase of separate financial products) remain part of financial regulation despite considerable skepticism about their effectiveness in non-financial product markets. Likewise, US financial law traditionally has relied upon rules designed to prevent the appearance of conflicts of interest, forbidding competitive tactics that would raise few concerns in other markets.

Chapter 6 explores the potential inconsistency between this commitment to fair process in retail markets and the US financial regulatory system's preference for free competition and innovation. For some scholars and policymakers, the solution to this conflict is to bifurcate financial product markets, and financial regulation, into retail and wholesale sectors, allowing deregulation to proceed in wholesale markets while regulation of retail markets remains intact. In US financial markets, however, bifurcation may be unsustainable. It is also likely to be viewed as fundamentally at odds with the level playing field's requirement that all players have an opportunity to participate equally in financial markets.

Finally, on the level playing field, the market, not the government, should pick the winners and losers.   This fourth element of fairness manifests itself in several ways in US financial regulation. For example, despite reliance on regulatory burdens and subsidies to ensure equal starts, the US regulatory system professes to abhor government bailouts to prevent financial failure. Of course, government bailouts have occurred in various forms, from Continental Illinois in 1984 to Long-Term Capital Management in 1998, but they have almost always provoked intense public criticism and occasionally adverse congressional reaction. In the early 1990s, for example, following the bailout of the failing thrift industry, Congress passed new legislation designed to make future rescues difficult if not impossible for financial regulators to accomplish.[14] Thus, although their actions may suggest otherwise, the players in US financial markets at least claim to disapprove of government intervention to save failing financial firms.

This attitude is not surprising: to the extent that the level playing field requires that players be left free to win or lose on their own, it follows that the government should not attempt to ensure equal outcomes. Government financial assistance to firms that are unable to compete with more efficient players may be criticized as both uneconomical and unfair. Further, in a financial regime that encourages free competition, any collusion or agreement among the players to ensure a particular outcome is also frowned upon. As a result, voluntary collective action by market participants to support a troubled financial institution tends to be infrequent in US financial markets.

This creates a dilemma for financial regulators. As Chapter 7 explains, the lack of a tradition of voluntary collective action by private competitors makes it virtually impossible for the government to maintain a hands-off attitude toward financial failure, particularly when there is a threat that failure will affect the smooth functioning of financial markets. Because the government cannot rely on private players to ensure orderly markets, public intervention to prevent financial crisis is inevitable; but regulators intervene reluctantly because they recognize that failure prevention is inconsistent with prevailing notions of fairness.

The desire to allow the market to pick the winners and losers also accounts for the unwillingness of the public sector directly to subsidize financial product development, a phenomenon that is explored in Chapter 8. Certain financial innovations such as electronic banking and 'smart cards' proved slow to launch in the US, in part because of the government's reluctance to predetermine the outcome of the competitive process by favoring one technology over another. To the extent that the government is itself a significant player in financial markets, its choices cannot avoid affecting competitive results, but the government has often acted at cross-purposes, with one agency endorsing a particular financial technology at the same time that another is discouraging it. Moreover, although coordinated action by private industry participants to ensure the successful development and marketing of particular innovative financial products might substitute for direct government subsidization, this kind of coordination among competitors is also discouraged by regulation.

Three caveats and three responses

These four rules of fairness – starting the players equally, rewarding innovation and competition, ensuring fair play and allowing the market to determine the winners and losers – provide a theoretical basis for understanding the values that inform US financial regulation. Nevertheless, like any attempt to provide a complete explanation of regulation, this approach opens itself to several objections. First, critics may point out that calls for fairness and a level playing field may be little more than a convenient rhetorical mask employed by players in financial markets to hide their genuine, less idealistic motives from public view. Financial firms and regulators who pay lip service to the level playing field may secretly be more interested in empire-building than in fairness.

Although this may be the case, the choice of rhetorical mask itself says much about the fundamental values that resonate in a society. The peculiar notions of fairness that find symbolic expression in the rhetoric of the level playing field explain how particular financial regulatory initiatives gain, retain or lose their legitimacy. Understanding the importance of these symbols to the process of regulatory legitimization will help observers to predict not only the future path of US financial regulation, including how particular interest groups may best promote their private goals through the regulatory process, but also the kinds of proposals that US players are likely to bring to the table when international regulatory schemes are debated.

Second, critics may warn that the ideal of the level playing field may be defined so inclusively as to lose any explanatory or predictive power. For example, it is likely that all financial markets to some extent aim to achieve the elements of fairness that have been identified here with the level playing field. For that reason, an effort will be made to narrow the concept by showing its peculiar manifestations in particular areas of US financial law, especially those that are less generalizable to other regulatory regimes. In the end, readers may make their own decisions as to the explanatory value of the level playing field as metaphor, but hopefully they will gain some insight into how US financial regulation works and how it is changing.

Finally, the concept of the level playing field offers support for a view of financial regulation that is controversial today, particularly in the academy – namely, that regulation matters and, through its commitment to guaranteeing a level playing field, may even contribute to the enduring popularity and vitality of US financial markets. This conclusion is supported by the apparent reluctance of US market participants to scrap their regulation too quickly. It is also recognized by non-US competitors who have come to perceive the advantages that US regulation traditionally has afforded US financial institutions.

That regulation still matters in US markets is suggested by recent financial reform that, far from abandoning the regulatory ideal of a level playing field, continues to rely on the regulatory process to achieve all four elements of fairness. In 1999, the impetus for financial modernization was the need to ensure that all financial firms, whether bank, securities organization or insurance company, had an equal starting position on a level playing field. Yet, as the following chapters describe, financial modernization is also preserving some role for regulatory competition and innovation, guaranteeing fair play by protecting retail investors in diversified financial product markets and allowing the market rather than the government to judge competitive outcomes. How successful the new regulatory regime ultimately proves to be in achieving these goals may determine its longevity.

The question remains whether, as markets integrate globally and pressure mounts for less national regulatory interference in international financial transactions, the US will be forced to abandon its regulatory system's commitment to ensuring fair play in competitive markets. Are US notions of competitive fairness so different from the international norm as to impede the development of uniform cross-border regulatory standards, or may a new global paradigm emerge that reflects these values? More fundamentally, in truly borderless financial markets, can any one regulatory scheme hope to have much influence over the structure and rules of the playing field? Will regulation matter in the markets of the future? Definitive answers to these questions must await the further evolution of truly transnational financial markets, which are in their infancy as the new century begins. Nevertheless, a better understanding of the values that have given US financial regulation its legitimacy may help observers to explain the past success of US regulation and to begin to predict its impact on future regulatory strategy.

1
How to Think About Financial Regulation

In the United States, explanations of the origins of financial regulation are often as complex and contradictory as the regulation itself. US financial regulation has been depicted at times as uniquely American, reflecting the peculiar qualities of domestic law and culture,[1] and at other times as derivative of the British experience;[2] at times as a genuinely public-regarding effort to respond to the definitive economic event of twentieth century America, the Great Depression,[3] and at other times as a private bargain that responded to nothing more than the needs of a few politically powerful interest groups;[4] at times as a reflection of rational economic theory[5] and at other times as an 'incoherent barbarism'.[6]

Given these contradictions, there is a strong temptation for the student of US financial regulation to ignore explanations of past regulation and to go on immediately to the pressing current question of whether and how regulation should be reformed. In fact, the inability of either policymakers or scholars to arrive at a consensus as to the original goals of financial regulation may be a good argument for deregulation. Certainly, the absence of a clear and widely shared vision of the historical purposes of regulation makes the status quo more difficult to defend.

Nevertheless, understanding how modern observers of US financial regulation choose to think about the origins of regulation is essential to understanding the cumbersome process of US financial reform. Although often presented as resting upon neutral principles, scholarly explanations of regulation actually have normative content, reflecting one's basic beliefs about the legitimacy of financial regulation and of the reform process. Simply put, the fact that US financial experts cannot agree on a definitive explanation of regulation's past explains their inability to agree on regulation's future, and whether, in the long run, regulation matters.

With this in mind, it is useful to review the leading modern explanations of US financial regulation that have dominated the scholarly literature and have influenced to some extent the political debate over deregulation. What is striking about these explanations is how distinct they are, reflecting differing perspectives on a common set of historical events. Each tends to begin with the same defining moment in US history, the Great Depression. Although financial law in America obviously predated the 1930s (for example, the National Bank Act was adopted some six decades earlier), the laws that emerged in the 1930s and succeeding years remained the source of the most important, and the most controversial, regulation governing US financial institutions in the late twentieth century. If the Great Depression was the defining event in US financial regulatory history, however, modern explanations of financial regulation view the impact of that event on the political and regulatory process very differently, and this in turn colors their analysis of the purposes of the regulatory regime that was enacted in its wake.

There is one common element uniting prevailing explanations of financial regulation: each in its own way is highly critical of regulation. Although this might suggest that a consensus does exist in favor of deregulation, different explanations of regulation lead to entirely different conclusions as to what should be done with the existing regulatory framework. As will be described, the principal point of disagreement is whether regulation matters, a question that is raised but not fully addressed by any of the standard explanations. As this chapter will conclude, using this question as a place to begin, rather than end, scholarly analysis may offer a better way to understand both US financial regulation and current attitudes toward regulation in both the academy and the marketplace.

Three theories of regulation

Explanations of US financial regulation tend to fall into three main schools of thought that may be categorized as political, ideological and market-oriented. Recently, for reasons that will become clear, political explanations of regulation have dominated financial scholarship, particularly the works of economists and legal scholars identified with the law and economics movement. In the past, however, ideological explanations were most common, and market explanations are probably still favored by bankers and other participants in the financial markets.

Regulation as politics

The political theory of financial regulation draws on the familiar public choice model of the regulatory process, which itself owes a debt to earlier 'capture' theories of regulation as well as to classical economic models of supply and demand.[7] At the risk of simplifying, the public choice model explains the origins of regulation by reference to the pursuit by interested actors of private goals through the political process. Regulation, like any product, will be supplied to the highest bidder. The suppliers of regulation, whether the legislators who adopt regulatory statutes or the agencies that administer them, will maximize their own advantages by protecting the interests of their constituencies in the political process.

Certainly, the economists who pioneered public choice theory were not the first to point to the influence of private interest groups in the political process, but they were instrumental in positioning rent-seeking as a plausible explanation of the decisions of regulatory agencies. Previously, economists had questioned the efficiency of regulation, particularly rules that interfered with the workings of competitive markets. Although traditional regulatory theory had presumed that government intervention in private markets was justified by market failure, economists argued that, in too many cases, market failure could not account for regulatory interference. Public choice theory, with its model of regulation as a consumption good to be supplied to the highest bidder, offered a view of the regulatory process that explained why regulation did not very often (in the economists' view) serve the public good.

To critics of financial regulation, public choice theory offered an appealing explanation of the status quo. First, historically, US financial regulation has been highly protectionist. Bank regulators took into account the supposed threat of 'overcompetition' in banking markets when ruling on applications to charter new banks[8] and when limiting the rates of interest that banks could offer retail customers when they competed for deposits.[9] Second, US financial regulation has provided competitive benefits to some financial firms at the expense of others. Regulation preventing banks from selling securities and insurance products created cartels in financial product markets, limiting entry by potential competitors. These consequences of financial regulation were consistent with the public choice model of regulation as a private interest group bargain designed to reward the successful rent-seeker.

A prime target of public choice theory was the Glass-Steagall Act, which until its repeal in 1999 limited the power of US commercial banks to participate in the securities industry. Glass-Steagall was adopted by Congress in 1933, as part of broader banking reform legislation that, notably, also created the federal deposit insurance program. The statute prohibited deposit-taking banks from acting as merchant bankers (investing in corporate equities as principal) or as investment bankers (placing corporate debt or equities with investors) and from affiliating with securities firms.

As a political matter, Glass-Steagall received relatively little attention until the 1970s, when a legal challenge to a regulation adopted by the Comptroller of the Currency (the chartering authority for national banks) prompted the first serious inquiry by the Supreme Court into the statute's purposes.[10] In the years following, Glass-Steagall attracted greater notice as rising interest rates and enhanced efficiencies in the securities issue process caused increasing numbers of corporate borrowers to defect from their banks in order to raise capital in the securities markets, threatening the profitability of the traditional corporate lending business. Glass-Steagall, which prevented banks from offering their customers securities underwriting services, came to be perceived as a significant competitive barrier, rewarding the securities industry at the expense of the banking industry. Public choice theory provided the theoretical explanation for this unfairness: Glass-Steagall must have been the product of rent-seeking by securities firms that successfully persuaded Congress to exclude banks from their turf.

In linking the origins of Glass-Steagall to its consequences for modern financial markets, the public choice explanation has functioned, albeit somewhat uneasily, on two levels, operating both as political theory and as history. Public choice is a child of the law and economics movement, which, as historians point out, tends to be deliberately ahistorical, basing its models on generalizable behavioral assumptions, such as rational actors' pursuit of profit maximization, rather than on historical contingencies.[11] Yet, to the extent that public choice models have been used to explain the origins of specific regulatory programs, they must seek support in the historical evidence. In the case of Glass-Steagall, however, the historical evidence actually undermines the public choice story in several key respects, a problem that ultimately diminishes the effectiveness of public choice as a political theory of financial regulation.

Certainly, the public choice story was correct to question the earlier conventional wisdom about the origins of Glass-Steagall. Remarkably, until relatively recently, the principal historical account of Glass-Steagall was the Supreme Court's look at the legislative history of the Act in its 1971 decision in *Investment Company Institute* v. *Camp.* Relying almost exclusively on a speech made on the Senate floor in 1932 by Senator Bulkley of Ohio, who was a member of the committee that had drafted the statute (and, incidently, a former college room-mate of President Franklin D. Roosevelt), the Supreme Court read Glass-Steagall as a form of consumer protection legislation that was designed to remedy the abuses, or 'subtle hazards', that supposedly had occurred in the 1920s when banks operated in the securities markets. According to the Supreme Court, Congress had been concerned with more than the danger that speculation in securities put banking assets at risk, leading to bank failure and depositor losses. In addition, bank involvement in the securities markets damaged public confidence in the independence and soundness of the banking industry as a whole, particularly if it were suspected that banks would readily lend their funds and their reputations to ensure the success of their securities operations. The Court concluded its historical reading of Glass-Steagall as follows:

> In sum, Congress acted to keep commercial banks out of the investment banking business largely because it believed that the promotional incentives of investment banking and the investment banker's pecuniary stake in the success of particular investment opportunities was destructive of prudent and disinterested commercial banking and of public confidence in the commercial banking system.[12]

The *Camp* decision suggests several motives for the Glass-Steagall Act that appear to be public-regarding, such as restoring confidence in banking markets, protecting consumers from improper sales tactics and preventing conflicts of interest. (Similar goals are associated with another example of Depression-era financial regulation, the Securities Act of 1933, which is viewed far more favorably by modern scholars than is Glass-Steagall.) Nevertheless, the Supreme Court's reading of history was, at best, woefully incomplete. For example, the floor speech by Senator Bulkley that the Supreme Court cited as the defini-tive legislative history of the Glass-Steagall Act was actually delivered over a year before final congressional consideration of a substantially modified bill took place, by which time Senator Bulkley's 'subtle hazards' were no longer of pressing concern to Congress. In fact, in

May 1933, just before the final vote, a congressman charged with explaining the legislation to members of the House of Representatives dismissed the provisions separating banking and securities as moot and therefore not worth even '19 seconds' of discussion.[13] Moreover, the legislation that was eventually enacted by Congress went well beyond what was required to redress the 'subtle hazards', barring banks from activities such as participation in wholesale securities markets that created no consumer concerns. All this suggests that something other than the 'subtle hazards' must have been driving the legislative process.

The public choice story, however, chooses to refute *Camp*'s version of history in a different way. *Camp*'s reading of history was faulty, according to public choice theory, because the reasoning that it imputes to Congress is economically flawed. The assumption that banks in the 1920s would have gambled their assets and reputations in support of their securities activities is unsupported either by evidence or by economic theory, since no rational banker would risk enterprise failure by diverting funds from financially sound to financially unsound operations. On the other hand, the consequence of the Act was to prevent competition in securities markets. Finding no economically rational public-regarding motive for Glass-Steagall's interference with free markets, the public choice story imputes causes from effects, suggesting as the most plausible explanation that Congress deliberately set out to hinder competition for the benefit of a favored interest group, in this instance, the securities industry. The public choice story supposes that congressional motive was economically rational and that the consequences of congressional action were fully foreseen: Glass-Steagall was a deliberate and successful experiment in private interest group legislation.[14]

This explanation of Glass-Steagall had considerable appeal to scholars, particularly to those who questioned *Camp*'s version of history. It also satisfied a banking industry that had come to view the securities industry as its direct competitor. Finally, it proved popular with politicians because it provided an elegant political rationale for regulatory reform. By making the case that Glass-Steagall had a private purpose (interfering with free competition) rather than a public purpose (correcting market failure), the public choice story undercut the legitimacy of Glass-Steagall. Why should a legislator continue to support a statute whose only goal appears to be to subsidize the securities industry? Why, for that matter, should the public support a legislator who does so?

The public choice story also provided a basis for the narrow, often highly legalistic, interpretation of Glass-Steagall that began to be employed in the 1980s by banks and bank regulators to punch holes in the statutory framework. As early as the 1970s, some bank regulators were already interpreting the language of Glass-Steagall in a light most favorable to the banking industry in an attempt to allow banks to re-enter some aspects of the securities business, but, as evidenced by the Supreme Court's *Camp* decision, this movement was originally rebuffed by the courts.[15] By the 1980s, however, in response to industry pressure, bank regulators became increasingly creative in their reading of statutory language, culminating in the Federal Reserve Board's 'Section 20' decisions permitting affiliations between banks and securities firms that were not 'engaged principally' (as defined by the Board) in underwriting and dealing. This time, reviewing courts were far more willing to defer to creative agency interpretation of Glass-Steagall despite protests from the securities industry.[16] That bank regulators would favor their constituency, the banking industry, at the expense of its rivals is perfectly consistent with public choice theories of regulatory action, but why were the courts willing to endorse this result? The public choice story's delegitimization of Glass-Steagall gave courts a reason to construe the statute narrowly, thereby partly righting the competitive imbalance that Congress had created.

As regulatory history, however, the public choice story of Glass-Steagall has several serious flaws, one of which is its insistence that rational economic motives be assigned to legislative action. For example, modern economists examining evidence from the 1920s have concluded that the alleged abuses by bank securities operations chronicled by Senator Bulkley and retold by the Supreme Court in the *Camp* decision occurred infrequently, if at all.[17] As a result, it is tempting for modern observers to assume that some other motive must have driven the legislative process, but this may not have been the case. Perhaps policy-makers in the 1930s did not have access to the same evidence as modern scholars, or perhaps they discounted it. Or perhaps they were acting rationally according to their limited understanding of financial economics. In either event, it may be shortsighted to look at historical purpose through the prism of modern economic theory.

This in turn raises another, more serious, problem with the public choice story as an historical explanation of regulatory purpose. To conclude that Glass-Steagall was the product of rent-seeking by the securities industry at the expense of the banking industry ignores the fact that the modern US financial industry structure looks entirely different from its 1933 counterpart. In the 1930s, for example, the institutional divide between 'commercial' banks (deposit-lenders) and 'merchant/investment' banks (underwriter-dealers) was not clear at all. The dominant securities firms of the era, such as J.P. Morgan and Kuhn Loeb, accepted deposits. Morgan called itself a bank, but, unlike rivals like Chase National Bank, was not subject to supervision by bank regulators. Nor was Morgan a 'universal bank' as that term is understood today, because Morgan had no retail operations. During congressional hearings on bank securities activities in the 1920s, legislators were amazed to learn that Morgan would not accept new customers without a formal introduction![18]

Morgan's refusal to deal with the public was not simply a business whim. Had Morgan solicited public depositors, it would have been required to obtain a banking license and to subject itself to government regulation. Morgan preferred to remain a private, or unregulated, bank. In fact, the principal institutional divide in the financial industry of 1933 was between unlicensed financial institutions that operated to some degree in both securities and traditional banking markets and licensed banks, the largest of which were also operating in both markets, often through the notorious securities affiliates criticized by Senator Bulkley and, later, by the *Camp* decision. The institutional divide was actually even more complex because the banking industry included both nationally chartered banks and large numbers of state-chartered banks that were not subject to any federal oversight and were just as opposed to the notion of uniform national bank regulation as were private banks like Morgan.

So who exactly were the securities firms that successfully bargained for Glass-Steagall? Morgan and other unregulated private banks were powerful players in the securities markets, but, as will be shown, they had strong reasons to object to the legislation. The Investment Bankers Association of America was, at the time, a leading trade organization for the securities industry, but in the early 1930s it was dominated by bank securities affiliates and took positions in opposition to the legislation. More generally, high failure rates among securities firms in the early 1930s had weakened the securities industry, making it less likely that securities firms could outbid still powerful banking firms like Morgan and Chase for favorable regulatory treatment from Congress. So no single firm or group of securities firms emerges as an obvious candidate for the role of successful rent-seeker.[19]

This apparent historical anomaly disappears, however, when Glass-Steagall is viewed in the context of the financial market structure that actually prevailed in 1933. In fact, the statute itself offers clues as to the complexity of that structure. The drafters of Glass-Steagall had to rely on four separate prohibitions in order to achieve their goal of dividing the banking and securities markets. First, federally regulated banks (which according to the plan adopted in 1933 would ultimately have included all licensed banking institutions that joined the federal deposit insurance system – and at the time it was expected that virtually every bank would join) were prohibited from merchant and investment banking. Second, these banks were restricted from affiliating with firms engaged principally in underwriting and dealing securities. Third, firms engaged in any securities business, as well as any private bank or other firm not regulated as a bank under national or state banking law, were no longer allowed to accept deposits. Finally, management interlocks between banking firms and securities firms were barred.

These provisions were not redundant, but addressed the complex financial industry structure that prevailed in 1933. Their effect was to simplify that structure by forcing financial firms to opt between deposit-taking, which henceforth would be subject to government banking regulation, and securities underwriting and dealing, which would be subject to a separate, disclosure-based regulatory scheme under the Securities Act of 1933, adopted just weeks before Glass-Steagall, and the Securities Exchange Act of 1934. By requiring financial firms to make that choice, Glass-Steagall originated the dual market structure that prevailed in the US for decades, pursuant to which banks and investment banks operated in separate, and separately regulated, financial arenas, the deposit-lending market and the securities market.

Interestingly, by the 1990s, this dual market structure threatened to break down as financial firms used creative legal interpretations to refashion themselves into hybrid institutions that could no longer be neatly categorized as 'bank' or 'securities firm'. Suddenly, banks once again were operating securities affiliates (through the Section 20 route) and securities firms once again were competing for deposits (through the money market mutual fund). US financial market organization was rapidly becoming as complex as it had been in the 1920s, a development that put enormous pressure on a regulatory framework that was premised on the continuation of the dual market structure. The result, eventually, was Glass-Steagall reform.

In 1933, the regulatory restructuring of financial markets mandated by Glass-Steagall affected every financial institution to some degree, but some were more affected than others. Among licensed banks, only the largest had established brokerage and underwriting operations, and by June 1933, when Glass-Steagall was enacted, many of these banks had voluntarily abandoned the securities business. Although the threat of legislation, as well as growing public outcry over the alleged abuses of retail customers by bank securities operations, may have influenced these banks' decisions, a number of banks had already left the securities markets as early as 1931, suggesting that banks were responding to business as well as political pressure.[20] In any event, by 1933, many bankers probably were no longer inclined to expend a tremendous amount of political capital to defeat Glass-Steagall. In March 1933, Winthrop Aldrich of the Chase National Bank, which had operated one of the largest securities affiliates, reversed his bank's earlier stance on Glass-Steagall and actually endorsed the legislation.[21]

In contrast, in 1933, unlicensed private banks, especially Morgan, had much to lose from the enactment of Glass-Steagall because it required them either to submit to government regulation as banks (and relinquish their securities business) or to give up deposit-taking. Morgan, whose corporate deposits totaled $500 000 000 in 1929, was the most seriously affected, and, after enactment of Glass-Steagall, the firm decided to retain its deposit operations and to spin off its securities business. Interestingly, the provision in the Glass-Steagall Act that forced Morgan to make this choice, namely, the prohibition on deposit-taking by private banks, did not appear until the final version of the legislation that was considered by Congress in May 1933, and it reportedly was drafted by Winthrop Aldrich – head of the Chase National Bank. Morgan viewed the provision as an attack by a competitor on its position as the leading US financial firm, a perspective that was shared by the press; one newspaper heralded Winthrop Aldrich as the 'First Challenger of [the] House of Morgan'.[22]

Thus, if evidence of rent-seeking can be found in the historical record, the winner was the largest bank of its era (Chase) and the loser was the largest securities firm of its era (Morgan). (That, after Glass-Steagall, Morgan chose to become a bank may account for some modern confusion over the identities of victims and victors.) Yet even if the public choice story is rewritten to reverse the winners and losers, the story still provides an incomplete explanation of regulation. For example, it begs the question why Chase, and not Morgan, prevailed in the legislative process. Senator Glass, a fierce and effective advocate of the legislation bearing his name, was far more intimate, politically and personally, with Morgan principals like Russell Leffingwell, who had been assistant Treasury Secretary under Glass, than with Winthrop Aldrich.[23] Moreover, Glass and his political allies, including Senator

Bulkley, had spent months attacking banks like Chase for contributing to speculation that had in their view caused the stock market crash and ensuing cataclysm.

Public choice theorists may respond that they never intended to write a complete history of Glass-Steagall. Regardless of the identity of the actual victors in the legislative process, the conclusion of the public choice story remains that Glass-Steagall must have responded to interest group pressure, not public need. At this point, the public choice story relies on the presumption that, so long as the effect of Glass-Steagall was to limit competition, then its purposes could not have been public-regarding. This argument then becomes a justification for narrow statutory construction or repeal. If regulation serves no public-regarding purpose, then any limitation on its scope, whoever may benefit in the short term, will enhance competition and therefore serve the public in the long term.

For this reason, public choice theorists probably were not particularly troubled by the complaint made by securities firms in the 1980s that creative regulatory and judicial interpretation of Glass-Steagall was rewarding the banking industry at the expense of the securities industry. Likewise, they probably were not concerned when, in the 1990s, many of the largest banks and securities firms joined together to urge repeal of Glass-Steagall over the objections of smaller financial firms. Presumably, rent-seeking, if it leads to the demise of private interest group regulation that restricts free competition, is tolerable – or at least more tolerable than the rent-seeking that produced the anticompetitive regulation.

If this is the moral to be drawn from the public choice story, however, the story loses its value either as an explanation of the regulatory process or as a political mandate. Although the public choice story teaches that past regulatory bargains are illegitimate, it offers no insights as to how and when regulatory reform becomes possible. If rent-seeking is the ultimate explanation of regulatory change, then Glass-Steagall should have been quickly repealed as soon as private interest groups supporting reform gained sufficient political clout to outbid groups that favored the status quo. Yet Glass-Steagall survived through most of the 1990s despite the existence of a politically powerful coalition in support of repeal.

Why Glass-Steagall retained its legitimacy for so long despite relentless assaults from interest groups and from the academy is the conundrum that is raised but not answered by the public choice story. Public choice offers an easy way to delegitimize regulation, but it cannot explain how regulation, or deregulation, manages to gain and retain legitimacy in the first place. Some other factor must be added to the story in order to account for when interest group bargains are likely to be successful and when they can be successfully overcome. A search for this factor leads the student of regulation on, or perhaps back, to an alternative explanation of financial regulation that directly addresses the question of how regulation is legitimized.

Regulation as ideology

Before public choice suggested that US financial regulation was the product of political bargaining by private interest groups, most financial scholars probably would have explained regulation by reference to cultural or ideological factors. This emphasis may have reflected the fact that the few scholars who were looking at the origins of financial regulation tended to be lawyers or historians, not economists. Lawyers and historians may be more sensitive than economists to the rhetoric used by policymakers to build support for their legislative programs, and, in the case of financial regulation, this rhetoric typically has relied upon ideological symbols rather than upon economic theory.

Nevertheless, it would be an oversimplification to conclude that economists see financial regulation as politics but historians and lawyers see financial regulation as ideology. Modern scholars are beginning to retell the political story by adding cultural elements that provide, if not an independent motive for regulation, a convenient rhetorical mask that may have been employed by legislators to build a public consensus in favor of financial regulation. Even some economists have added the notion of ideological 'slack' to their public choice analysis, suggesting that, to the extent that private interest groups have difficulty monitoring and policing their bargains with legislators and regulators, those policymakers have some freedom to indulge their personal ideological biases, a factor that may influence regulatory outcomes.[24]

Thus, ideological explanations of regulation may be complementary to political explanations, and, in fact, the two approaches have a lot in common. Each starts from the same place, focusing on 1930s-era regulation such as Glass-Steagall, and arrives at the same conclusion, raising doubts about the legitimacy of regulation. Nevertheless, the theme of the ideological story is quite different from that of the political story and in some respects the two stories are inconsistent.

The ideological story of financial regulation is in essence a story about the populist movement in twentieth century America. The use of the term 'populism' is somewhat problematic because the term potentially covers many very different political and ideological move-ments in US history. For example, the populist label is frequently applied to the anti-monopoly, anti-bigness legal theories of Louis Brandeis, adviser to President Wilson and later Supreme Court justice, whose famous attack on Wall Street and its concentration of financial power, entitled *Other People's Money and How the Bankers Use It*,[25] remains a populist bible; several of his intellectual followers were involved in crafting major pieces of New Deal financial legislation such as the Securities Act of 1933 (but *not*, significantly, the Glass-Steagall Act and other banking legislation). Yet the populist label is also applied to the Depression-era anti-government diatribes of Senator Huey Long of Louisiana, who shared with Brandeis his distrust of Wall Street but little else. Significantly, some historical scholarship on the ideological roots of 1930s-era legislation has avoided use of the term 'populist', defining the anti-monopoly move-ment more narrowly as 'a form of democratic collectivism in which the monopoly power of businessmen would be transferred to the state or to other economic groups'.[26]

In contrast, the modern ideological explanation of financial regulation tends to employ the populist label quite broadly to include virtually all anti-bank or anti-Wall Street sentiment, whether derived from specific economic theory of competition or from popular prejudice against 'financiers'.[27] Although this broad-brush approach is helpful in demon-strating that both formal scholarly theory and informal popular senti-ment may become driving forces in shaping the ideological foundations of public policy, it runs the danger of making political allies out of the most unlikely pairs, such as Louis Brandeis and Huey Long. Nevertheless, the decision to define populism as broadly as possible may be quite con-scious, because, as will be described, it supports the ideological story's conclusion that financial regulation is fundamentally flawed.

For the ideological story as well as for the political story of financial regulation, the Glass-Steagall Act has become an instructive case study. In its search for statutory motive, the ideological story relies heavily on rhetoric, drawing on literature, political speeches and popular culture to provide evidence that Glass-Steagall, as well as other bank regulation, responded to populist suspicion, even fear, of the power of large finan-cial firms. Certainly, in the 1930s, anti-bank and anti-Wall Street rhetoric reached new heights. Financial firms were blamed first for causing the Depression by speculating in securities and then for falling victim to it themselves, thereby destroying the savings of ordinary Americans. Those financial firms that survived the crash of 1929 and the subsequent banking crisis were faulted for not lending freely to help spur economic recovery. Even politicians who were working furiously to save the banking system indulged in anti-bank rhetoric, as evidenced by President Franklin Roosevelt's famous warning that the 'money changers have fled their high seats in the temple of our civilization'.[28]

This rhetoric might have had little impact on the regulatory process but for two concurrent developments. First, although Louis Brandeis' denunciation of the so-called 'Money Trust' – the Wall Street bankers who had dominated US capital formation in the years before World War I – had been all but forgotten during the 1920s, when capital was suddenly cheap and US securities markets were highly competitive, his ideas began to resonate in the 1930s as policymakers looked for explanations of what had gone so wrong. Second, from January 1933 through July 1934, a Senate subcommittee known as the Pecora Committee conducted a highly publicized investigation of the alleged abuses of financial firms in the 1920s stock market that claimed to uncover widespread instances of conflicts of interest, unfair sales tactics directed at retail investors and stock price manipulation.

Against this backdrop, the ideological story paints Glass-Steagall as an assault on Wall Street generally, designed in the short run to prevent consumer abuses by removing commercial banks, widely assumed to have been the most egregious offenders, from the retail securities brokerage business, and in the long run to limit financial monopoly by preventing combinations of banks and securities firms. The ideological story does not really care whether a specific legislative provision hurt Morgan, Chase or some other firm. The targets of regulation were any and all financial firms that were thought collectively to have dominated credit and capital. Moreover, the ideological story accounts for the enduring popular support for Glass-Steagall as well as for financial regulation generally. Regulation that weakens the competitive positions of financial firms is popular because the public, still suspicious of Wall Street, continues to demand tight governmental control over the size and power of the financial industry.

As mentioned, economists have pointed out that, despite the revelations of the Pecora committee, financial firms participating in 1920s securities markets were not engaged in widespread speculation and consumer abuses. Moreover, by the 1920s, financial markets were anything but monopolistic. Enhanced competition in the underwriting business had lowered spreads, new competitors were entering the securities markets and the volume of corporate securities issues had skyrocketed from $2.7 billion in 1919 to $9.4 billion in 1929.[29]

Nevertheless, the ideological explanation addresses these inconsistencies by arguing that, regardless of the actual state of markets, policymakers and the public believed that financial concentration was to blame for their problems. This belief, even if mistaken, explains the regulatory response.[30]

This gap between ideology and reality provides the ideological explanation with its normative content. At first read, the ideological story may appear to offer a public-regarding motive for financial regulation like Glass-Steagall insofar as its creators believed that preventing financial conglomeration would enhance competition in financial markets and protect consumers. Nevertheless, to modern scholars, this Brandeisian fear of a Money Trust is both exaggerated and based upon economic theories that have been discredited. Therefore, although previous generations of policymakers may have thought that they were serving the public interest when they regulated financial markets, they based their policy on false assumptions.

In contrast, today's policymakers, armed with modern economic theory, should know better. Therefore, deregulation is now the truly public-regarding policy. In this way, the ideological story, like the political story, begins to delegitimize financial regulation. This delegitimization is complete when populist sentiment that motivated financial regulation is defined more broadly to include not just Brandeisian economics but also the more extreme and irrational anti-Wall Street political rhetoric that was common in the 1930s but that sounds so anachronistic to the modern listener.[31]

The ideological story may be somewhat better than the political story at accounting for the uniqueness of the US approach to financial regulation. Ideology offers an explanation of regulation that is culturally bound, serving to distinguish US regulation from other national regulatory regimes. This distinction is less clear in the political story: there is no reason to assume that rent-seeking by private interest groups seeking to influence financial regulation is confined to the US, although perhaps America's fragmented political and regulatory structure makes interest group bargaining more likely. In contrast, US populist sentiment has no counterpart abroad. Moreover, populist fear of bigness, whether in business or in government, may itself explain the US preference for a decentralized, pluralist model of government that encourages the proliferation of interest groups.

As an explanation of financial regulation, however, the ideological story greatly overstates the impact of populist sentiment on the development of the law. In fact, the influence of populist ideology on financial regulation has been so slight, particularly in comparison with its impact on other areas of the law, such as antitrust law, that a more historically accurate conclusion would be that the US financial regulatory structure has evolved *despite* the strength of public anti-bank sentiment. That Wall Street has flourished under the yoke of regulation, often even outperforming Main Street, is neither subject to dispute nor accidental. Far from punishing the hated financial industry, regulation has protected and subsidized it. Moreover, populists have recognized this, and have more often opposed financial regulation than they have favored it.

The history of Glass-Steagall provides compelling evidence of populist opposition. When Senator Glass proposed the separation of investment and commercial banking, populists strongly condemned his legislation as an 'iniquitous bankers' proposal'. Their hostility was not surprising, because Glass-Steagall's attempt to divide financial markets was expected to do exactly what populists feared most, to permit greater financial concentration and monopolization of the securities markets by a few large firms. Congressional critics of Glass-Steagall, including Senator Huey Long, who staged a twenty-one day filibuster in an effort to defeat the legislation, repeatedly complained that bifurcating financial markets would allow firms like Morgan once again to dominate the capital raising process, to the detriment of small business and local government. Other critics, such as columnist Walter Lippmann, warned that the legislation would further deflate the securities market, denying Main Street much needed access to securities credit.[32]

Main Street agreed. The US Chamber of Commerce argued that small business seeking access to capital in the 1920s had greatly benefited from the competition in the underwriting business provided by bank securities operations. Interestingly, the Chamber of Commerce also disputed the proposition that banks had foisted worthless securities on retail customers, asserting that default records of bank-underwritten securities were actually better than those of other securities and that the 'best interests of the investing public' had been served by bank involvement in securities markets.[33] Thus, the prevailing wisdom among 1930s populists and their Main Street constituents was that Glass-Steagall was an unwelcome assault on democratized financial markets. This is precisely the opposite reaction from that predicted by the ideological story, which assumes that populists welcomed Glass-Steagall as a deconcentration statute.

If populists opposed Glass-Steagall, their ideological enemies supported it. The statute was drafted not by the neo-Brandeisians who were responsible for New Deal legislation such as the Securities Act of 1933, but by Senator Carter Glass, a supporter of nationwide banking who dismissed the small independent bank idealized by followers of Brandeis as 'the little pawnshop that topples over and creates a psychology that eventually topples over the larger and sounder banks'.[34] Senator Glass' closest academic adviser was Parker Willis, a Columbia University professor with ties to Wall Street and the European financial community. President Roosevelt actually warned Senator Glass to disassociate himself from Willis, accusing the professor of belonging to 'that little group of Americans who are appendages or appendices – whichever part of the anatomy that you prefer – on the large body of international bankers of London, Paris, Shanghai, etc'.[35]

Glass and Willis, therefore, were hardly icons of the populist movement. Moreover, their mission was to end what in their view had been dangerous overcompetition and speculation in 1920s securities markets that had caused the stock market crash and threatened the stability of the financial system. Their solution was to slow the expansion of credit and to raise entry barriers in the securities markets, precisely the opposite prescription for financial reform from that favored by the populists.

Finally, the prototype for Glass-Steagall's functional separation of financial markets was found not in the US populist tradition but in the British experience. Until recently, UK financial markets (and, for that matter, markets in Australia, Canada and Japan) were characterized by a demarcation between investment banking and commercial banking functions roughly comparable to that prevailing in US markets from the 1930s until the 1990s. Scholars have pointed out that, in the UK, this market structure was the product of tradition and practice rather than legal mandate.[36] If US market structure and regulation reflected a prevailing political ideology that was uniquely American, then it is difficult to explain why the same model could be found in very different national markets.

Of course, the ideological story may still be relevant as an expression of basic American cultural values that have shaped how regulation is legitimized. For example, perhaps Glass-Steagall was not intended by its authors to satisfy populist goals, but it has been portrayed as such – and its subsequent characterization as an attack on Wall Street may have been a deliberate effort by its supporters to attain legitimacy by appealing to widely held populist values. Senator Glass certainly recognized the political appeal of populism; although an opponent of federal deposit insurance, he eventually allowed his legislation to be linked to the House of Representative's popular federal deposit insurance proposal as perhaps the only way to guarantee enactment of his own reform (both became part of the Banking Act of 1933). Likewise, in the long run, public perception of the purposes of Glass-Steagall may be more important than the actual motives of its drafters. If, for example, Glass-Steagall was (incorrectly) viewed as an anti-bigness statute, this might have accounted for public reluctance to tamper with it for so long. Perhaps populists feared that deregulation would result in the re-emergence of the hated 'Money Trust'.

Nevertheless, populism as a core American cultural value is far more malleable, or perhaps less deeply ingrained, than the ideological story presumes. Viewed historically, the US financial industry has undergone succeeding waves of conglomeration and deconglomeration that appear to be driven more by competitive factors than by popular sentiment. In 1983, for example, two US banks ranked within the top ten in the world measured by assets. In 1991, no US bank was in the top ten, but by year end 1997, pending mergers returned two US banks to the ranking, in positions two and five.[37] Given that these shifts occurred within a short period of time, it seems highly unlikely that they reflected any sea change in popular sentiment toward financial conglomeration.

Moreover, if Americans are fearful of financial conglomeration, where was their outrage when huge financial combinations like Citicorp/Travelers and Deutsche/Bankers Trust were announced? How strong was populist sentiment in 1994, when Congress legalized interstate banking after years of opposition from local banks and their populist congressional supporters (such as Senator Huey Long) who argued that large multistate banks are more likely to treat consumers unfairly than the friendly local bank? Finally, and perhaps most curious, what happened to the populist distrust of Wall Street in the late 1990s, when the faith of individual Americans in the stock market was probably greater than their faith in any other national institution?

Finally, if populist sentiment is hostile to financial firms, why, as mentioned earlier, have US financial institutions thrived? This is perhaps the greatest weakness in the populist story, which presumes that financial regulation responded to public demand to limit the power and influence of Wall Street. If so, however, the regulation that was supplied failed completely. US financial firms prospered despite their regulatory burden. Were regulators ineffectual, or were regulated firms just remarkably resilient? At least one answer is provided by the third explanation of US financial regulation.

Regulation as market driven

The market-based account of the origins of financial regulation is difficult to characterize because it does not purport to attribute a specific purpose to the regulatory regime. In fact, this explanation is more concerned with the evolution of markets than with the evolution of regulation, because its premise is that regulation has very little impact on markets. Markets evolve through competition and innovation to arrive at the structure that is most efficient for their participants. To the extent that regulation tries to interfere with that structure, market players find ways around regulatory impediments, making them superfluous. Therefore, US regulation has really had very little to do with determining the structure of US markets. Likewise, deregulation, if it occurs, is unlikely to produce any radical transformation of US financial market structure.

To the extent that this story offers an explanation of US financial regulation, that explanation is economic determinism. Rather than defining financial market structure, regulation is reactive and most successful when it codifies market developments. To the extent that regulation tries to reverse market trends, markets will innovate their way around regulation, forcing regulators to play catch-up to reassert their authority.[38] Eventually, however, regulators must concede defeat, returning to their primary function of codifying market trends. As a result, market innovation that challenges existing regulation is eventually legalized through the political process.

Market-driven stories of regulation view the cataclysm of the 1930s and the subsequent enactment of legislation such as Glass-Steagall completely differently from other regulatory stories. According to the market story, the defining event was neither the legislative bargaining process in 1933 nor populist anger at Wall Street after the stock market crash and banking crisis, but the transformation of financial markets that occurred in the 1920s. Although Louis Brandeis had complained that a bankers' oligopoly had dominated the financial markets of the early 1900s, by the 1920s, the oligopoly had been weakened, not by regulation but by growing competition in the US securities markets. The 1920s witnessed the first substantial individual participation in US securities markets, both directly and through collective investment vehicles such as mutual funds. It also saw the emergence of an active secondary trading market for corporate securities, the development of innovative securities distribution techniques and the restructuring of the financial services industry. Main

Street finally had access to the securities markets and no longer needed to borrow from banks. Banks followed their clients into the securities markets, increasing the competitiveness of the securities underwriting business. Yet despite new entrants, older securities houses like Morgan continued to thrive. Capital flows into US markets were substantial enough to allow for multiple players.[39]

Moreover, in the 1920s, market evolution challenged existing financial regulatory barriers, rapidly rendering them obsolete. At the time, the question whether national banks had legal authority to operate in securities markets was a hotly debated issue, and it is generally assumed that banks placed their securities operations in separate affiliates in order to avoid legal restrictions.[40] By the end of the 1920s, however, any legal barriers to bank entry into securities markets had become irrelevant as regulation lagged behind market change.

As noted earlier, the stock market crash and banking crisis threatened to put an end to the competitiveness of financial markets. Many commercial banks abandoned the securities business, lenders fled to quality and the cost of capital increased. As a result, markets might have returned to their pre-1920s state, dominated by a few financially powerful firms. Or the government might have taken control, nationalizing the banking system and shutting down the securities markets.

In comparison, Glass-Steagall hardly represented a radical restructuring of financial markets. Rather, it was a profoundly conservative solution to the financial crisis, designed to restore the competitiveness of 1930s markets by affording financial institutions an opportunity to regroup and recover. In part, regulation was irrelevant, merely codifying the business decision that most banks had already made to abandon the securities business. To the extent that regulation did affect the business practices of some individual competitors, such as Morgan, the aim was market preservation rather than market restructuring. By splitting Morgan into two powerful competitors operating in separate and competing markets, Glass-Steagall prevented Morgan from using other firms' weakness to reestablish its dominant position in US capital markets and thereby return markets to their pre-1920s state.

Economic determinism also explains what happened to financial regulation decades later, as market evolution put pressure on the regulatory framework. Although for many years banks and securities firms coexisted peacefully and profitably, by the 1970s, the expansion of securities markets once again was encouraging corporate borrowers to bypass the banking industry, threatening the traditional lending business and pressuring banks to follow their clients into the securities markets. As in the 1920s, banks were forced to innovate their way around regulatory barriers, in this case, Glass-Steagall itself. Once market innovation had made Glass-Steagall obsolete and regulators were no longer willing or able to plug the holes that had emerged in the regulatory structure, the stage was set for deregulation to codify market gains.

The market explanation of regulatory evolution is helpful to understanding why US financial institutions, the most heavily regulated in the world, also may be the most innovative. Regulation fosters innovation as firms seek to escape regulatory controls in order to improve their competitive positions. In addition, the market explanation accounts for congressional inaction in the face of apparent defiance by the financial industry, their regulators and judges who tolerated creative readings of regulatory statutes that rendered them ineffectual. The market explanation suggests that, in dynamic markets, regulatory obsolescence is to be expected. Once market evolution is complete, Congress will perform its usual mopping up effort, codifying and rationalizing market developments.

Congressional passivity has a rational explanation. Financial markets are complex and constantly changing, frustrating attempts by the legislature to impose a static structure. Allowing market innovation to occur under the watchful eyes of the regulatory agencies provides useful experimentation before regulatory structure is hardened into law. As a result, regulatory change is less likely to have a radical dislocative effect on markets. Of course, some firms will still have difficulty adjusting to the new financial order, but these firms presumably were inefficient competitors and would have failed even without legal change. Most firms will adjust quickly and accept the legitimacy of the new regulatory regime.

Nevertheless, as regulatory theory, the market story of regulation has several shortcomings. For example, it fails to explain why a particular market structure emerges in the first place. One must simply assume that any market structure that has evolved and stood the test of time must be efficient. (On the other hand, if that structure changes, then presumably the new structure must be even more efficient.) Further, the story begs the question whether notions of market efficiency are culturally bound. For example, if bifurcated US financial structure is most efficient for US markets, is the more unified European structure the most efficient for European markets? If so, are the reasons cultural and historical, or are US and European markets in different stages of development on an identical continuum? The market story cannot answer this except to conclude that, in the US at least, regulation was not the defining factor in market evolution.

Yet regulation may have been key to market evolution because of what it did not do: It did not prevent the growth of active and competitive markets. Economic historians have documented the fundamental shift in financial market structure that occurred in the US between roughly 1910 and 1929 as a bank-dominated financial oligopoly (Brandeis' Money Trust) gave way to highly competitive securities markets. This shift may be characterized as an evolution from bank-dominated finance to market finance, or alternatively, as a devolution of market power from lenders to borrowers. In either case, market structure changed profoundly.

What was the principal catalyst for this change? Some scholars have argued that individual investors made the difference. Individuals had participated in the Liberty Bond campaigns that helped the government to finance World War I and had become accustomed to investing in securities; after the war, these investors were looking for new opportunities for profit. Corporations seeking funds to finance post-war expansion discovered that these investors, often their own employees and customers, were more willing to invest than their traditional pre-war sources of capital. By the mid-1920s, the US public's demand for securities apparently exceeded domestic firms' need for external funding: securities of non-US issuers accounted for almost one-fifth of all new issues in the US.[41]

Initially, this reading of the historical evidence seems consistent with the market story, since it presumes that private demand for investment opportunities (rather than government policy) led to the expansion of the securities market. Nevertheless, the question arises why a similar process did not occur in other bank-dominated national financial markets, such as the German market. One explanation that has been given for the survival of bank-dominated markets in Germany is that the growth of securities markets was actively discouraged by a regulatory environment that imposed special burdens on non-bank finance.[42]

This then raises the question why, in the US, the bankers' oligopoly that had dominated finance in 1910 did not successfully use its political clout to persuade the US Congress to impose regulatory burdens on fledgling securities markets in the early 1920s. Costly regulation might have deterred corporate issuers from using the securities markets and prevented entry into the underwriting business by new competitors such as the commercial banks. Aided by a regulatory environment that was hostile to expansion of the securities markets, the Money Trust might have continued to control all avenues to capital, resulting in a very different financial market structure from that which has prevailed in the US since the 1920s.

Perhaps this effort to turn back the clock would not have succeeded, even with the assistance of regulation. The Money Trust may not have been able to supply sufficient capital by itself to meet the demands of post-war expansion. Regulation might have delayed, but might not have prevented, the opening of US markets. Nevertheless, it is significant that, through the 1920s, no effort was made to use regulation to discourage securities market growth. Moreover, when market structure was regulated, beginning in 1933, the effect was to preserve securities markets from the re-emerging financial oligopoly. As the market story recounts, regulation such as Glass-Steagall that bifurcated the financial industry created new competitors (like the two Morgans) operating in separate and competing markets. In addition, regulation such as the securities disclosure laws aided in the recovery of the securities markets by improving the transparency and liquidity of securities investments. Thus, regulation was not irrelevant. The decision to regulate, or not to regulate, was more influential in setting the course for financial market evolution than the market story admits.

Further, although the market story discounts the impact of regulation, even the minor function that the story assigns to the regulatory process may be anything but benign. According to the market story, regulation encourages innovation as regulated firms try to evade regulatory restraints. Yet regulatory-driven innovation may have some significant costs if it imposes an additional level of complexity on financial products that responds solely to the need to escape regulation. This raises the question whether, without the need for regulatory avoidance, certain financial innovations that are common in the US would have succeeded. For example, money market mutual funds were developed in order to avoid regulation that restricted deposit-taking to licensed banks and imposed limits on the interest that banks could pay retail depositors. As interest rates rose in the 1970s, these funds allowed non-bank securities firms to compete successfully for bank deposits. Without the twin pressures of rising interest rates and bank regulation, however, it is unclear whether money market mutual funds would have gained market acceptance.

Finally, although the market story of regulation assumes that market change leads to regulatory change, the time frame for this evolution is unclear. By the 1980s, for example, US financial market structure had already changed radically, yet regulatory reform did not follow for years. It is unclear why this was so, or how it may have affected market evolution. Did the slow pace of regulatory reform interfere with the movement of financial markets to a more efficient structure? Or is the lesson of the market story that regulation is so irrelevant that regulatory reform, or lack thereof, has little or no impact on the growth of US financial markets? This raises a fundamental question posed by attempts at regulatory explanation: how much does regulation really matter?

The normative power of regulatory explanation

As previously noted, the explanations that US observers offer for their own financial regulation reflect their normative judgments about the efficacy and desirability of that regulation. It is no accident that all three explanations of financial regulation that have dominated modern scholarship are, in their own ways, regulatory critiques. In the late twentieth century, the legitimacy and desirability of the US regulatory structure was undergoing the most serious re-examination perhaps since Glass-Steagall was adopted in 1933, and regulatory explanation reflected this introspection. Nevertheless, what is more revealing about regulatory explanations is where they part company. Their differences reflect an ongoing and fundamental disagreement in the US about the nature of the financial regulatory process that may explain some of the contradictions that are apparent in the US regulatory system.

As previously described, both political and ideological explanations delegitimize financial regulation by questioning its motives. The political explanation rejects any public-regarding purpose for regulation, instead attributing regulatory outcomes to private interest group bargaining. Although the ideological explanation allows that widely shared cultural values may account for regulation, it suggests that rhetoric that draws on ideological prejudices, such as populist fear of Wall Street, may be used to justify regulatory outcomes that are inefficient and based on erroneous assumptions about markets or economics. Thus, populist financial regulation may, in the name of preventing monopoly, hinder competition in financial markets.

Although both explanations provide a theoretical basis for attacking the legitimacy of existing regulation, both assume that regulation matters. Regulation, whether the product of private interest group bargaining or populist ideology, has shaped financial industry structure and remains of key importance to the future of US financial markets. Thus, it is not surprising that political and ideological explanations appeal to lawyers and others who believe that it is essential that deregulation takes place through the political process in order to preserve the competitive positions of US financial institutions in global markets. Moreover, regulatory explanation plays a key role in the reform process. To the extent that the longevity of regulatory schemes reflects either the residual power of interest groups or the lingering appeal of ideological prejudice, these forces can best be overcome by scholarly elucidation of the questionable origins of regulation. Once these origins are fully understood, an enlightened public consensus in favor of reform may be achieved.

In contrast, the market explanation, although also critical of existing regulation, views its impact as relatively benign, since market developments are more important than political developments in determining the competitiveness of the US financial industry. This may increase the appeal of the market explanation to bankers and other market participants who are more concerned with developing new products than with lobbying Congress for financial reform. These players suspect that markets will continue to outpace regulation, and that, regardless of what policymakers do, forces such as global competition and technological development will continue to drive markets.

Nevertheless, this difference in outlook among critics of regulation may produce its own form of political gridlock, which in turn may account for the apparent lack of urgency about financial reform that characterized the US for so many decades. The standard explanation for the failure of the US Congress to act to repeal Glass-Steagall when its legitimacy was first called into question in the 1970s and 1980s was that regulatory critics differed as to the precise form that deregulation should take. Yet this inability to reach some acceptable compromise as to details seemed to belie the claim, made by many parties, that some regulatory reform was essential in order to save US financial institutions from competitive ruin.

The problem may have been that, for those reformers who believed that regulation matters, the precise form that deregulation took was as important as the fact of deregulation itself. At the same time, for those reformers who believed that regulation does not matter, there was no reason to invest resources to support one alternative over another when financial institutions could always continue to innovate around regulatory barriers. The result, for the regulatory reform process, was continued disagreement over how to construct legislation that would have both legitimacy and market significance. Although, in the case of Glass-Steagall, a consensus may have been reached, the same disagreement is likely to complicate future attempts at regulatory reform.

Finding common ground

Despite their differences, the divergent stories of regulation that dominate today's discussion of financial reform do share some themes that may help to reconcile otherwise conflicting accounts of regulatory origins. One similarity in all three stories is the premise that financial markets should remain unregulated absent a compelling public-regarding justification for intervention. This may seem obvious, but it is not so clear why it should be. In the 1930s, for example, nationalization of the US banking system was seriously considered by at least some reformers. From time to time, suggestions have been made for turning at least the retail banking function into a public or a not-for-profit business as the best way to ensure the protection of deposits or the money supply. Yet these proposals ultimately have been rejected and the preference for free financial markets has prevailed. This preference, in turn, shapes public debate over financial regulation. The question underlying all regulatory explanations is whether the goals of regulation, which vary from story to story, provide a sufficient reason to overcome the presumption that competitive markets best serve the public interest.

In addition, all three explanations depend in their own way on the assumption that dynamic competition produces regulatory change. In the political story, competing interest groups shape regulatory outcomes, but in a pluralistic society the possibility always exists that regulatory bargains will be renegotiated as interest group preferences shift and new coalitions are formed. In the ideological story, the populist vision dominates, but approaches to the problem of conglomeration may change as different economic theories compete to capture the public imagination. In the market story, competition occurs between market participants and regulators, creating innovation and ultimately regulatory change. Thus, the notion of regulation as at least somewhat responsive to competitive forces does seem to inform all views of the regulatory process.

Finally, all three explanations presume that regulatory change requires some sort of legitimation in order to succeed. The political story asserts that private interest group bargains are made to be undone; it defends the regulatory and judicial assaults on Glass-Steagall that occurred in the

1980s and 1990s on the ground that regulation that promotes private rather than public interests lacks legitimacy and should be construed narrowly. The ideological story presumes that regulatory programs require some grounding in widely held public or cultural values in order to survive. And the market story claims that regulatory legitimation demands that innovations be tested in the field and accepted by the markets before being codified into law.

Do these three themes contribute to our understanding of US financial regulation, or do they simply raise new questions about the US regulatory regime? For example, in a regulatory environment in which the overwhelming preference is for free markets and the regulatory status quo is subject to constant competitive challenge, how does any regulation achieve the legitimacy that is essential to its survival? Put another way, when does regulation matter?

The answer may be simpler than past regulatory explanations would suggest. Regulation matters to US financial markets, their regulators and their participants to the extent that it facilitates fair play on a level playing field. As the Introduction suggested, the ideal of a level playing field has had considerable rhetorical power in the recent debate over financial regulatory reform, providing a metaphor for certain standards of competitive fairness that are widely shared in US financial markets. Moreover, as a historical matter, these standards have remained relatively constant, even as their expression through specific regulatory programs has altered. Thus, reference to this fairness quotient as the source of regulatory legitimacy may offer a new way to look at both the goals of US financial regulation and the process of financial regulatory evolution that, by the end of the twentieth century, was producing changes in US financial regulatory structure.

How may regulation contribute to fair play on a level playing field? Consider, for example, a relatively rare case of financial *re*regulation that took place in the early 1990s involving the deposit brokerage business. Deposit brokerage was a financial market innovation of the 1980s that began when brokers, often representatives of large Wall Street securities firms, began to assist large investors to split their deposits into fully insured pieces that could be placed with multiple banks located anywhere in the US. Investors could rest assured that, although their total investment in deposits far exceeded $100 000, their exposure to any single bank would fall within the $100 000 insurance limit.

At the time, US policymakers appeared remarkably reluctant to halt any financial market innovation even when that innovation was designed to evade regulation (for example, Congress had ignored the securities industry's complaints about bank securities affiliates and the banking industry's complaints about money market mutual funds although both innovations circumvented Glass-Steagall). Yet, in this case, Congress acted with unusual rapidity to discourage deposit brokerage on the ground that it amounted to a willful evasion of the deposit insurance ceiling. In doing so, Congress even resorted to a regulatory strategy that it had rejected a decade earlier, imposing new interest rate ceilings on brokered deposits.[43]

Why in this instance were policymakers able to reach a consensus for regulatory change when in so many other areas, notably Glass-Steagall reform, consensus proved so elusive for so long? At the time, the economic case against deposit brokerage was not universally accepted. Although some experts complained that brokered deposits were permitting financially troubled banks to attract funds nationally when they had exhausted their local deposit base, others, including Federal Reserve Board Chairman Alan Greenspan, argued that, on balance, brokered deposits could strengthen the banking industry, enhancing liquidity and facilitating the efficient flow of funds.[44]

Moreover, the decision to regulate deposit brokerage did not fit any of the traditional explanations of the US regulatory process. Neither banks nor securities firms as a group appeared to benefit from the imposition of regulatory burdens on the deposit brokerage business. The regulation had no obvious appeal to populist opponents of banks and probably disadvantaged many small local institutions that had relied upon brokers to gain access to wholesale deposit markets. Finally, the regulation did not codify market evolution but actually halted innovation and free competition in deposit markets.

So what was the source of support for regulation of brokered deposits? The common concern may have been one of simple fairness. Most participants in financial markets probably would have agreed that the real problem associated with deposit brokerage was the extension of the deposit insurance subsidy to large, and largely undeserving, wholesale depositors. Deposit brokerage permitted these sophisticated depositors to convert what otherwise would be risky investments into fully insured deposits, allowing them to enjoy the same insurance protection as the small investors who were the intended beneficiaries of the deposit insurance program. The perception that deposit brokerage was allowing large depositors unfairly to exploit the deposit insurance subsidy may have overcome policymakers' natural reluctance to intervene in free markets.

Another basic rule of fairness may have been violated by deposit brokerage. Although deposit brokerage was the product of competitive market innovation, it did not necessarily contribute to competitive equity among capital-seeking firms. In competitive wholesale money markets, weaker banks ordinarily must pay premiums for large wholesale deposits that reflect the degree of risk associated with the investment. Although above market rates may appeal to certain depositors, at some point the degree of risk associated with investment in the weakest banks should eventually deter all but the most risk-averse depositors. Deposit brokerage allowed the weakest banks to promise high rates plus government protection in the event of failure, giving them an unfair advantage in funding markets over more prudent banks. Thus, regulation of brokered deposits was needed to correct the competitive imbalance that existed in wholesale deposit markets by virtue of weak banks' exploitation of the deposit insurance guarantee.

As subsequent chapters describe in greater detail, much of US financial regulation may be explained by reference to these and other basic notions of fair play on a level playing field. At times, concern for competitive fairness has legitimized forms of regulatory intervention in financial markets that must appear surprisingly intrusive to outside observers. Historically, Glass-Steagall comes to mind; more recently, as Glass-Steagall has been dismantled, new financial consumer protection rules have proliferated even as US policymakers have promised to deregulate financial product markets. At other times, concern for competitive fairness has been the excuse for the failure of the US government to intervene in situations in which other regulatory regimes might have taken a more active approach, such as government subsidization of financial technologies. In both cases, regulatory policy is rooted in the peculiar notion of fairness that provides US financial regulation with its legitimacy among financial market participants. Understanding this fairness quotient, and how it historically has shaped attitudes toward the US financial regulatory process, is essential to appreciating the ways in financial regulation continues to matter very much to US markets, their regulators and their players.

2
Is Regulation Beneficial?

When do regulatory subsidies become regulatory burdens? That question is central to the debate over financial regulatory reform in the US. The prevailing wisdom among advocates of deregulation is that US financial regulation, although in many cases originating as subsidy, now imposes significant burdens on US financial institutions that have disadvantaged them when competing in global markets. For example, US regulation has kept financial firms small and specialized in a world in which diversified universal banks dominate; as a result, many US financial institutions may lack the size necessary to compete in global markets. US financial firms have proved skillful at using innovative legal structures to evade regulatory restrictions, but the high transactions costs associated with this strategy eventually may take their toll on the US financial industry, injuring its competitive position.

The logic of this argument appears to offer an irrefutable case for radical financial deregulation. Nevertheless, one of the defining characteristics of late twentieth century US financial markets was the frustratingly slow pace of regulatory reform, especially at the national congressional level. Although financial markets were experiencing rapid and profound transformation, fueled by the economic dislocation of the 1970s, the restructuring movement of the 1980s and the industry consolidation of the 1990s, regulatory transformation lagged behind, fueled more often by agency reinterpretation of old statutes than by bold new legislative initiatives. Even Glass-Steagall, although thoroughly discredited, continued to maintain legal barriers between banking and securities markets during much of the 1990s. And other traditional elements of the US financial regulatory scheme, such as the virtually total separation of banking and commerce, remained intact.

Yet another defining characteristic of late twentieth century US financial markets was the vitality of the US financial industry. Despite their regulatory burden, US financial firms prospered. In fact, US financial institutions were widely viewed as better positioned to succeed in global financial competition than their less regulated rivals.[1] This was not just the opinion of the US financial press, which might be expected to favor the prospects of domestic firms. Non-US observers apparently agreed: a 1993 survey of global capital market users ranked US firms at the top of global investment banks in trading, underwriting and advisory services.[2]

Given the success of US financial firms, competitors may have wondered whether US financial markets were in urgent need of deregulation after all. This raises an important but often overlooked question about the nature of regulatory burden and subsidy: was there a link between the slow pace of financial regulatory reform in the US and the relative strength of US financial firms in global markets? If there was a connection, then the conventional wisdom in the US that regulatory subsidies have become regulatory burdens may not be entirely correct, a possibility that may explain why US financial institutions did not try harder and earlier to achieve the repeal of supposedly burdensome regulatory statutes such as Glass-Steagall.

Regulation and the theory of equal starts

As was suggested in Chapter 1, the legitimacy of US financial regulation may be measured by its contribution to promoting fair play on a level playing field. As recent scholarly critiques of regulation make clear, the philosophical preference of US market participants is for open and competitive markets subject to as little government interference as possible. Yet the practice in US financial markets has been for participants to accept significant regulatory burdens and subsidies that affect the starting positions of financial competitors. What explains this contradiction? The answer may be found in the peculiar American conception of competitive fairness. On a level playing field, fairness requires that all competitors enjoy an equal start. Regulatory intervention, in the form of burden and subsidy, is tolerated insofar as it guarantees this equal starting position to all players.

Why is equality of starting position so important to US markets? Equal starts provide competitive markets with their legitimacy, thereby eliminating the need, and public demand, for government regulation of the competitive process itself. So long as every player has an equal opportunity to participate in competitive markets, the results of unfettered competition are more likely to be accepted. The market will be allowed to pick the winners and losers without the necessity for government intervention to ensure a fair outcome.

This commitment to equal starts informs social as well as economic philosophy in the US; as a political matter, it explains why government policy that aims to eliminate competitive inequalities, whether in markets or in society at large, tends to be more successful than government policy that seeks to predetermine the results of competition. Government intervention to ensure equal starts promotes fair competition; in contrast, government intervention to ensure equal outcomes is antithetical to competitive fairness. This distinction is particularly important in the sphere of business regulation, where the goal of ensuring equal starts finds expression in a variety of regulatory programs. For example, through the antitrust laws, the government seeks to discourage anticompetitive behavior, such as the exploitation of monopoly power, by which one competitor gains an unfair starting advantage over its rivals. Likewise, the government has sought to eliminate insider trading in US securities markets in order to prevent one investor from exploiting an informational advantage to earn higher trading profits than less informed investors. In both cases, regulatory intervention in free markets is justified as necessary to equalize the players' starting positions and thereby ensure that competition proceeds on a level playing field.

When implemented through specific regulation, the goal of equal starts has had its critics. For example, both scholars and policymakers have recognized that informational asymmetries in securities trading markets are inevitable and are not always undesirable. A flat rule of equal information that prohibited all securities trades made on the basis of superior knowledge would itself be unfair if, for example, it denied analysts and other market professionals (and their paying clients) the opportunity to profit from their own investments in research and analysis.

Nevertheless, critics of insider trading law probably would not deny that equal starts may be a legitimate regulatory goal, but would simply point out that guaranteeing market players an equal starting position does not necessarily mean that their starting positions must be identical. How equality should be defined in the context of market competition is a very difficult question that elicits very different responses from different players, which explains why US policymakers often take so long to build a consensus for regulatory reform. Yet, as an expression of the values that inform and legitimate the regulation of markets, the ideal of equal starts has considerable resonance and is embraced to some extent by most policymakers and market participants. Put another way, regulatory intervention in markets is more likely to be regarded as legitimate when it arrives at a balance of burden and subsidy that, in the eyes of market participants, ensures that all competitors are starting equally on a level playing field.

Regulatory handicapping in financial markets

Perhaps nowhere is the legitimacy of regulatory handicapping as well accepted as in the domain of regulation of financial institutions. This may reflect a sense in the US that financial markets are different from other markets, and more vulnerable to competitive inequalities that require regulatory handicapping. Certainly, the significant level of individual participation in US financial markets may justify more active regulatory intervention to ensure equal starts than in markets in which the players appear more equally matched. Nevertheless, regulatory handicapping in US financial markets goes far beyond protection of individual investors and affects virtually every player, including the most sophisticated of market participants.

An alternative explanation of the widespread acceptance of regulatory handicapping in financial markets is that the US government's participation in those markets, especially the implementation of national monetary policy through the private financial sector, produces competitive inequalities that must be eliminated in order to level the playing field. For example, federal insurance of bank deposits, although considered necessary to promote monetary stability, has the unintended effect of subsidizing the private banking industry by giving banks a funding advantage over rival financial firms that do not have access to insured deposits. As is detailed in Chapter 3, this implicit regulatory subsidy has justified the imposition of special regulatory handicaps on the banking industry that are not imposed on rival financial firms.

Although deposit insurance is perhaps the most obvious case, regulatory handicapping provides a useful way to understand the complex balance of burden and subsidy that characterizes most US financial regulation. For example, when viewed as regulatory handicapping, the goals of Glass-Steagall become more focused and more comprehensible than traditional theories of regulation reviewed in Chapter 1 would admit. Was Glass-Steagall a subsidy to the financial industry or a burden on Wall Street? Regulatory handicapping suggests that most likely it was both, confining banks and securities firms to their own markets but also protecting them from competitive threat from their rivals. Moreover, regulatory handicapping accounts for Glass-Steagall's original legitimization and its ultimate delegitimization. The balance of subsidy and burden created by Glass-Steagall produced an equilibrium that remained relatively stable for many decades until, eventually, market evolution turned subsidy into burden, upsetting the balance and creating pressure for rehandicapping.

Of course, even in 1933, not all players in US financial markets immediately embraced Glass-Steagall's allocation of burden and subsidy as creating a perfectly level playing field. Private banks like Morgan that were forced to chose between deposit banking and investment banking probably found regulation more burdensome than commercial banks like Chase that had voluntarily abandoned the securities business. As early as 1935, Congress considered amending Glass-Steagall to ease the regulatory burdens on both banks and securities firms, although in the end neither reform proposal became law.[3]

Yet, gradually, regulatory handicapping did gain legitimacy, a process that was accelerated by some important early compromises that re-adjusted regulatory burdens in ways that made them more tolerable for both rival industries. For example, Glass-Steagall sought to bar banks from the securities business, but banks had always been major players in government securities markets. Removing banks from these markets would have eliminated a significant profit source and potentially threatened the liquidity of the government securities markets. So Glass-Steagall incorporated an exception that allowed banks to continue to invest and deal in government securities. Likewise, securities firms had traditionally used cash credit balances in customers' brokerage accounts to maintain securities positions, to fund margin loans and for other general corporate purposes. If credit balances were treated as 'deposits' that could no longer be 'received' by securities firms, the negative impact on the securities industry and securities markets would have been substantial. So securities firms were allowed to keep their credit balances, but they agreed not to compete with banks by offering higher rates of interest on credit balances than the comparable rates on bank deposits.[4] These accommodations helped to maintain a regulatory equilibrium that was acceptable to both industries and preserved the statute from attack.

Regulatory equilibrium was also maintained because, for many decades, the dual market structure created by Glass-Steagall worked to the advantage of both the banking and the securities industries.

Obviously, the two markets were not at all times equally profitable. But the markets were sufficiently different, and self-contained, that the regulatory subsidy provided by entry barriers apparently outweighed the regulatory burden created by diversification restrictions. For at least four decades, both industries apparently were content to honor what some scholars have called the 'informal live-and-let-live compact ... that had evolved as an implementation of – and a complement to – the reform legislation of the 1930s'.[5]

By the 1970s, however, markets were changing, implicating both the banking and the securities industries. High inflation, rising interest rates and altered investment patterns adversely affected both businesses, albeit in different ways. Banks were squeezed by regulation restricting the maximum interest rates that they could pay on their deposits. As bank depositors defected to higher yielding investments, a new term, 'disintermediation', entered the public lexicon. At the same time, on the asset side of their balance sheets, banks were threatened by the loss of their corporate borrowers to the commercial paper and short-term debt markets. But securities firms were experiencing problems of their own as high interest rates caused a decline in stock and bond prices and brokerage profits fell. In response, both industries began to look for new revenue sources. To the extent that regulation interfered, some adjustment of regulatory burden took place, either through industry innovations that exploited regulatory loopholes, such as the development by securities firms of the money market mutual fund to compete with bank deposits, or through regulatory reinterpretation of statutory prohibitions, such as the Federal Reserve's Section 20 decisions that allowed banks to establish limited-purpose securities affiliates.[6]

Still another market change that affected all segments of the US financial industry was the growing competitive challenge from non-US financial firms as financial markets became globalized. In theory, globalization should have altered the stakes for US financial firms that already were engaged in internecine warfare to preserve and extend their own market boundaries. Glass-Steagall did not just burden US financial firms competing in domestic markets; it also burdened US firms competing in global markets with non-US rivals, most of which were free under their own national laws to engage in universal banking.

Thus, the handicapping function of Glass-Steagall, and of US financial regulation generally, came to have implications not only for domestic financial competition but for global financial competition as well. In the 1930s, policymakers probably did not contemplate the integration of international financial markets when they attempted to design a level playing field for US financial competitors. By the 1990s, however, the relevant playing field had expanded, and US firms faced a formidable new opponent, the giant universal bank. The presence of this new player might have been expected to lead individual financial firms to reassess their positions on regulatory handicapping. Although banks and securities firms probably disagreed over how regulatory handicaps should be reallocated between their two industries, they were likely to concur that, in competing with non-US firms, all US firms were unfairly burdened. Regulatory cartelization, although perhaps workable in purely domestic markets as a way to achieve competitive equality, disadvantaged US financial institutions confronting a competitive challenge from unregulated non-US rivals.

Simply put, globalization might have been expected to encourage US financial firms to abandon domestic turf wars and arrive at a consensus in favor of rapid deregulation. That, as of the 1990s, the US was virtually alone among industrialized nations in severely restricting permissible bank powers was a cause for considerable concern among policymakers, bankers and scholars. Two elements of the US regulatory system were thought to put US financial institutions at a special disadvantage. First, regulatory cartelization had kept US financial institutions relatively small. Through most of the 1990s, no US bank ranked among the top ten in the world in asset value,[7] giving rise to fears that no US firm would have the size necessary to compete with global megabanks. Second, regulatory compliance imposed significant costs on US financial institutions. Although in domestic markets every competitor faced high compliance costs, the compliance burden was expected to emerge as a significant factor in global competition, putting US firms at a disadvantage.

These concerns suggest that US firms would have been wise to join forces early on to lobby for rapid and radical deregulation of US financial markets. Such a joint effort might have been expected to influence policymakers motivated either by the desire to please the powerful financial lobby or by the fear of a decline in US influence in international financial markets. Certainly, by the 1990s, most financial regulators were calling for deregulation, and a powerful coalition of large banks and securities firms had emerged in support of financial reform. Even Citigroup, which in its earlier incarnation as Citicorp had opposed pending legislation to repeal Glass-Steagall, had a change of heart once Citicorp's merger with Travelers converted what had been a regulatory subsidy into a regulatory burden.[8]

Nevertheless, despite these forces in favor of deregulation, through most of the 1990s, the pace of regulatory reform in the US did not accelerate significantly. Even Glass-Steagall, whose demise had been confidently predicted since at least the 1980s, survived until 1999, far longer than most critics thought possible. What stymied regulatory reform? Most observers blamed ongoing domestic turf wars among financial institutions and among their regulators who could not agree on a single plan for financial modernization. Splits occurred between large and small financial firms, between proponents of the bank holding company structure and proponents of the unitary bank structure, between banks desiring to become securities underwriters and banks desiring to become insurance underwriters. Everyone wanted deregulation, but no one could agree on its ideal form. How the new US universal bank should be structured and who should regulate it were the questions that divided financial market participants through the 1990s.

In retrospect, it seems puzzling that these seemingly minor disagreements proved so hard to resolve. If, as critics contended, the regulatory burden was rapidly eroding the competitive position of the US financial industry, then quick triage was needed. Financial firms and their regulators, confronted with an international competitive challenge, could no longer afford to quibble over details. In global financial warfare, presumably, any deregulation was better than the status quo.

The explanation of the seemingly slow pace of financial deregulation in the US requires a return to the question asked at the beginning of this chapter: when do regulatory subsidies become regulatory burdens? Although it has long been assumed that, in global competition, US financial regulation has been a significant handicap for US firms, this may not be the case. US financial regulation, even Glass-Steagall, may have provided some lingering subsidy to US firms embarking on global financial competition, a subsidy that continued to be significant in global markets long after it had disappeared from domestic markets. So long as regulatory subsidies retained some value for US firms in the global marketplace, US firms had little reason to object to the slow pace of regulatory reform. In fact, US firms probably benefited from a gradual reform process that succeeded in reducing regulatory burdens in domestic markets in ways that preserved the regulatory subsidy enjoyed by US firms in global competition.

Moreover, through the 1990s, US firms and policymakers remained convinced that at least some regulatory subsidy was still necessary to overcome the competitive disadvantages that US financial firms faced in global markets as a result of their significant regulatory burden. If this argument sounds a bit circular, it may be, but it illustrates the profound significance of the handicapping function of US financial regulation. Regulation retains its legitimacy so long as market participants perceive that the subsidies and burdens that it creates are necessary to compensate for competitive inequalities that affect the players' starting positions. In this case, special subsidization of US institutions and special burdening of non-US institutions were viewed, at least by US market participants, as a way to maintain a level playing field in global financial markets.

Did US financial players really need this special subsidy? Did unregulated non-US universal banks really enjoy a competitive edge over US firms, either in their own domestic markets or in US markets? If so, what explains the apparent success of US financial players in global competition in the 1990s? These questions suggest the difficulty confronting policymakers who are required to decide when regulatory subsidies actually become regulatory burdens, requiring rehandicapping through the regulatory reform process.

Regulatory subsidy and global competitiveness

In theory, the transformation of regulatory subsidy into regulatory burden should have several discernable consequences for financial markets. First, the competitive positions of one or more players should suffer as regulation begins to interfere with profitability and growth. Second, those players that are disadvantaged should recognize that the playing field is no longer level and call for a reallocation of regulatory handicaps to reflect their changed circumstances. These two developments were evident in US financial markets beginning in the 1970s as banks and securities firms, facing declining profitability in their protected markets, complained that the regulatory subsidies created by Glass-Steagall had become burdens. As a result, Glass-Steagall lost its legitimacy, paving the way for reform.

Theoretically, the integration of international financial markets should have exacerbated the competitive problems of US financial firms. Hobbled by an unequal regulatory burden, US firms should have experienced difficulty competing with their less regulated rivals, particularly large universal banks. Yet, surprisingly, US firms did not appear to suffer in international competition. To the contrary, they were competing in global financial markets from a position of strength. Perhaps they were simply lucky. In the 1990s, the US economy was strong relative to other industrialized nations and

US financial markets continued to thrive. Nevertheless, it is significant that the US regulatory burden apparently did not operate as much of a drag on US financial markets or US financial institutions. In fact, there are reasons to believe that regulation may have even contributed to their success.

Certainly, US financial regulation prevented US financial institutions from reaching the size of their universal banking rivals (although, by the late 1990s, US firms were catching up at a surprisingly rapid pace). Nevertheless, in the 1990s, many observers were concluding that, contrary to conventional wisdom, size, at least when measured by assets, was not key to success in global financial markets.[9] When rankings were made on the basis of market value, US financial firms scored consistently high. As of 30 September 1998, measured by global market value, US firms held the top three positions; of the top 100 firms, 44 were US financial institutions.[10]

Moreover, between 1987 and 1996, despite their regulatory burden, US financial institutions led the world in revenues, profits and shareholder returns. During this period, returns to shareholders of US financial firms grew at a rate of 11.3 percent per year. The next strongest performers were UK firms, with an annual growth rate of 10.4 percent. In contrast, firms from nations with traditional universal banking structures lagged far behind.[11]

That US institutions were highly profitable despite their relatively small size may not have been accidental. Asset growth may actually be a liability unless new assets can be employed profitably. And, although conventional wisdom suggests that universal banks benefit from the ability to diversify, too much diversification may increase operational risk. Managers may be unable to monitor risk-taking adequately or to exploit synergies to their fullest potential. Worse, they may be tempted to use earnings from profitable activities to subsidize losing businesses. And worst of all, diversification may be motivated by 'empire building' on the part of managers who pursue costly and ultimately unprofitable acquisition strategies.

In the US, the costs and benefits of corporate diversification have long been the subject of lively academic debate. Some scholars argue that the beneficial discipline imposed by competitive capital markets should be sufficient to deter managers from making diversification 'mistakes' like inefficient empire building. Nevertheless, market discipline tends to be ex post rather than ex ante. Capital suppliers have occasionally penalized inefficiently diversified commercial conglomerates, but market discipline did not prevent their formation in the first place. Ironically, in financial markets, regulation that restricted opportunities to diversify may have saved some financial firms from succumbing to the temptation to build inefficient conglomerates that they eventually would have been forced to dismantle.

Finally, asset size may be an advantage principally in financial markets that depend primarily on domestic bank credit. The rise of the European universal bank in the nineteenth century has been associated with deliberate government policy that encouraged the growth of large banks that could finance domestic industry, freeing companies from reliance on foreign capital and foreign control.[12] Ownership links between financial and industrial concerns ensured a steady flow of credit to business as well as mutual support in the event of financial crisis. Now that global financial markets are becoming more integrated, however, financial opportunities are increasing for both capital users and capital suppliers. Given the array of available financial products and financing techniques, borrowers no longer must rely on a single bank for financing. When borrowers are able and willing to employ multiple financial service providers, financial firms may not need to maintain sufficient size and capacity to satisfy all of their large clients' financial needs.

This trend in global financial markets is often described as a shift from bank-dominated finance to securities finance, but another way to characterize the change is to view it as a transition from relationship-based markets to transaction-based markets. As capital flows freely across national borders to find its highest valued use, long-term financial relationships are simply less important, resulting in a sea change in the business of financial intermediation. Once capital-seeking firms have the option of selecting the most efficient financing technique, financial firms must compete on the basis of superior skills and products rather than their ability to maintain stable alliances with client firms.

Interestingly, in the US, domestic financial markets underwent a similar metamorphosis in the 1920s, when the growth of securities markets challenged traditional capital raising techniques. Before World War 1, domestic capital shortages allowed a small group of financial firms that could tap foreign capital to function as gate-keepers to the financial markets, using their control of funding sources as a way to sell other financial products to a stable client base. Adolf Berle, who later become famous for documenting the separation between ownership and control in the modern American corporation, described private banks like Morgan as occupying the center of a 'web of economic interests' that bound businesses that relied on external sources of capital to their bank, which provided for all of their financial needs.[13]

By the 1920s, however, US financial markets were changing. The expansion of domestic funds available for investment in securities, in many cases in the form of individuals' savings, allowed corporations to break stable banking relationships and to turn to the securities markets to raise funds. The new-found ability of business borrowers to escape from their web of economic interests led to the emergence of the modern US corporation that, as Adolf Berle described in 1932, was no longer defined by its ties to a single powerful financial institution.[14] The growth of US securities markets in the 1920s was a profoundly important development in the history of US finance, and US financial institutions were forced to learn to adapt. Their decades of experience with operating in competitive capital markets probably put them ahead of their universal banking counterparts in understanding and adapting to the increasingly competitive and increasingly securitized global financial markets that were emerging in the late 1990s.

Moreover, US regulation contributed to their ability to adapt. In 1933, Glass-Steagall, by bifurcating financial markets, prevented the securities markets, devastated by the stock market crash of 1929, from returning to their moribund pre-1920s condition, when they were easily dominated by a few private banks like Morgan. Breaking up Morgan ensured that two strong competitors would henceforth operate in two competing markets.[15] Mandatory securities disclosure regulation, adopted in 1933 and 1934, restored investors' confidence in securities markets by improving the transparency of securities investments, while, in banking markets, federal insurance of deposits allowed banks to regain the public's trust in the safety of bank deposits, ensuring the return to the banking system of small savings that could be used for lending. Thus, US regulation played a role both in restoring financial markets to health and in maintaining competition between those markets.

That regulation facilitated the growth of active and highly competitive financial markets explains a contradiction that may puzzle non-US observers: US financial institutions are the most heavily regulated in the world, but US financial markets are highly competitive and largely unrestricted, particularly compared with rival national financial markets. This pattern reflects the regulatory philosophy, described at the start of this chapter, that views the proper role of regulation as guaranteeing competitors equal starting positions so that, in the ensuing competition, government can adopt a hands-off attitude, allowing free markets to determine competitive outcomes. This approach characterized the regulation of the 1930s, which served the dual goals of preserving competitive financial markets and handicapping the players to ensure that markets would remain competitive.

Regulation also encouraged financial firms to adopt survival strategies that have positioned them well for global competition. For example, most observers agree that US markets and financial institutions are characterized by a high degree of specialization and innovation. Scholars argue that the link between specialization and innovation is not coincidental. Financial innovation is generally associated with the introduction of new financing techniques, usually through the securities markets, that challenge traditional financial intermediation. In oligopolistic financial markets dominated by universal banks, however, incentives to innovate are weak because universal banks must be concerned about the competitive impact of innovation on their traditional financial products. Unless anticipated revenues from innovation exceed anticipated losses on the sale of existing bank products, the universal bank will not invest in innovation. The opposite is true in specialized financial markets where financial firms rely on innovation to lure customers away from other specialized financial firms.[16]

Applied to US financial markets, this argument suggests that specialized financial firms had strong incentives to innovate in order to entice customers to cross the market boundaries created by regulation. Securities firms developed deposit substitutes, commercial banks developed insurance substitutes and so on. Had financial conglomeration been permitted, this product innovation would have been less likely to occur because a universal bank would have less incentive to develop new products that would compete directly with existing profit sources.

Another piece must be added to the puzzle in order fully to explain incentives for innovation. Certainly, regulation that bifurcated financial markets set the stage for competition between markets. Nevertheless, other financial regulation gave US financial firms a reason to engage in cross-market rivalry. Without this regulatory impetus, managers of specialized financial institutions may not have felt the need to expand their customer base through constant innovation. For example, by virtue of deposit insurance, the banking industry enjoyed a stable, low-cost source of funds that it could invest conservatively (for example, buying a portfolio of government securities) yet still cover interest expense and other charges. Because regulation also limited entry into the banking business and imposed ceilings on the rates of interest payable on retail deposits, banks were protected from competitive challenge. Why, then, would the banking industry feel the need to increase returns (and risks) by innovating?

At least prior to the 1970s, critics did accuse the banking industry of lacking creativity and the will to innovate.[17] Perhaps only the crisis produced by rising interest rates in the 1970s, which caused even retail depositors to defect to higher yielding investments and led to the removal of deposit interest rate ceilings, aroused bank managers from their lethargy. Nevertheless, financial institutions did face affirmative regulatory pressure to improve their profitability. Because regulation discouraged the formation of large financial–industrial conglomerates, most financial firms were forced to rely on the competitive capital markets, particularly the equity markets, for at least some of their funding. Interestingly, the banking industry, which enjoyed access to subsidized deposits, experienced the most intense regulatory pressure to submit itself to market discipline. Alliances between banks and commercial firms that might have provided banks with a stable source of capital were forbidden, and, beginning in the 1980s, banks were subjected to minimum capital requirements that compelled them to increase their equity levels. This forced reliance on outside capital, particularly capital supplied by the equity markets, is significant because, in theory at least, equity holders will require managers to maximize profits, encouraging competition and innovation.[18]

Moreover, deposit insurance, although providing banks with a subsidized funding source, was actually designed to encourage banks to take more risks. After the banking crisis of the early 1930s, banks appeared eager to abandon not just the securities business but also the lending business, preferring the safety of the government securities markets. Giving banks a stable and inexpensive funding source, deposit insurance, its supporters hoped, would allow the banking industry to lend more freely to private borrowers, thereby speeding economic recovery.[19]

Years later, this consequence of subsidizing deposits came to be regarded less favorably by policymakers who feared that banks were taking too many risks in their lending business. Moreover, by the 1970s, rising interest rates and competition from money market mutual funds (a deposit substitute developed by the securities industry) had reduced the significance of insured deposits as a funding source for many banks. Regulators then began to rely increasingly on capital regulation to subject banks to the discipline of market investors who, unlike insured depositors, would bear the cost of bank failure and therefore would encourage more responsible risk-taking. Yet this also made banks more sensitive to the stock market's demand for profits.[20] Thus, regulatory policy may be responsible in part for US banks' recent concern with improving shareholder returns.

Of course, US financial institutions as a group have not been consistently profitable, as the thrift crisis of the 1980s proved; weakened by poor investments, liquidity problems and some insider fraud and mismanagement, the US savings and loan industry virtually disappeared, forcing government intervention to protect insured depositors. Nevertheless, the thrift crisis does provide additional evidence of a link between regulation, shareholder returns and innovation. Before 1981, for example, regulation required federally insured thrift institutions to have at least 400 shareholders and no single shareholder was permitted to own more than 10 percent of the institution's stock. Although this rule probably was intended to bind thrifts more closely to their local communities (regulation also required over 25 percent of thrift shareholders to live locally), it also ensured that thrifts would have a significant number of unaffiliated owners who presumably would monitor thrift managers to ensure that they maximized profits. In 1981, the law changed, allowing thrifts to be purchased by single owners, such as real estate developers, many of whom treated their thrifts as their personal banks, using subsidized thrift deposits to fund their own speculative and often unsuccessful ventures. In hindsight, the 400 shareholder rule made sense, since it subjected thrifts to beneficial market discipline.[21]

Likewise, much of the deregulation of the thrift industry that took place in the early 1980s was designed expressly to allow thrifts to boost profits by making high-risk investments that promised higher returns than traditional home mortgage lending. This regulatory strategy backfired when many of these new investments resulted in significant losses. Although this experience discouraged US policymakers from relying on asset diversification as a magic tonic for unprofitable financial institutions, policymakers are still convinced that subjecting financial institutions to the discipline of the competitive capital markets will encourage managers to develop more successful and ultimately more profitable business strategies. Success, in US financial markets, is measured by return on equity. And in highly competitive financial markets producing higher returns to shareholders requires constant innovation.

As US firms compete in increasingly globalized financial markets, however, the question arises whether specialization and innovation will offer US firms any advantage over their larger rivals. Will global competition in financial markets turn out to be principally transaction-based, as in the US, or relationship-based? Interestingly, many observers are coming to the conclusion that the ability to offer distinctive and innovative products will count more in international financial markets than the ability to leverage stable client relationships. For example, recent strides in information technology should permit financial consumers to identify and choose among the best and most efficient financial products available anywhere in the world. As markets become increasingly transparent, the standard economic benefits derived from maintaining stable long-term financial relationships with a single firm, such as lowered search and monitoring costs, will diminish. Although reputation will always matter in financial markets, as financial products become increasingly complex, specialized firms may be more successful in advertising themselves as leaders in particular product lines than generalist firms that run the danger of becoming known as institutions that do everything but excel at nothing.[22]

Regulatory subsidy and market integration

There is danger in generalizing about winning strategies for financial firms in future global market competition. In the past, predictions have often proved wrong, and many firms have suffered when they have fallen into the trap of believing that a single strategy is the winning one. In the US, the duel between the 'specialist' model and the 'financial supermarket' model of financial product delivery has been going on for decades, and there is still no victor. Of course, next to the European universal bank, all US financial firms look like specialists, but, by the late 1990s, conglomeration, in the form of both domestic and cross-border combinations, was proceeding at a rapid pace in the US. The combination of Travelers and Citicorp to form Citigroup, for example, may have been the prototype for the US financial firm of the future, which, by loosely combining multiple functions under one corporate roof, will have the ability to deliver a package of linked financial products, such as banking and insurance, to a broad market base. On the other hand, the late 1990s trend toward the megabank may not last if management and risk control problems prove insurmountable.[23] Paradigm shifts have been the norm in US industry structure, in both financial and non-financial markets. Between 1970 and 1999, for example, many US industrial firms first fashioned huge diversified conglomerates, later dismantled them and eventually began combining once again.

Nevertheless, the frequency with which US financial firms, like other US companies, have been forced to re-invent themselves may offer them an advantage in future global competition. US institutions have already experienced the dislocation that occurs when formerly separate financial markets begin to integrate. As the barriers between securities and banking markets began to fall in the 1970s and 1980s, financial firms had to develop transitional strategies in order to survive the deterioration of their traditional businesses. The traditional financial firm had offered a limited product line (for example, deposit banking or securities underwriting and brokerage) to a broad customer base of individuals, businesses and institutions. When walls between product markets deteriorated, some firms made the decision to offer more products to fewer customers, for example, abandoning retail consumer banking to concentrate on wholesale financial services. Others took the opposite route, beginning aggressive acquisition programs to gain adequate size to operate in larger markets.[24] Whatever route was taken, by the late 1990s, most US firms had adjusted to the integration of domestic markets and had selected the strategy that they intended to pursue in the coming global competition.

US firms were helped by the fact that, because of the persistence of regulation, market re-integration proceeded slowly. There was no 'Big Bang' in US markets; securities and banking markets consolidated gradually, often guided by friendly regulators. The Federal Reserve's Section 20 rulings, which initially allowed banks to engage only in limited amounts of previously impermissible corporate securities underwriting, meant that banks would enter a new and unfamiliar business slowly without making a major commitment of resources. Once banks gained experience, restrictions on their investment in underwriting were relaxed over time. Moreover, the necessity to obtain Federal Reserve approval before entering the underwriting business meant that banks that in the view of the regulators lacked the managerial or financial capacity to diversify were not permitted to do so, protecting them from failure.

In contrast, the pace of integration of international markets may be less amenable to the control of one or more friendly regulators. In the late 1990s, observers of globalization were predicting that innovations such as the adoption of a single European currency would speed the integration of national financial markets and favor the growth of large, liquid regional securities markets. Universal banks that were accustomed to operating in bank-dominated financial systems with thin public securities markets were expected to have the most difficulty adjusting to new market structures. Some responded by acquiring international investment banks with established experience and reputations in securities transactions and related businesses, such as asset management and mergers and acquisitions. Interestingly, US commercial banks were once in the same position, having been barred by regulation from participation in securities markets. Yet, by the late 1990s, regulatory barriers had been relaxed sufficiently to allow a number of large US banks to gain a toehold in the securities business. They, along with their investment banking rivals, were well positioned to move into newly expanded European securities markets.[25]

At the same time, however, financial institutions seeking to compete globally are likely to encounter at least some national and cultural resistance to integration. For example, will customers, especially retail customers, be receptive to unfamiliar financial products offered by unfamiliar financial firms? Because of their long experience with fragmented domestic financial product markets, however, US firms have become expert at crashing market barriers, enticing consumers to cross market lines by creating products that are the financial equivalents of traditional products but that offer something better. (In the US, the highly successful money market mutual fund, which was targeted to retail bank customers who, many pundits thought, would never be willing to give up the safety of bank deposits, is a prime example.) Tailoring products for cross-market appeal has become a mainstay of the US financial industry, and presumably this talent will be exportable.

Regulatory subsidy and US markets

Another reason why, in the late 1990s, US financial firms were well positioned for global competition was the continuing significance of US financial markets to international capital raising. It is important to note that the primacy of US markets does not necessarily guarantee the global success of US financial firms. In fact, under different circumstances, US firms might have been eclipsed by non-US banks in their own home markets. In the late 1990s, US markets remained dominant in part because foreign capital flows into US markets remained strong. Non-US capital seekers and capital suppliers continued to favor US markets, but they were not obligated to employ US financial firms as their intermediaries when they engaged in US market transactions. Many may have preferred to rely on a financial intermediary from their home country that was familiar with their particular financing needs. Non-US financial firms had incentives to follow their customers into US markets in order to maintain and expand their business.

Moreover, non-US financial firms brought their own unique strengths to US markets. In the late 1980s and early 1990s, non-US banks were able to exploit their superior credit ratings to win a significant share of the US market for standby letters of credit and other financial guarantees. By 1994, branches and agencies of non-US banks accounted for half of the market for standby letters of credit. Even US debt issuers, especially state and local governments, were major purchasers of financial guarantees from non-US banks. In the same period, non-US banks also captured a significant share of the US market for interest rate swaps and foreign exchange commitments, accounting for 23 percent of this market at the end of 1994.[26]

Finally, most non-US financial firms operating in the US enjoyed a lighter regulatory burden under their home country's laws than did their US counterparts. Because conglomeration was generally permitted outside of the US, most were larger than their US rivals, and most engaged in a variety of financial activities. At least prior to 1978, non-US banks that operated in the US through branches or agencies were not subject to US national banking laws preventing diversification and often could offer both commercial and investment banking services in the US.

As a result, US financial firms complained that non-US firms enjoyed significant competitive advantages when operating in US markets. Beginning in the late 1970s, the US adopted regulation designed to level the playing field by imposing new regulatory handicaps on non-US firms to ensure that they would start equally with their US competitors. In 1978, the International Banking Act subjected the branches and agencies of non-US banks to many of the regulatory burdens that at the time were imposed on domestic banks, such as reserve requirements, limits on geographic expansion and interest rate ceilings. In addition, restrictions on diversification into non-bank financial and non-financial businesses were extended to non-US banks entering US markets. As a result, Glass-Steagall's prohibition on the combination of banking and securities became applicable to the US operations of non-US universal banks, forcing these firms to choose, in their US business, to become either commercial banks or investment banks.

In 1991, the Foreign Bank Supervision Enhancement Act increased the regulatory burden on non-US banks doing business in the US. In addition to augmenting US government oversight of the US banking operations of non-US firms and requiring that those operations meet financial, managerial and operational standards identical to those applicable to US banks, the new regulation prohibited branches of foreign banks from accepting insured deposits. As a result, non-US banks choosing to engage in retail banking in the US were forced to organize a separate US bank subsidiary.

As previously noted, these regulatory burdens were justified politically as necessary to remove the competitive advantage that non-US banks were perceived to have in US markets. The principle of 'national treatment' embodied in the new regulation was intended to level the playing field by ensuring that all competitors started equally when operating in US markets. Nevertheless, although making non-US entrants abide by the same rules that govern US players may at first glance seem to be fair, in practice, this national treatment may have provided a subsidy to US financial firms. For example, by increasing the cost of operating in US markets, regulation may have discouraged non-US financial firms from establishing or expanding US operations. A 1996 US General Accounting Office (GAO) study found that, after two decades of rapid growth, by 1990, non-US bank expansion in the US had slowed. Although economic and business factors may have accounted for some of this slowdown, the GAO study noted a strong perception on the part of non-US bankers that, as a result of the regulatory burden placed on non-US entrants, the US had become a hostile environment in which to operate.[27]

US bankers may reply that they are subject to the same regulatory burden. Nevertheless, as a practical matter, compliance costs may have been higher for non-US firms that were unfamiliar with the US regulatory structure and practices. Moreover, as the GAO study revealed, at least in the 1990s, applications for entry or expansion by non-US banks were delayed by the requirement that US bank regulators evaluate the quality of the applicant's comprehensive consolidated supervision by its home country. Thus, equal treatment may have unintentionally imposed unequal transactions costs on non-US banks operating in US markets.

As mentioned, some non-US banks may have responded to these costs by cutting their losses and curtailing their US operations. Nevertheless, because of the continued significance of US markets in global capital formation, major international banks could not afford to abandon their US presence. By doing so, they would have ceded their own corporate customers, who were still raising funds in US markets, to their US rivals. Thus, in order to compete globally, non-US banks were forced to continue to navigate the often hostile waters of the US regulatory system.

Of course, the principle of national treatment also has meant that non-US banks share the benefits of deregulation equally with their US counterparts. When restrictions on interest rate ceilings on deposits and barriers to interstate branching disappeared, non-US entrants theoretically enjoyed the same regulatory relief as US banks. Again, however, in practice, the benefits of deregulation may not have been shared equally. The GAO's 1996 study found that few non-US banks maintained full service retail banking operations in the US. Moreover, although non-US banks were major lenders to commercial and industrial borrowers, they usually were not loan originators, instead purchasing participations in credits originated by US banks.[28] Since interest rate ceilings and interstate banking restrictions principally burdened full service banks engaged in traditional deposit-taking and lending through branch networks, removal of these particular regulations probably was of greater moment to US banks than to largely wholesale non-US institutions

Non-US banks were more interested in reform of Glass-Steagall and other restrictions on diversification that prevented them from combining investment and commercial banking and other financial activities, such as insurance, in the US. These restrictions were of particular concern for non-US financial institutions because they forced them to adopt unique organizational structures in the US to comply with regulation. Yet, in this key area, the regulatory reform process probably benefited US banks more than their non-US rivals.

Glass-Steagall reform began seriously in the 1980s when the Federal Reserve Board interpreted the statute to permit bank holding companies to set up separate securities affiliates (the Section 20 affiliates) that were allowed to engage in limited amounts of securities underwriting and dealing. Although this approach was required by the language of Glass-Steagall (which barred banks from engaging directly in any corporate securities underwriting but barred banks from affiliating only with firms 'engaged principally' in underwriting), the Federal Reserve favored the use of separately incorporated affiliates for securities activities because the affiliate structure facilitated the policing of interaffiliate funds transfers and the imposition of prudential 'firewalls' designed to shield the bank from financial difficulties experienced by an affiliate. (The affiliate structure also guaranteed the Federal Reserve a continued supervisory role in regulating bank securities activities, as is explained in Chapter 4.)

From the perspective of US banks, the requirement for a separate securities affiliate was neither unusual nor overly burdensome. Most US banks had already adopted the holding company structure for a variety of legal and business reasons. In 1998, for example, banks with holding company structures controlled 96 percent of total US bank assets.[29] In contrast, the separate affiliate requirement forced many non-US banks to adopt a special structure for their US financial operations. Non-US banks probably would have been better off had Congress simply repealed Glass-Steagall in its entirety, allowing new entrants to replicate their home organizations in the US.

Moreover, any advantage that universal banks might have had over US banks and securities firms as a result of their greater experience in combining commercial and investment banking meant little in US markets because of the slow pace of regulatory reform. The original bank securities affiliates were permitted by the Federal Reserve to engage in only limited amounts of corporate securities underwriting – first, 5 percent of revenues, then 10 percent and then 25 percent. These limits, although again responsive to the literal language of Glass-Steagall, had the effect of tying the hands of non-US banks, preventing them from exploiting either their superior size or experience in order to dominate US securities markets. In addition, banks operating in the US generally were not permitted to engage in merchant banking (holding corporate equities for investment purposes) as was their standard practice in their home financial markets. In contrast, US banks, new to the investment banking business, benefited from the opportunity to build their securities operations slowly.

Finally, before commencing securities operations in the US through affiliates, banks faced a lengthy regulatory approval process. For US bank holding companies, the application process was familiar, and any resulting delays gave managers time to prepare for entry into an entirely new business. For non-US banks seeking to do in the US what they already did at home, the application process was simply costly and time-consuming. From the perspective of US banks, equal regulatory treatment of non-US banks simply leveled the playing field. From the perspective of non-US banks, however, the playing field was anything but level.

Thus, the slow pace of regulatory reform may have subsidized the US financial industry by giving it an opportunity to adjust to market changes before being subjected to the full force of competition from universal banking rivals. By the end of the 1990s, US financial firms appeared ready to compete in deregulated markets, and a process of inter-industry consolidation had begun that was making some US firms as large and diversified as their non-US rivals. And, perhaps not coincidentally, Glass-Steagall was finally repealed.

Subsidy to burden – a reprise

The process by which Glass-Steagall was ultimately vanquished provides an illustration of how regulatory reform tends to take place in the US. Beginning in the 1970s, Glass-Steagall began to lose its legitimacy when the banking and securities industries pointed out that the regulatory subsidies that the statute had created had become burdens. Nevertheless, regulatory relief did not come immediately but took place gradually over three decades, suggesting that the transformation of subsidy to burden was not as complete as critics of Glass-Steagall had often argued. As late as the 1990s, the regulatory handicapping initiated by Glass-Steagall may have provided some lingering subsidies to US financial firms in their competition with non-US rivals. This may account for Glass-Steagall's longevity even after its delegitimization in domestic markets.

In some ways, this story parallels the public choice story told in Chapter 1, which suggests that politically powerful financial firms will support regulation so long as it benefits them. Yet the public choice story fails to explain why US financial firms often tolerate regulation that appears to impose significant burdens on their operations. Regulatory burdens as well as subsidies are accepted as legitimate (and are likely to survive assault even by the most politically powerful of interest groups) so long as they are perceived by most players in financial markets as ensuring equal starts for all competitors. When regulatory handicapping no longer guarantees a level playing field, then regulation is vulnerable and the process of regulatory rehandicapping begins.

This theory helps to explain why regulatory reform appears more likely to be successful when it proceeds slowly. Gradual reform, which permits the informal reallocation of regulatory burdens among players, allows competitors to reposition themselves on the playing field so that they may be ensured an equal start in the future. For example, had Glass-Steagall been repealed too early, US financial firms would not have had the time to adjust to the reintegration of US financial product markets. Moreover, they would have been at a competitive disadvantage with non-US universal banks that already had a presence in both securities and banking markets.

Of course, as noted at the beginning of this chapter, when the playing field is level is a matter of perception. In 1978, US financial institutions successfully persuaded US policymakers that, without regulatory handicapping, non-US financial firms would have enjoyed a superior starting position in US markets. Non-US firms disagreed, and, eventually, their complaint that the playing field was not level may finally have resulted in some readjustment of their regulatory burden. In 1999, financial modernization legislation permitted freer combinations of banking and other financial activities, including merchant banking, allowing non-US banks more flexibility to export their home financial businesses to the US. By the late 1990s, new investments in US markets by some major non-US banks indicated that non-US firms' perception of a competitive imbalance created by US regulation may have softened somewhat, although some non-US banks still complained that US regulation unfairly burdened them.[30]

Again, this suggests that the process of regulatory transformation is more complex than interest group bargaining for private political advantage. Regulatory legitimization depends on a perception that the handicapping function of regulation is working to ensure equality of starting position for all competitors. As a result, how players in financial markets measure the relative weights of their subsidies and burdens and, perhaps more important, how they articulate that assessment in the political arena are likely to determine regulatory outcomes. In fact, as Chapter 3 describes, success in the war over deregulation may depend less on the political influence of a particular industry than on the way in which that industry is able to make its case to other players in financial markets that the playing field is no longer level.

3

Deposit Insurance and the Politics of Regulatory Subsidy

In US financial regulation, deposit insurance is the quintessential regulatory subsidy. The insurance guarantee, which covers deposits in banks (and certain other depository institutions) up to a maximum of $100 000 (since 1980), may appear to be a straightforward consumer protection scheme, designed for the benefit of small depositors who otherwise would suffer financial loss in the event of bank failure. And certainly deposit insurance is not unique to the US. In recent years, some form of deposit guarantee has become a part of many national bank regulatory regimes.

In the US, however, deposit insurance is far more than simply a government consumer protection program. The impact of deposit insurance on the banking industry, its funding and its competitive position has proved central to the evolution of US financial regulation and has played a major role in recent debate over deregulation. The existence, or non-existence, of the so-called deposit insurance subsidy is a conundrum that has complicated the progress of regulatory reform on a number of fronts, including repeal of the Glass-Steagall Act, that seem to have little or nothing to do with the insurance plan. In redesigning the level playing field, therefore, deposit insurance remains a substantial, and perhaps insurmountable, obstacle.

Why has the deposit insurance subsidy become something of a smoking gun in the debate over financial regulatory reform in the US? The answer is to be found in the handicapping function of US financial regulation, which aims to ensure that competing financial players enjoy equal starting positions on a level playing field. If deposit insurance provides an unique regulatory subsidy to the banking industry (and to its fellow depository institutions, thrifts and credit unions), then banks enjoy an inherent competitive advantage over other financial players. This advantage must be neutralized by special regulatory handicapping of banks in order to guarantee fair starts to uninsured rivals. Conversely, to escape this special burden and to achieve deregulation of their industry, banks must convince policy-makers that the regulatory subsidy traditionally associated with deposit insurance is no longer real, or at least is not sufficiently valuable to legitimate the degree of regulatory handicapping to which depository firms as a group have been subject.

Recently, the US banking industry, and even some of its regulators, have been making this argument, and in so doing have challenged a fundamental premise of US financial regulation – that banks and their fellow depository firms require more, and more intense, regulation than do financial institutions such as securities and insurance firms that do not accept insured deposits. This premise is deeply ingrained in the US financial regulatory scheme: for example, regulatory supervision of depository firms typically has been prudential in orientation, frequently relying on substantive regulatory control of private risk-taking (such as the laws restricting permissible bank investments and activities), in contrast to the disclosure-based schemes associated with regulatory supervision of broker-dealers, mutual funds and other securities firms.[1] Likewise, US politicians and the public typically have looked to banks, but not to non-bank financial institutions, as owing a special duty to the US economy and financial markets, including an affirmative obligation to provide for the credit needs of business and individuals, especially in times of economic stress.[2] Both of these motives for bank regulation, although different, are based upon the premise that the subsidy provided by deposit insurance must be balanced by special regulatory responsibilities.

If banks are able to refute this premise, then the basis for much of the special regulation of banks disappears. Thus, in this particular rehandicapping process, the stakes are high. The challenge being mounted to the notion of deposit insurance as subsidy could change the dynamics of financial regulation in the US, delegitimizing large portions of the traditional regulatory framework.

Deposit insurance as subsidy

Interestingly, from the beginning, the subsidy created by deposit insurance was recognized by policymakers and influenced political debate on bank regulation. The federal deposit insurance program was created by the Banking Act of 1933, the statute that also gave US financial markets the Glass-Steagall Act (which, as previously described, prevented a single organization from both taking deposits and engaging in securities activities). Like Glass-Steagall, deposit insurance was a political response to the banking crisis of the early 1930s, which had produced widespread bank failure, government mandated bank 'holidays' and loss of public confidence in the banking system. Unlike Glass-Steagall, however, deposit insurance was a reform that the average bank customer was likely to understand and to welcome. Many state governments had already experimented with deposit protection programs, and numerous congressional proposals had already been made for a national deposit insurance scheme. Between 1886 and 1933, 150 separate bills providing for some form of federal deposit insurance had been introduced in the US Congress. By 1933, the idea of protecting small depositors from bank losses had broad bipartisan support, although, notably, not from Senator Carter Glass (of Glass-Steagall fame), who reluctantly attached the House of Representatives' deposit insurance plan to his own legislation, and, interestingly, not from President Franklin D. Roosevelt, although he later embraced deposit insurance as his accomplishment.[3]

Nevertheless, despite its consumer appeal, deposit insurance was designed with broader goals in mind than simply to protect small retail depositors. These broader goals, and the plan's success in attaining them, account for the widely held view that deposit insurance provides a significant subsidy to the banking industry. For example, perhaps the most important accomplishment of the deposit insurance program was to provide the banking industry with a long-term stable and inexpensive source of funds. Insured deposits would be stable because insured depositors would no longer fear for the safety of their investments and would leave their savings in their banks. Insured deposits would be inexpensive because insured depositors would not demand high premiums to compensate them for the risk of loss in the event of bank failure.

Why was the stability of the bank deposit base of such concern to national policymakers? Understanding their motives requires a return to the banking markets of the early 1930s. Bank runs, in the form of rapid and unpredictable outflows of funds from the banking system, had periodically plagued the US banking industry, but the problem was never so severe as between 1929 and 1933, when widespread deposit withdrawals affecting multiple banks, system-wide liquidity crises and high failure rates eventually forced the declaration of a national bank holiday from March 5–9, 1933. Between December 1932 and March 15, 1933, the deposit base declined by roughly one-sixth (this reflected both net outflows of deposits and frozen deposits in banks that were unable to reopen for business after March 9, 1933).[4] In contrast, in 1934, the first year of operation of the deposit insurance program, deposits rose 22 percent, returning to the banking industry roughly half of all funds lost between 1931 and 1933.[5]

The significance of this accomplishment was twofold. First, deposit insurance greatly contributed to long-term monetary stability by solving the problem of bank panics; for this, insurance has been called the 'most important structural change in the banking system to result from the 1933 panic'.[6] Second, deposit insurance restored to the banking system a stable and inexpensive supply of funds that would be permanently available for lending to individuals and business. Encouraging banks to lend, thereby alleviating credit shortages and stimulating economic development, was urgent government policy in the early 1930s, but deposit insurance had a longer term effect on credit availability, solving the age-old banking problem of how to borrow short and lend long without risking liquidity crises and insolvency.[7] Because of deposit insurance's impact on deposit pricing and volatility, banks could afford to invest short-term deposits in long-term, often illiquid loans.

Other elements of the story of the origins of deposit insurance are less well known but also help to explain the modern view of deposit insurance as subsidy. Contrary to conventional wisdom, the deposit runs that ravaged the banking industry during the 1930s cannot be blamed entirely on small unsophisticated depositors. In fact, withdrawals by large depositors had a far more devastating effect on the banking system than small retail runs. Statistics collected by the Federal Reserve show that, between 1930 and 1933, large deposit accounts of $100 000 or more declined by 70 percent. In comparison, withdrawals of small accounts of $200 or less were insignificant.[8] Anecdotal evidence tends to confirm these statistics. For example, in early 1933, Henry Ford's threat to withdraw some $20 million of deposits from a Detroit bank frustrated government-coordinated efforts to prop up Michigan's troubled banking system. Some observers have cited this event as precipitating the final banking crisis that forced President Roosevelt to declare the nationwide bank holiday in March 1933.[9]

The creators of deposit insurance were certainly aware of the disproportionate impact on the banking system of large deposit runs. They created an insurance scheme that, from its inception, protected what at the time would have been considered large deposit accounts.

Under the temporary deposit insurance scheme that began operation on January 1, 1934, deposits up to $2500 were protected in full. This ceiling was quickly raised to $5000. The permanent plan, which was scheduled to take effect on July 1, 1934, was even more generous, protecting 100 percent of deposits up to $10 000, 75 percent of the next $40 000 and 50 percent of all amounts over $50 000. The permanent plan eventually was scrapped and the temporary plan was made permanent, yet, even under the less generous $5000 insurance limit, as of October 1, 1934, 98.5 percent of all depositors were insured in full.[10] Thus, in context, the current $100 000 ceiling, which is often criticized for protecting more depositors than it should, does not look so generous.

Further, although the deposit insurance plan as originally conceived was to have been a bona fide insurance scheme, complete with rather rigorous entry qualifications for banks, the plan was rapidly transformed into a deposit *guarantee* program when bank regulators became convinced of the necessity of allowing as many banks as possible to qualify for admission. The June 1933 legislation creating deposit insurance specified that the program would be open only to banks that by the end of the year had been certified as 'solvent' by a federal bank regulator. After the March 1933 bank holiday, almost 15 000 banks had reopened for business, but many were technically insolvent. In December 1933, roughly one-seventh of all operating banks still could not meet the basic solvency test. Yet, just two months earlier, President Roosevelt had reassured the public that all operating banks would be in sound condition once deposit insurance took effect in January 1934.[11]

So political considerations dictated that insolvent banks be certified as sound so that they might join the deposit insurance system, with the assistance of some $1 billion of government-supplied capital.[12] Although the government's action may have been justified in order to prevent a renewed crisis of confidence in the banking system, this shift in policy had a profound effect on the administration and goals of the deposit insurance scheme. Simply put, deposit insurance became a way to protect banks, not just to protect their depositors.

Critics may conclude that this was the beginning of the moral hazard problem that has long been associated with the deposit insurance program.[13] So long as deposits are guaranteed regardless of the riskiness of a bank's assets, bank managers can afford to gamble with depositors' money without fear of retaliation by either risk-averse depositors or a disapproving insurer. This was also the beginning of the deposit insurance subsidy. By guaranteeing the deposits of all participating banks (but no non-banks) regardless of individual financial strength or managerial competence, deposit insurance provided the banking industry as a whole with a special funding advantage over unsubsidized rivals.

Another accomplishment of the deposit insurance program, which again was probably intentional and which reinforced the notion of a deposit insurance subsidy, was the preservation of the unit banking system. As mentioned, even after the banking crisis, as of June 1933, the US still had roughly 15 000 operating banks, many in precarious financial condition. Policymakers were considering various alternatives to strengthen the banking industry, one of which was to encourage bank conglomeration (and thereby shrink the number of independent banks) by legalizing interstate branching and acquisitions. Nationwide branch banking was viewed as a threat by small independent banks that feared competitive challenge from, or takeover by, the large city banks. Deposit insurance became a more politically acceptable alternative,[14] strengthening small banks by allowing them to compete for funds on an equal footing with the larger, better diversified banks that were likely to be favored by the deposit market. (In fact, interstate bank branching was not permitted in the US until federal legislation in 1994.[15]) Thus, deposit insurance provided a special subsidy to small banks, lowering their funding costs and allowing them to compete in funding markets with both larger banks and non-bank financial firms.

Interestingly, in the 1930s, most banks did not appear to welcome the subsidy provided to them by deposit insurance, perhaps because they recognized that any regulatory subsidy would inevitably be accompanied by a corresponding regulatory burden. For small unit banks, for example, accepting the benefits of deposit insurance meant submitting themselves to new and potentially costly federal regulatory oversight. As originally conceived, the deposit insurance scheme would have required all banks with insured deposits eventually to join the Federal Reserve system, thereby subjecting many state-chartered banks to national bank regulation for the first time. As might be expected, state-chartered banks objected vehemently to this requirement, and it was eventually eliminated.[16]

Nevertheless, insured state banks did not thereby avoid all federal bank regulation. The Federal Deposit Insurance Corporation, created to administer the insurance program, quickly assumed the role of bank regulator, examining and supervising all insured state-chartered banks that did not voluntarily join the Federal Reserve system. This regulatory oversight was justified as necessary to enable the deposit insurance administrator to protect the insurance fund from the danger of moral hazard created by the insurance scheme.[17] So the link between regulatory subsidy and regulatory burden was established early in the life of the deposit insurance program. The Federal Deposit Insurance Corporation became a federal bank regulator, sharing responsibility with the Federal Reserve (chief regulator of Federal Reserve member banks) and the Comptroller of the Currency (chief regulator of nationally chartered banks) to administer and enforce substantive federal bank regulation.[18]

Yet the deposit insurance subsidy also legitimated the imposition of regulatory burdens on insured banks that went far beyond the basic prudential regulation required to protect the insurance fund from moral hazard. This additional regulatory handicap may be understood as addressing the concern, fundamental to US financial regulation, that all competitors in financial markets enjoy equal starting positions. If deposit insurance gives banks a starting advantage over rival financial firms by subsidizing bank funding costs, then banks must be specially handicapped in order to level the playing field.

This theory may offer the most satisfactory rationale for traditional rules limiting the power of banks to diversify into certain non-bank financial businesses, such as securities underwriting or insurance. Many students of bank regulation have assumed that the motive for these anti-diversification laws was entirely prudential: for example, diversification-minded banks might venture into new risky financial markets, fail and require assistance from the deposit insurance fund. What if, however, rather than failing, diversified banks were able to reduce their overall risk by combining traditional banking functions with other financial activities? If so, then prudential considerations would justify government policy that encouraged rather than restricted bank diversification.

Whether conglomerate diversification really is as efficient as standard securities portfolio diversification in reducing risk is not free from doubt. (Chapter 2 suggested several reasons why, in the real world, conglomerate managers may diversify inefficiently). Nevertheless, even retail depositors were empowered to move freely between banking and securities markets, converting deposits into money market mutual funds and back into deposits. Yet, until 1999, regulation continued to prevent banks from operating in both markets.

Historical evidence suggests that anti-diversification regulation may have reflected something other than policymakers' concern that banks would diversify inefficiently. Even before passage of the Bank Holding Company Act of 1956, which restricted the permissible activities of non-bank affiliates of banks, few if any US banks had been part of huge overdiversified conglomerates. Rather, many affiliations between banks and non-banks apparently had been formed to ensure a stable flow of credit from the bank to its affiliated non-bank business.[19]

The desire to restrict this cross-funding may offer a better explanation of longstanding US regulatory policy against bank diversification, even into financial businesses such as securities and insurance that are functionally quite similar to banking. The problem, again, is the deposit insurance subsidy, which is assumed to give banks an unfair funding advantage over unsubsidized financial firms. If banks are permitted to invest their inexpensive subsidized deposits in non-bank ventures, they may be able to underprice non-bank competitors and monopolize non-bank financial markets. The regulatory solution to the problem of subsidy has been to limit the power of banks to compete in non-bank markets, or, more recently, to allow them to compete in those markets only through special organizational structures, such as separately incorporated affiliates or subsidiaries, that do not have access to insured deposits.[20]

Special regulatory handicapping of insured banks has taken another, more subtle form, justifying the imposition of an affirmative legal duty on the banking industry (but not on other financial firms) to ensure the availability of financial services to under serviced markets. As previously mentioned, the creators of deposit insurance expected, or at least hoped, that subsidizing bank deposits would lead to easier bank credit. Nevertheless, what if banks accepted the subsidy yet still chose not to lend freely? In at least one instance, regulation has mandated bank lending. The Community Reinvestment Act, enacted by Congress in 1977, obligates insured banks (and insured thrifts) to meet the credit needs of their local communities, especially low and moderate income neighborhoods.

Originally, this requirement may have been justified as a form of recycling: if banks took deposits out of their home communities, it was only fair that they reinvested at least some of those deposits in loans to those communities. Alternatively, past lending discrimination and 'red-lining' by the banking industry may have provided a basis for remedial legislation that made community lending a legal requirement. In modern financial markets, however, many banks are no longer community financial institutions, geographically tied to particular neighborhoods, but compete in national or even global markets. Mutual funds and insurance companies also take funds out of local communities, but they are not obliged to reinvest them in those communities. Non-bank lenders, such as finance companies, may also have poor track records as lenders to low-income customers, yet these financial firms are not subject to the Community Reinvestment Act. An explanation of this disparate treatment may be that, unlike banks and thrifts, these firms do not benefit from the deposit insurance subsidy. This public subsidy, unique to depository institutions, justifies the imposition of special obligations to serve the public.

It is important to note that the regulatory subsidy accruing to banks may derive not just from federal deposit insurance but also from other parts of the so-called bank 'safety net', such as banks' ability to borrow, often at below market rates, from the Federal Reserve's discount window. Further, at least in the past, US bank failure policy resulted in the preservation of bank franchises whenever possible through regulatory assisted mergers or recapitalizations of troubled banks, which dispositions protected even uninsured bank depositors from losses.[21] This implicit deposit insurance guarantee subsidized large uninsured depositors (with investments over $100 000), potentially providing banks with a funding advantage over non-banks even in wholesale money markets. More generally, any regulation that decreases bank operating costs (such as government check clearing and other transactions services that are offered at a discount to banks) may be viewed as subsidizing the banking industry, thereby providing banks with a competitive edge over rival financial firms. Nevertheless, when US policymakers talk about the bank subsidy, they are usually referring just to those three parts of the bank 'safety net' – deposit insurance, Federal Reserve discount window lending and government rescues of failing banks – that may reduce or eliminate the ordinary risks associated with investing in banks. As a result, risk averse investors may feel safer putting their money in banks, giving the banking industry an unfair advantage over its non-bank rivals.

Because this bank subsidy is a creature of regulation, the imposition of corresponding regulatory burdens to neutralize the banks' advantage may seem both fair and necessary to level the playing field. Recently, however, banks have argued that the playing field is not level because banks are over handicapped. Their argument is twofold: first, they assert, the deposit insurance subsidy, even when defined to encompass the entire bank safety net, is far less valuable to the banking industry than is commonly supposed; second, even if some subsidy remains, it is outweighed by the heavy regulatory burden that is shouldered by the banking industry.

These kinds of arguments are likely to be made by any financial competitor seeking regulatory relief through the political process. In this instance, however, the banking industry is seeking relief not just from a specific rule or rules but from a entire body of regulation that, since 1933, has been premised on the existence of the deposit insurance subsidy. In fact, it may not be an exaggeration to assert that this subsidy is the single most important issue complicating the financial reform process in the US. The problem, for policymakers, is how to regulate banks that operate in financial markets that are increasingly integrated and diverse. If banks still enjoy a competitive funding advantage by virtue of deposit insurance and other elements of the safety net, then constructing a level playing field will require the retention of some special regulatory burden on banks and banks alone. If the bank subsidy no longer exists, however, then there is little remaining justification for a regulatory scheme that, despite progress toward deregulation, continues to treat banks differently from other financial firms.

The case against the bank subsidy

Initially, the existence of some deposit insurance subsidy appears irrefutable. By virtue of insurance, depositors do not have to worry about losing their savings in the event of bank failure. As a result, they will not expend resources to monitor the financial condition of their bank, they will not demand risk premiums to cover monitoring costs (or to compensate for monitoring failure) and they will not abandon their bank at the first sign of trouble. Put another way, banks are freed from the necessity of raising funds in the competitive money markets, whose participants impose harsh discipline for mistake or mismanagement and occasionally even panic and flee to quality.

Bankers may respond that these advantages are not so great as they appear to be. Not all bank deposits are insured, and not all bank liabilities are deposits. In any case, deposits, particularly demand deposits (that may be liquidated by the holder without prior notice to the bank), are inherently more volatile than other funding sources, such as short-term debt. If insurance simply compensates for the volatility of deposits, then banks enjoy no net benefit over non-banks. Finally, the banking industry, not the government, pays for deposit insurance coverage through risk-based premiums assessed against and collected from insured banks.

Non-bankers may reply that, in the past, uninsured deposits (and occasionally even non-deposit bank liabilities) enjoyed de facto deposit insurance protection by virtue of failure resolution techniques employed by the US government that prevented troubled banks from closing.[22] Moreover, all creditors benefit from other parts of the safety net, such as the ability of banks to borrow from the Federal Reserve's discount window, that reduce the risk that the bank will experience a liquidity crisis and fail. As a result, deposit markets, even uninsured deposit markets, may actually be less prone to panic than other short-term money markets. For example, the commercial paper market experienced a textbook run in 1970 when the unexpected default by Penn Central Transportation Company caused worried investors to demand repayment of maturing short-term paper issued by scores of corporate borrowers.[23] Finally, although banks do pay for their own deposit insurance, and insurance premiums are now tied to the riskiness of participating banks, the thrift crisis of the late 1980s demonstrated that the US government will never allow the bank insurance fund to become insolvent. This implicit government backing gives the deposit insurance guarantee greater credibility than purely private insurance schemes.

These kinds of arguments have appeared in the scholarly banking literature for decades, but recently they have entered the political discourse, fueling debate over the existence, or non-existence, of the deposit insurance subsidy. The debate has become more intense as financial markets integrate and as the issue of regulatory cost emerges as a concern in global financial competition. It is in the interest of the US banking industry to make the case politically that the bank regulatory subsidy is not as significant as it once was if the industry hopes to gain any relief from its lingering regulatory burden. Moreover, as cross-industry financial combinations become possible, non-banks considering affiliations with banks have a reason to join the banking industry's cause in order to minimize their own future regulatory costs when they enter the banking business. Finally, non-US banks operating in the US also have a stake in the debate. Some own US banking subsidiaries, or would like to. Although others may not maintain insured deposit-taking facilities in the US (and therefore do not enjoy the full benefit of the deposit insurance subsidy), to the extent that their US branches are regulated as banks they are subject to at least some of the corresponding regulatory burden.

So how convincing, politically, is the bankers' argument? Recent changes in bank funding patterns do indicate that insured deposits have become a less significant source of funds for banks, particularly large banks, then they have been in the past. For example, statistical data collected by the US General Accounting Office and published in 1991 show that, during the 1980s, insured deposits decreased slightly as a percentage of bank assets, reflecting growing reliance on non-deposit liabilities, such as repurchase agreements, as well as equity capital. As of mid-1990, the 46 largest insured US banks (with assets over $10 billion) held only 22 percent of total insured deposits but 59 percent of uninsured deposits.[24] More generally, all domestic deposits, both insured and uninsured, have declined as a percentage of bank assets. A study by the Federal Deposit Insurance Corporation found that the ratio of domestic deposits to assets had fallen from a high of 94 percent in 1945 to a low of 66 percent in 1998. Again, the most significant decline occurred at the largest banks.[25]

Moreover, despite insurance, deposit volatility may be increasing. Between 1970 and 1990, average yearly deposit turnover grew ten-fold for the banking system as a whole and fifteen-fold for major banks in New York City. Higher volatility reflected improvements in cash management techniques available to retail depositors (such as sweep accounts that automatically transfer excess deposit balances to higher yielding uninsured mutual funds).[26] As a result, deposits, even insured deposits, appear to be a less stable source of funding for banks than they once were.

Finally, changes in bank failure policy dating from the early 1990s may have reduced the value of the implicit deposit insurance guarantee. As previously mentioned, this implicit guarantee arose from investors' assumption, based on past regulatory practice, that the US government would whenever possible resolve troubled banks in ways that protected uninsured as well as insured depositors. This implicit guarantee reached its highest value in 1984, when the government promised that all creditors, even non-depositors, in ailing Continental Illinois, the huge Chicago bank, would be protected in any future regulatory disposition. Even before Continental, however, many bank failures were resolved through government-assisted mergers of troubled banks with healthy banks in which the healthy bank typically assumed all of the troubled bank's deposit liabilities, shielding uninsured as well as insured depositors from losses associated with bank failure.

In 1991, after the thrift industry crisis raised concerns about the viability of the deposit insurance scheme (and the potential cost to the government of bailing out an insolvent insurance fund), the US Congress adopted legislation designed to alter traditional bank failure policy in order to ensure that insurance funds would be used for the narrow purpose of reimbursing insured deposit accounts. Bank regulators were encouraged to resolve most bank failure by closing the troubled institution, paying off insured depositors out of the insurance fund and relegating uninsured depositors and other creditors to liquidation proceedings to recover some portion of their investment.[27] (Congress also limited the discretion of the Federal Reserve to lend through the discount window to troubled banks and required the regulators to intervene promptly to force weak banks to raise private capital.) The unambiguous intent of these changes was to subject uninsured depositors to the risk of bank failure and liquidation. As a result, in theory at least, the perceived benefit of the bank subsidy to uninsured depositors should have declined considerably, removing any implicit bank funding advantage in uninsured wholesale money markets.

How much has the total value of the bank subsidy declined? Bankers like to point out that, if any significant funding advantage remained, one might expect diversified banking organizations to raise most of their funds (to the extent legally permissible) through their bank subsidiaries. Yet many bank holding companies choose to fund their operations, including their bank subsidiaries, through commercial paper issuances at the holding company level. Although the reasons for this choice of funding strategy may vary, factors other than the deposit insurance subsidy appear to be driving bank funding decisions.

Even if some subsidy remains, the banking industry argues that there is no net subsidy: in other words, any subsidy is outweighed by the high cost of complying with special bank regulation. Although quantifying regulatory compliance costs on an industry-wide basis is difficult, case studies and surveys have attempted to estimate the burden. A 1998 review of these studies by the Federal Reserve concluded that compliance costs accounted for as much as 12–13 percent of total non-interest expense.[28]

Although this amount seems substantial, without any quantification of the remaining value of the bank subsidy, it is impossible to say whether or to what extent regulatory costs actually exceed regulatory benefits. Moreover, there are reasons to suspect that the calculation may differ for different segments of the banking industry. If, as statistics suggest, large banks rely less heavily than small banks on insured deposits (and on domestic deposits generally) for funding, then it is logical to conclude that the value of the bank subsidy may decline with bank size, with large banks enjoying little or no subsidy. Yet studies of bank regulatory costs indicate that economies of scale may exist in regulatory compliance.[29] Moreover, deposit insurance premiums are assessed against banks in proportion to their domestic deposit base. So large banks may derive less value than small banks from the regulatory subsidy, but they also may shoulder less of the regulatory burden.

Further, despite congressional changes, bank failure policy remains a wild card. Before 1991, the conventional wisdom in US markets was that large banks were simply too big to fail – in other words, because of the potential impact of the failure of a large bank on its correspondents, its community and the financial markets, the bank regulators would always resolve problems at the biggest banks in ways that avoided closing and liquidation. For example, the government's recapitalization of ailing Continental Illinois in 1984 was viewed as proof that a troubled large bank (and its creditors) would be rescued even when a merger with a healthy bank could not be arranged. As a result, the implicit deposit insurance guarantee was of greater value to large banks (that never were liquidated) than to small banks (that might be liquidated if no acceptable merger partner could be found).[30]

As mentioned, in 1991, Congress sought to alter bank failure policy to discourage rescues of large banks, thereby subjecting uninsured bank creditors to liquidation risk. Nevertheless, Congress did not preclude all bank bailouts.[31] Some observers, including many bank investors, probably remain convinced that, despite legal changes, the US government still will not permit a megabank to close its doors. If this assumption is widespread, influencing investors' decisions, then some part of the implicit subsidy may still benefit the largest banks.

Happily for the bank regulators (and the banking industry), the profitability of the banking business in the late 1990s limited opportunities to test the government's resolve to liquidate even large banks. If investors believe that some US banks are still too big to fail, they may be right, or they may be wrong. Nevertheless, there is reason to believe that, for all banks except a handful of huge megabanks, the implicit deposit insurance guarantee is gone. Smaller banks, that tend to rely more heavily than larger banks on domestic deposits for funding, are now virtually certain to be liquidated in the event of failure, resulting in losses for their uninsured creditors. This factor, together with smaller banks' relatively higher regulatory compliance costs, suggest that, contrary to conventional wisdom, the net deposit insurance subsidy may actually be worth less to small banks than to the large banks that typically have taken the lead in making the case that their regulatory burdens outweigh their benefits, a possibility that further complicates the net subsidy debate.

A slightly different approach to the net subsidy debate focuses on the increasingly blurred lines between banks and non-banks in the US. In a famous essay published in 1982, Gerald Corrigan, who at the time was president of the Federal Reserve Bank of Minneapolis, argued that the special functions performed by banks justified the special regulatory treatment of the banking industry. These special functions – issuing transaction accounts (demand deposits), acting as the back-up source of liquidity for other financial and non-financial entities and serving as the 'transmission belt' for government monetary policy – provided the rationale for both regulatory subsidies such as deposit insurance and regulatory burdens such as the anti-diversification laws. Viewed this way, the continued legitimacy of regulatory handicapping ultimately depends upon whether banks are 'special', performing unique functions that demand special regulatory subsidy and burden.[32]

Do banks still perform special functions? Some experts would say no. The money market mutual fund, a securities product, has become the functional equivalent of a bank deposit, offering comparable liquidity and convenience to retail investors. Banks share their lending function with non-bank firms, many of which have better credit ratings and may be able to fund their loans more cheaply than most banks. And, in modern financial markets, monetary policy may no longer be implemented exclusively through the banking system.

To some observers, this blurring of distinctions among financial firms may be a compelling argument for ending special regulatory treatment of banks. To others, however, it may be a reason to extend the special regulatory treatment accorded banks to non-bank entities that perform the same functions as banks. Most would agree that there is a strong possibility that, as a consequence of the blurring of functional distinctions within the financial industry, non-banks may become the unintentional beneficiaries of some part of the bank regulatory subsidy without becoming subject to corresponding regulatory burdens. Should this occur, banks will have a compelling case that the playing field is no longer level.

To some extent, non-banks have always derived indirect benefits from the safety net, but these benefits have flowed through the medium of banks. For example, participants in the uninsured commercial paper market addressed their market's volatility and vulnerability to runs by turning to the banking industry to provide lines of credit to commercial paper issuers to secure repayment in the event that market panic prevented issuers from rolling over maturing paper. Banks served as backup sources of liquidity for the commercial paper market, but their own liquidity was guaranteed by the bank safety net, particularly their borrowing privileges at the Federal Reserve's discount window. This was demonstrated in 1970, when, to quell the panic in the commercial paper market that followed Penn Central's unexpected default, Federal Reserve officials announced that, until the crisis ended, advances would be made to any bank desiring to lend to creditworthy commercial paper issuers.[33] If this commitment reassured commercial paper investors and allowed issuers to roll over their paper, then participants in the commercial paper market were indirectly benefiting from the bank subsidy.

May non-banks exploit the bank subsidy more directly? Theoretically, the Federal Reserve may lend to non-bank financial firms in order to avoid a liquidity crisis that threatens financial markets. In practice, the Federal Reserve may prefer to operate through the banking system, lending to banks so that they might lend to avert the failure of a large non-bank financial firm. Nevertheless, there is growing awareness that, as financial markets and firms integrate, the failure of a large securities firm may be just as devastating to US financial markets as the failure of a large bank once was thought to be. Whether or not this danger of financial market disruption warrants government intervention to prevent failure, the question arises whether there is any remaining justification for the government to treat banks and non-banks differently.

This question was posed in 1998 in the aftermath of the financial crisis at the hedge fund Long-Term Capital Management. Long-Term Capital Management was not a bank subject to federal regulatory oversight, yet the Federal Reserve Bank of New York played an integral role in arranging private sector financing to avert the failure and involuntary liquidation of the fund. Although the regulators were quick to assure the public that neither government monies nor government pressure played a part in the hedge fund's bailout, the bank regulators' public involvement in a non-bank crisis was sufficient to invoke comment and complaint that the bank safety net was being extended to non-bank firms.

Why did the Federal Reserve take any notice of problems at Long-Term Capital Management? Certainly, some banks had large exposures to the fund, but it is unclear whether the failure of one or more of these banks was imminent; even if it had been, it is also unclear whether the best way to resolve the banks' difficulties was to insist that the lenders refund their borrower. In any event, the Federal Reserve's stated rationale for its involvement in the bailout had less to do with the domestic banking system than with the broader international financial markets in which the hedge fund operated. According to Federal Reserve Board Chairman Alan

Greenspan, the rescue was necessary to prevent serious disruption of global financial markets: 'The scale and scope of LTCM's operations, which encompassed many markets, maturities and currencies . . . made it exceptionally difficult to predict the broader ramifications of attempting to close out its positions'.[34]

The Federal Reserve's concern with preventing global financial market disruption may signal a de facto extension of some portion of the safety net to cover non-bank as well as banking markets. This does not necessarily mean that, in the future, the US government will bail out failing securities firms (or failing banks, for that matter). Nevertheless, it may mean that, as government policy toward financial failure resolution evolves, the government is likely to treat banks and non-banks more equally. This may add support to the banking industry's argument that, as financial markets integrate, any special subsidy deriving from banks' exclusive access to the safety net is rapidly disappearing.

The politics of subsidy

Who is actually making the argument that the bank subsidy no longer exists, and what has been its effect on the rehandicapping process? Initially, the answer may seem obvious. Banks and their regulators are making the case as a way to justify deregulation of the banking indus-try. In fact, however, the politics of subsidy have been more subtle, in some cases dividing bank regulators from their constituents and from each other. These conflicts reflect the intricacies of the regulatory rehandicapping process, but they also signal some ambivalence, even within banking ranks, about the implications of the bank subsidy argument. Taken to its logical conclusion, the argument challenges the legitimacy of all special regulation of banks. Yet not all those who argue that there is no special bank subsidy are willing as yet to advocate the end of all regulatory distinctions between banks and non-banks.

One point of difference that emerged in the late 1990s concerned whether and to what extent banks entering the securities and insurance businesses might be able to export any residual deposit insurance subsidy into these new financial markets. In the past, this possibility provided a rationale for laws restricting bank diversification, of which the best known were the Glass-Steagall Act, barring banks from the securities business, and the Bank Holding Company Act, limiting bank affiliations with insurance and other non-bank firms. To the extent that banks could diversify, regulation traditionally restricted their ability to use subsidized deposits to fund their non-bank enterprises. For example, Section 23A of the Federal Reserve Act placed quantitative limits on loans and other financial accommodations by a bank to its affiliated non-bank entities, such as holding company securities affiliates. Section 23B required that interaffiliate asset transfers and other transactions be on terms and conditions at least as favorable to the bank as comparable arms-length dealings between unaffiliated firms.

Like anti-diversification laws, these anti-funding rules may have responded in part to prudential concerns (such as the danger that bank managers would unwisely divert funds from the bank to prop up inefficient or failing non-bank enterprises) but they also were designed to prevent banking organizations from exploiting the deposit insurance subsidy by utilizing below-cost deposits to fund non-bank businesses. As restrictions on diversification disappeared in the 1980s and 1990s, restrictions on interaffiliate funds transfers became increasingly important as a way to neutralize banks' supposed funding advantage. Yet these restrictions presumed that banking organizations would diversify by placing their new activities in separately incorporated affiliates of the bank rather than in the bank itself.

Thus, the existence or nonexistence of the deposit insurance subsidy became central to the debate in the 1990s over financial deregulation, especially Glass-Steagall reform. If the deposit insurance subsidy gave banks a funding advantage over non-bank rivals, then fairness dictated that banks be required to enter non-bank businesses only through separate affiliates subject to interaffiliate funding restrictions (such as holding company affiliates). If banks no longer enjoyed any real funding advantage over non-bank rivals by virtue of the subsidy, however, then there was no need to couple deregulation with new restrictions on funding or on organizational structure. The bank of the future might freely combine deposit banking, securities and insurance within a single unified corporate structure (such as a national bank) without thereby obtaining any unfair competitive edge over non-bank rivals.

This debate over how diversified banks should be required to organize themselves pitted the Federal Reserve, chief supervisor of holding companies, against the Comptroller of the Currency, chief regulator of national banks. In part, their differences reflected an ongoing competition for regulatory authority over the banking industry. In the 1980s, the Federal Reserve had been the architect of the Section 20 revolution when it interpreted the Glass-Steagall Act to permit bank holding companies to establish securities affiliates to engage in limited amounts of securities underwriting and dealing. The Federal Reserve became the regulator of these securities affiliates, and it is understandable that the agency desired to retain regulatory authority over bank securities activities even after Glass-Steagall was repealed. In contrast, legislative reform that permitted nationally chartered banks to engage directly in securities activities rather than using holding company securities affiliates would expand the supervisory authority of the Comptroller of the Currency.

Nevertheless, in this competition for regulatory authority, the question of the bank subsidy also played a role, influencing both the rhetoric and the substance of financial reform. Supporters of the holding company argued that this structure would best address the problem of the deposit insurance subsidy, while proponents of unitary banks disputed that any special subsidy still existed. At least in 1999, however, the majority view appeared to be that some bank regulatory subsidy might remain (or perhaps policymakers were simply unwilling to take the chance that it did not). Financial modernization legislation adopted in 1999 required diversified banks to place most of their securities and other non-bank financial businesses either in holding company affiliates or in separately incorporated financial subsidiaries of the bank that were subject to the same funding restrictions that governed holding company affiliates.

In 1999, policymakers were also reluctant to accept the argument that, because banks no longer enjoyed any special regulatory subsidy, they should be relieved of their special regulatory burden under the Community Reinvestment Act to supply credit to under served lending markets, or, at least, a similar obligation should be imposed on their non-bank rivals. Although the latter option probably had some political appeal, it also ran counter to longstanding US aversion to government mandated credit allocation. In the case of banks, credit allocation has been legitimated by the existence of the deposit insurance subsidy, which provided the banking industry with regulatory benefits that justified the imposition of regulatory burdens.

The lesson is that the crafters of US financial regulatory policy are not ready to accept the full implications of the argument that the deposit insurance subsidy no longer exists. For now, financial regulation will continue to be guided by the notion that banks enjoy some special regulatory advantage that justifies some special regulatory burden. This bodes ill for the banking industry's argument that banks should be regulated just like other financial firms. Yet even the banking industry occasionally has been willing to admit that regulatory subsidies do exist.

In these instances, however, banks have employed the subsidy argument offensively to justify the imposition of special regulatory burdens on their competitors.

Yes, there is a regulatory subsidy (at least for credit unions)

Thus far, this chapter has focused exclusively on banks, ignoring the other insured depository institutions, thrifts and credit unions. These firms also have access to the deposit insurance subsidy, but, because each is governed by its own regulatory regime, its regulatory handicapping is different from that associated with bank regulation. Credit unions in particular enjoy a very different mix of burdens and benefits. Traditionally, these depository institutions have provided limited banking services exclusively to their members, who are connected by a common bond of occupation or community (for example, many credit unions are organized by large corporations to provide basic banking services to their employees). Credit union deposits are insured, but under a separate plan from that governing insured banks and thrifts. Because credit unions serve only a circumscribed group of customers, they are not subject to the lending obligations of the Community Reinvestment Act. They also enjoy certain special tax benefits not available to banks.

Credit unions found themselves at odds with the banking industry when, in the 1980s, they, like other financial firms, began to look for ways to expand their customer base. Federal law limited membership in credit unions to groups that shared a common bond of occupation or geographic location. In 1982, the National Credit Union Administration, supervisor of federally chartered credit unions, interpreted this 'common bond' requirement to permit a single credit union to serve multiple employee groups working for two or more unrelated employers. This interpretation allowed credit unions to increase their size and customer base, bringing them in direct competition with small community banks that operated in the same deposit/lending markets.

Arguing that the playing field was not level, the banking industry cited the special regulatory subsidy enjoyed by credit unions. This subsidy derived not just from deposit insurance (which banks enjoyed as well) but also from their favorable tax treatment and their exemption from the Community Reinvestment Act, both of which gave credit unions an unfair advantage when competing with small banks. The credit unions' special regulatory subsidy had once been balanced by special regulatory burdens such as the common bond requirement that had prevented credit unions from expanding their client base beyond a single employer group. By reinterpreting this requirement to benefit its constituents, the National Credit Union Administration had unfairly altered regulatory handicaps, giving credit unions a starting advantage over small banks.

Eventually, the banking industry brought a legal action challenging the National Credit Union Administration's reinterpretation of the common bond requirement. The Supreme Court agreed with the banks, reading the common bond requirement to limit credit union membership to employees of a single firm.[35] Credit unions then appealed to Congress, which partly reversed the Supreme Court's decision by amending federal credit union law to permit some multi-employer credit unions. During congressional negotiations, lobbyists for the banking industry argued that, to compensate for this reduction in the credit unions' regulatory burden, small banks should be relieved from their special regulatory burden under the Community Reinvestment Act, but Congress refused.[36]

The credit union war is a minor footnote to the story of US financial reform in the 1990s, but it offers several insights into the politics of regulatory handicapping and the net subsidy debate. For example, the Supreme Court's decision in the banks' favor was a relatively rare instance in which the US judiciary has prevented a federal financial regulatory agency from interpreting statutes creatively in order to lighten the regulatory burden on its constituent industry. As the next chapter describes, during the 1990s, the Supreme Court routinely accepted creative statutory readings by the bank regulators that authorized banks to compete with securities and insurance companies.

Likewise, Congress' rapid response to the Supreme Court's action was highly unusual. For decades, the Glass-Steagall Act had undergone significant transformation at the hands of the bank regulators and the judiciary, yet Congress remained silent. In both instances, however, Congress may have been expressing a consistent preference for deregulation. So long as the bank regulators were achieving de facto deregulation by creative statutory interpretation that allowed banks access to new markets and the courts were not stopping them, Congress had no reason to act. In the credit union area, however, the Supreme Court's decision had stopped progress toward deregulation and market integration, necessitating a legislative response.

More generally, it may be significant that Congress refused to rely on the existence of a special regulatory subsidy to legitimate regulation that would have restricted competition by eliminating a potential competitor from integrated financial markets. The competitive benefits to be gained by permitting credit unions to serve broader markets apparently were more important than any possible starting advantage that credit unions might enjoy when entering those markets by virtue of their special regulatory subsidy. This suggests that, although ensuring equal starting positions is an essential goal of US financial regulation, the regulatory system is also committed to the separate but equally important goal of promoting competition in financial markets. As the next few chapters show, especially recently, this goal has been reflected in the regulatory scheme's tolerance and even active encouragement of industry and agency innovation and rivalry that expand and diversify financial markets.

The future of regulatory handicapping

So where does this leave the commitment to equal starting positions on a level playing field? Certainly, the existence of regulatory subsidies suggests that some regulatory handicapping will always be part of US financial regulation. As a result, ensuring equal starts may never mean that every financial firm will be subject to an identical regulatory regime. And banks may never succeed completely in convincing policymakers, or their competitors, that deposit insurance and the safety net no longer offer any lingering subsidy to the banking industry, justifying removal of special regulatory burdens, such as banks' obligations under the Community Reinvestment Act.

Of course, the regulatory handicapping process would be far simpler were financial and regulatory structure in the US less fragmented than it is. As the credit union war suggests, the argument over regulatory subsidy and burden is complicated by the sheer number of different financial firms, with different regulators and different regulatory burdens and subsidies, that operate in the same financial markets. This financial industry balkanization, which encourages competition among financial firms and among financial regulators, is not accidental but is a deliberate part of the US regulatory plan, playing an integral role in ensuring fairness on the level playing field. The next few chapters explore how this US regulatory structure has encouraged competition and innovation but at the same time has complicated the process of regulatory reform.

4
Results Matter

The initial reaction in the financial press and on Wall Street to the stunning announcement in April 1998 of the impending merger between Citicorp and Travelers Group was to ask, 'How did they do that?' At the time, Citicorp was the third largest commercial banking organization in the US, with over one thousand branches and offices in the US and overseas; its flagship bank was New York-based Citibank, one of the best known banking names in the world. Travelers, a major US insurance firm engaged in both insurance underwriting and agency, had already diversified into a variety of financial businesses, including real estate management and investment, commodities trading and mutual fund distribution. It owned two securities companies, Salomon Smith Barney Inc., one of the largest securities brokerage firms in the US, and The Robinson-Humphrey Company, LLC. The combination of Travelers, with consolidated assets of $420 billion, with the $331 billion Citicorp would create the largest financial services company in the world.[1]

Citicorp was a bank holding company regulated by the Federal Reserve, and its diversification potential, like that of other banking organizations operating in the US, was limited at the time by two federal laws, the Glass-Steagall Act, which, as readers are aware, prohibited affiliations between banks and securities firms, and the Bank Holding Company Act, which prevented non-bank companies, including non-bank financial concerns such as insurance companies, from owning or controlling banks. In the 1980s, the Federal Reserve had interpreted Glass-Steagall to permit banks to affiliate with firms engaged in limited amounts of corporate securities underwriting (at the time, up to 25 percent of revenues), and Citicorp had taken advantage of this interpretation to set up its own securities affiliate. And, despite the Bank Holding Company Act, bank holding companies and other non-bank affiliates of banks were permitted to engage in a select 'laundry list' of financial activities that had been determined by the Federal Reserve to be 'closely related' to banking. But certainly insurance underwriting (as well as many other businesses conducted by Travelers) did not appear on the laundry list. (In fact, businesses not yet open to bank holding companies represented 25 percent of Travelers' assets.[2]) And, through its control of Salomon Smith Barney, Travelers was one of the largest securities firms in the US. Yet Travelers was now proposing to become a bank holding company by acquiring Citicorp,[3] bringing Citicorp's substantial banking operations under its very large and diversified umbrella.

Moreover, this proposed acquisition could not take place without the acquiescence of the Federal Reserve. Under the Bank Holding Company Act, regulatory approval had to be explicit: in other words, the Federal Reserve had to rule on a formal application by Travelers to become a bank holding company and to state its reasons for approving or rejecting the application pursuant to the standards set forth in the statute.[4] Thus, in contrast to the procedures allowed by some other regulatory regimes applicable to business combinations (such as the federal antitrust laws) that permit the government to remain silent, here, the Federal Reserve had to go on record to bless the transaction. For that reason, it was common practice for applicants in bank merger transactions, particularly large deals, to vet their proposal with the regulators informally before commencing the costly application procedure – and, of course, before making the all important public announcement of the deal. So, in this case, presumably, Citicorp and Travelers had checked with the Federal Reserve, and the Federal Reserve had not vetoed the acquisition for non-compliance with either the Bank Holding Company Act or any other law.

This latter point was of particular interest to banking lawyers, as well as to members of Congress who, coincidentally, were considering legislation to amend the banking laws to permit the very kind of affiliation that Citicorp and Travelers were proposing. At the time, however, the chances for legislative reform that would be sufficiently broad to allow this particular combination seemed slim to none. Although the Federal Reserve was supporting a reform proposal sponsored by Congressman Jim Leach, chairman of the House Banking Committee, that would have allowed the formation of financial holding companies to engage in banking, securities and insurance activities, this proposal had encountered strong political opposition, even from the ranks of the banking industry and, at least before the announcement of its proposed combination with Travelers, from Citicorp itself.[5]

To be fair, the banking industry's opposition to deregulation was based on form rather than on substance. Nationally chartered banks like Citibank and their chief regulator, the Comptroller of the Currency, preferred reform that would leave banking organizations free to locate their new securities and insurance businesses within the bank itself (regulated by the Comptroller of the Currency) rather than requiring that securities and insurance be contained within separate holding company affiliates (regulated by the Federal Reserve) as Congressman Leach's 1998 bill was proposing. Now, however, Citicorp and Travelers were planning a combination that would follow the blueprint of the Leach bill, except that the Leach bill was not yet law, and had not even been voted on by the full House of Representatives. Moreover, the Leach bill faced major obstacles in the Senate as well as a hostile president who had already threatened to veto it.

Further, if the acquisition did have the imprimatur of the Federal Reserve, then that agency was reversing what had been a long-standing government policy against the combination of banking and insurance. Decades earlier, the US Congress had made the legislative decision to leave regulation of the insurance business up to the states,[6] and many states had tried to outlaw affiliations between insurance firms and banks.[7] In 1982, Congress had amended the Bank Holding Company Act to make clear that the non-bank financial activities permitted to bank holding companies did not include the insurance business.[8]

The Federal Reserve itself had tended in the past to take a dim view of attempts by non-banks to employ creative statutory interpretation to gain or retain control of banks, condemning these moves as evasions of the Bank Holding Company Act. In the early 1980s, for example, a number of non-bank financial firms acquired 'non-bank banks' – institutions that performed standard banking functions, including accepting insured deposits, but that technically were not considered banks, at least for the purposes of the Bank Holding Company Act's prohibition on corporate ownership of banks, because they did not fit within the peculiarly narrow definition of 'bank' contained in that statute. According to that definition, a bank was a firm that accepted deposits legally entitled to repayment upon demand and that engaged in the business of making commercial loans. Non-bank banks escaped coverage either by not offering traditional checking accounts (instead they offered so-called NOW accounts that were functionally equivalent to demand deposits but that technically required notice of intent to withdraw, notice which was deemed to be given when the check was presented) or by spinning off their commercial lending operations.

The Federal Reserve had attempted to halt this evasion of the Bank Holding Company Act by adopting regulations that broadened the definition of bank to cover most non-bank banks, but the Supreme Court invalidated these rules, insisting on a literal reading of the statutory language.[9] Congress responded by rewriting the Bank Holding Company Act to include within its definition of 'bank' any institution that benefited from federal deposit insurance,[10] a change that allowed the Federal Reserve to stop non-bank firms, including insurance companies, from going into the banking business. Now, however, Travelers Group was about to receive the blessing of the Federal Reserve to acquire one of the leading banks in the US, creating the largest diversified financial services company in the world.

In September 1998, just five months after the deal was announced, the Federal Reserve approved Travelers' application to become a bank holding company by acquiring Citicorp. Although in May the House of Representatives had passed Congressman Leach's financial modernization bill by a one vote margin, in October, as had been predicted by many observers, the legislation died in the Senate. Congressman Leach vowed to try again, and in early 1999, a new regulatory reform plan that would legalize the formation of diversified financial services firms was introduced in Congress and began to make its way through the legislative process. In the meantime, Travelers and Citicorp completed their merger, creating the giant Citigroup.

Why did the Federal Reserve approve this combination? And what were the implications of the Federal Reserve's actions for the future of US financial regulation? The answers say much about the values that shape the US financial regulatory process and that give content to the ideal of the level playing field. As explained in previous chapters, the first step in creating a level playing field is to ensure, through regulatory handicapping, that players in financial markets enjoy equal starts. Once regulatory handicapping is in place, however, competition on the level playing field should proceed with a minimum of government interference. Unfettered competition is essential to achieving a truly level playing field because it is the best way to ensure that the results of play are both fair and efficient, goals which, in US financial regulation, are typically viewed as synonymous. Simply put, on the level playing field, the best players win.

At first, the high value that US financial market players accord to free competition in financial markets may seem somewhat at odds with their apparent tolerance of a legal regime that, despite deregulation, remains remarkably intrusive, particularly compared with non-US financial regulatory models. In fact, however, this faith in the competitive process to ensure the most efficient (and therefore the fairest) outcomes provides an explanation of the anomaly that US financial markets are at once highly regulated and highly competitive. Regulation is intense, but regulation itself is the product of a competitive process. Competition among different regulators and among different regulatory regimes is an accepted part of the US financial system and is viewed as a significant catalyst for regulatory reform. The Travelers/Citicorp combination offers an interesting and highly instructive example of the fruits of this regulatory competition.

Some theorists may view the rivalries that exist among financial regulators in the US as an inevitable consequence of the plethora of governmental agencies with overlapping and occasionally even conflicting responsibilities for regulation of financial markets. The average financial firm considering doing business in the US must take into account both state and federal laws and, within each layer of government, separate and often seemingly autonomous regulatory regimes governing banking or insurance or securities or commodities or occasionally all of the above. Fragmentation of regulatory responsibility for financial markets may simply reflect the general preference in the US for decentralization of political power that is designed to ensure that no single agent of government becomes too big or too powerful. Yet competition among regulatory authorities appears to be an affirmative goal, rather than simply an unintended byproduct, of the federal state. Certainly, in financial regulation, regulatory competition is an important norm, contributing to the creation and maintenance of a level playing field.

How does competition among regulators level the playing field for financial firms? First, regulatory competition makes possible the competitive innovations by regulated firms that, as previous chapters have described, help to equalize regulatory burdens and benefits, ensuring all players a fair starting position. For example, if Regulator A prevents its regulated firms from offering innovative Product X, the availability of an alternative and competitive regulatory regime will allow firms that want to sell Product X to switch to the jurisdiction of more permissive Regulator B so that innovation may proceed. Second, regulatory competition ultimately results in the survival of the fittest regulatory regime – and the fittest regulator. If Product X turns out to be a winner, every firm subject to Regulator A's authority eventually will switch to Regulator B in order to have the opportunity to sell Product X. Regulator A will have no constituency left and will either disappear, or relent and allow its regulated firms to innovate. If, however, Product X turns out to be a financial 'bubble', proving that Regulator A was right all along, risk averse investors will reward firms that chose to remain under the supervision of prescient Regulator A instead of switching to incompetent Regulator B. In either case, the most efficient regulation will prevail.

Finally, allowing this regulatory competition to proceed ultimately lets the market determine the outcome. Whether Regulator A or Regulator B wins depends on the market's judgment as to the worth of Product X. This may help to resolve the conundrum, faced by US financial policymakers, of how to reconcile their legal regime's heavy reliance on regulatory handicapping with its professed commitment to free competition. Regulatory competition provides a way to test regulation in the market to determine whether in fact it is providing equal starting positions to all competitors. If not, regulatory competition allows financial players to make some readjustments to their regulatory burdens with the help of friendly regulators. These regulators have incentives to be sensitive to industry complaints of competitive imbalance because players unfairly overburdened by one regulatory regime may switch to a more helpful regulator. Thus, competing regulators strive to maintain a rough equilibrium so that no player may obtain a starting advantage by defecting.

Of course, this description of perfectly functioning regulatory competition may be more ideal than real. In 1998, the Citicorp/Travelers combination offered a rare opportunity to examine regulatory competition in practice. Understanding how regulatory competition shaped the outcome of this transaction requires some consideration of the earlier battles among bank regulators that culminated in the Federal Reserve's groundbreaking decision, as well as a look at the actions of two other participants, Congress and the judiciary, that functioned as umpires of regulatory competition. Before the stage is set for the telling of this particular story, however, it may be helpful briefly to review the general theory of regulatory competition and to explain how it has provided political legitimacy for the division of supervisory authority that traditionally has characterized US financial regulatory structure.

Regulatory competition in theory

The theory of regulatory competition has profoundly influenced modern corporate legal scholarship in the US, providing the leading explanation of the evolution of American corporate law. In the US federalist system, corporation law is largely state law: individual states (and not the national government) charter corporations, and corporations are governed by the legal regimes adopted by their chartering states. A key element of the state chartering system is that corporations have freedom of choice as to their chartering authority. Because most firms are not required to locate their business operations within their states of incorporation,[11] they may switch chartering states without incurring relocation costs. As a result, the choice of chartering authority tends to be dictated largely by the particular regulatory climate that each state offers through its corporation laws.

States, on the other hand, have a motive to compete for corporate charters in order to maximize chartering fees. The state's pecuniary stake in corporate chartering, together with the corporation's freedom to choose among chartering authorities, are preconditions to effective charter competition. To attract and retain charters, presumably, states will adopt legal regimes designed to appeal to corporations. The state with the most desirable regulatory regime will win the most charters. To prevent further defections, states that value corporate charters will reform their own regulatory regimes to provide the same or additional benefits to corporations. The result, eventually, will be some form of equilibrium in which a particular model of corporation law will prevail in most if not all competing states.

Whether this model is likely to be efficient, reflecting what some corporate scholars have termed a 'race to the top', or lax, reflecting what other scholars have called a 'race to the bottom', continues to be a subject for debate. Ideally, charter competition will result in the dominance of a legal framework that maximizes shareholder value, since this model is most likely to appeal to the owners of the corporation. On the other hand, chartering decisions are often made by corporate managers rather than by corporate owners, and agency problems may prevent shareholders of large firms from monitoring their managers' decisions. If this is the case, then it is possible that corporate managers will look for state corporation laws that favor their own personal interests even at the expense of shareholders' preferences. For example, a state that offers its corporations legal protection from hostile takeovers may appeal to corporate managers, who fear losing their jobs, but not to shareholders, who welcome the potential financial gain to be made from the sale of their company. Whether this state eventually wins the competition for corporate charters, or loses to a state that gives shareholders' interests greater weight, may provide some evidence as to whether charter competition tends to detract from or contribute to the efficient evolution of corporate law.[12]

Regardless of how scholars view the evidence, however, most corporate experts presume that at least some interstate competition for corporate charters does take place. Moreover, despite growing appreciation among scholars of the potential for agency problems that may occasionally produce corporate legal regimes that are more beneficial to managers than to shareholders, there is remarkably little political will to scrap charter competition entirely, for example, by legislating a uniform national corporation code that preempts state corporation law. Periodically, there is pressure for a national standard to address a specific problem in corporate law (for example, the federal securities laws, which date from the 1930s, represent an important exception to state autonomy in the corporate field), but, in general, the competitive model has prevailed and is accepted, if not embraced, by most corporate players.

Interestingly, US bank chartering is often cited by corporate scholars as a special example of charter competition in action. Banks, unlike other corporations, have the option of choosing a national charter in lieu of a state charter. Moreover, unlike most non-bank corporations that may engage in any lawful business, banks derive their permissible powers from their chartering authority's banking laws. This factor adds a new and potent element to standard charter competition: the legal climate, and in particular the mix of powers allowed to banks by a chartering authority's banking laws, will determine a bank's future business opportunities, especially its diversification potential. Assuming that banks will seek to maximize this potential, regulatory competition theory suggests that both the states and the national chartering authority (the Office of the Comptroller of the Currency, which is part of the US Treasury Department) will compete for bank charters by expanding the menu of powers available to their banks.

Is this the case? There is some evidence that bank charter competition does occur: for example, as a preemptive strike against the Comptroller of the Currency, several state legislatures have adopted 'wild card' statutes automatically empowering their own state-chartered banks to engage in any new activity that becomes legal for national banks. For its part, the Comptroller of the Currency has used the doctrine of preemption to exempt national banks from restrictive state consumer laws such as usury ceilings, thereby extending business opportunities available to national banks beyond those available to their state-chartered rivals. These moves are consistent with the theory of charter competition described in the corporate and banking literature.[13]

As in the case of corporate chartering, however, charter competition in bank regulation, both in theory and practice, has generated some dissenting opinion. Because bank charter competition is presumed to focus on bank powers, the impact of charter competition on bank safety and soundness must be considered. Presumably, bank managers and bank shareholders alike will opt for permissive chartering regimes that allow banks the maximum flexibility to diversify with the minimum regulatory oversight. Thus, bank charter competition, if real, may precipitate a particularly dangerous race to the bottom, increasing the riskiness of banks as well as the risk of bank failure.

In practice, however, this danger may be mitigated by the likelihood that bank chartering authorities will be forced to consider factors other than maximizing chartering fees when drafting their banking laws. For example, if a state's lax banking laws result in sharply increased bank failure rates, then regulatory competition may prove counterproductive, leaving the winner with fewer active bank charters rather than with more. Moreover, bank chartering authorities appear to be at least somewhat sensitive to the demands of constituencies other than bank managers and shareholders, such as bank customers who may insist on tough consumer protection laws. State legislatures in particular may be vulnerable to pressure from local consumer interests, resulting in state law that is more restrictive and less friendly to banks than might otherwise be expected given the threat of charter competition.[14]

Finally, bank charter competition may be frustrated by the actions of other regulatory agencies that, although not chartering authorities, do have considerable say over the extent of permissible bank powers. For example, if a state-chartered bank chooses to become a member of the Federal Reserve system, it becomes subject to regulation by the Federal Reserve.[15] Non-member state-chartered banks that have federal deposit insurance (which, as a practical matter, includes virtually every bank that deals with the public) are regulated by the Federal Deposit Insurance Corporation. If a bank is controlled by a holding company, then that holding company is regulated by the Federal Reserve. Moreover, as banks increasingly diversify into other financial fields, such as securities and insurance, they come into contact with new regulatory agencies; for example, the securities affiliates operated by financial holding companies come within the jurisdiction of the Securities and Exchange Commission.

This rather confusing and overlapping regulatory structure has been simplified somewhat by a division of authority among the three federal bank supervisory agencies. Although all nationally chartered banks are required to join the Federal Reserve system and qualify for federal deposit insurance, national banks do not have to deal with three separate federal regulators; instead, the Comptroller of the Currency takes precedence, acting as principal federal banking regulator for all national banks. Likewise, the Federal Reserve serves as chief federal regulator of state-chartered banks that are members of the Federal Reserve system although these banks also must obtain federal deposit insurance. This leaves to the Federal Deposit Insurance Corporation all remaining state-chartered banks that have federal deposit insurance but do not have another federal regulator. (State-chartered banks still must deal with both their principal federal regulator and their state chartering authority, but accords among state and federal officials to share certain examination and oversight responsibilities have minimized some costly and duplicative aspects of dual regulation.)

Thus, as a practical matter, virtually every bank in the US reports to some federal bank regulator regardless of its charter. The question then arises whether this overlay of federal regulation short circuits regulatory competition or actually fosters competition by adding a new layer of regulatory rivalry. For example, although the states and the Comptroller of the Currency may have incentives to compete for charters by giving their banks new powers, the Federal Reserve, or the Federal Deposit Insurance Corporation, might halt the competition by adopting regulation that prohibits all member banks, or all insured banks, from exercising their new powers. Alternatively, these agencies might join in the competition, adjusting their own regulation in order to persuade banks to choose them as their principal federal regulator. This latter possibility raises the broader theoretical question of whether agencies that do not vie for chartering fees have any incentives to compete for expanded regulatory jurisdiction, and, if they do, whether the resulting competition is likely to contribute to or detract from regulatory efficiency.

Interagency competition

Do all regulatory agencies compete like chartering authorities, seeking to grow their stable of regulated firms by offering an hospitable regulatory environment? Some scholars may reject this analogy on the ground that, unlike chartering authorities, non-chartering agencies generally do not have to vie for jurisdiction over regulated firms. For example, if the Securities and Exchange Commission claims the power to regulate any product that it defines as a security, then financial firms that want to offer securities products are subject to the Commission's jurisdiction with no credible threat of exit. The agency has no incentive to modernize its regulation in order to satisfy regulated firms. To the contrary, the more restrictive its regulation (for example, the more products that it is able to include within its definition of a security), the larger its stable of regulated companies. Hence, agency rivalry, rather than facilitating desirable financial and regulatory innovation, may lead to overregulation as agencies act unilaterally to expand their jurisdiction to reach ever increasing numbers of firms.[16]

Moreover, regulatory competition among chartering authorities presumes that chartering agencies behave as profit maximizing entities, driven by the desire to increase revenues in the form of chartering fees or taxes. This assumption may be somewhat problematic even when applied to chartering authorities (for example, state banking departments may not profit directly from the proceeds of increased chartering fees but may depend for funding on appropriations by state legislatures). It is even more strained when applied to non chartering regulators. Some federal regulatory agencies, such as the Federal Reserve, do fund themselves, and a portion of their revenues derives from fees paid by their stable of banks for regulatory examinations and other services. Nevertheless, common sense suggests that, if interagency competition occurs, the average bureaucrat is likely to be motivated as much, if not more, by non-pecuniary considerations, such as the desire to expand regulatory jurisdiction and prestige (empire building) than by expectation of fee income. Of course, empire building is a powerful motive for action, but it is unclear what action it motivates. Agency employees seeking to expand their agency's jurisdiction (and justify their continued employment) may adopt unnecessary regulation that prevents innovation. Certainly, they will resist deregulation that shrinks their regulatory power.

Nevertheless, despite these theoretical objections, there is evidence that competition among financial regulators does occur under certain circumstances. Moreover, particularly recently, that competition is resulting in the diminution of regulatory burdens on the financial industry. The best example of this regulatory competition may be the rivalry that arose in the 1990s between the Comptroller of the Currency, chief regulator of national banks, and the Federal Reserve in its capacity as regulator of bank holding companies. How this rivalry became a catalyst for regulatory change is discussed later in this chapter, but first it may be useful to consider why, in this particular case, the preconditions for effective competition were in place, turning interagency rivalry into true regulatory competition.

One explanation is that, by virtue of deregulation, the banking agencies' power to prevent defection by regulated firms was diminished. This was not always the case: before the 1990s, the conventional wisdom was that all large banking organizations doing business in the US, particularly those with nationwide operations, would come within the jurisdiction of the Federal Reserve regardless of their choice of charter. Although many large US banks had national charters and were regulated by the Comptroller of the Currency, virtually all were owned by holding companies, and all of these holding companies were regulated by the Federal Reserve.

Thus, the Federal Reserve and the Comptroller of the Currency shared supervisory responsibilities over most major US banking organizations. This regulatory overlap might have created opportunities for the Federal Reserve to block the Comptroller of the Currency's efforts to compete with the states for charters by facilitating product innovation by national banks. As previously suggested, the Federal Reserve could have used its regulatory authority to prevent national banks that were part of holding companies from exercising new powers granted by the Comptroller, thereby frustrating the competitive process.

This, however, did not occur, for two reasons. First, the Federal Reserve itself conceded that, under the Bank Holding Company Act, it had no regulatory authority over *bank* affiliates of holding companies as opposed to non-bank affiliates.[17] For example, the Federal Reserve regulated the pre-merger Citicorp, a bank holding company, as well as its affiliates that did not have bank charters, but did not control the powers of Citibank, a nationally chartered bank, or of any other bank within the Citicorp constellation.

In theory, of course, the Federal Reserve could always have taken steps to penalize a holding company if it was unhappy about the activities of a subsidiary bank. So long as holding companies could not escape regulation by the Federal Reserve, the threat of retaliation alone might have had a chilling effect on regulatory competition. And escape was difficult: although the holding company structure was not legally mandated for US banking organizations, at least before 1994, as a practical matter, large banking organizations needed the holding company form of organization in order to avoid interstate banking restrictions. Before 1994, interstate bank branching was prohibited, even by national banks, but holding companies could diversify geographically by owning separately incorporated bank subsidiaries in different states so long as state law permitted such ownership. By the early 1990s, many states had relaxed their laws to permit such acquisitions, leading to the formation of large multistate holding companies such as Citicorp with multiple bank subsidiaries.[18]

In 1994, however, Congress passed the Riegle-Neal Interstate Banking and Branching Efficiency Act, which removed legal barriers to interstate bank branching. As a result, banking organizations were free to consolidate their separate subsidiary banks into a unified banking entity with branches in multiple states. Although the holding company structure still offered banking organizations the opportunity to establish non-bank affiliates to engage in non-bank businesses that were 'closely related to banking', so long as the Comptroller of the Currency was willing and able to expand the powers of national banks to equal or exceed those made available to holding companies by the Federal Reserve, the holding company structure no longer offered legal advantages to banks.

In sum, the repeal of restrictions on interstate branching lessened the value of the holding company structure, making the threat of exit from holding company regulation a real possibility even for large banks. Banks could escape the Federal Reserve's oversight completely by consolidating their operations into a single 'universal' bank with a national charter. Thus, at least one of the preconditions to effective regulatory competition between the Federal Reserve and the Comptroller of the Currency was satisfied. The Federal Reserve could maintain its regulatory authority over the largest banking organizations only by persuading them that it was in their interest to retain their holding companies. The Comptroller could expand the number and size of its own regulated entities by encouraging large banking organizations to consolidate their operations within a nationally chartered bank. What could the regulators offer banking organizations to gain their favor? For most of the 1990s, the main concern, especially of the largest banks, was the power to diversify into new financial businesses. The organizational form, and regulatory scheme, that offered the greatest diversification potential was likely to prevail.

Why did these regulatory agencies care about attracting large banks to their fold? Interestingly, in the 1990s, increasing political pressure for regulatory reform created incentives for both agencies to compete for constituents in order to justify their very existence. Deregulatory fever threatened the banking agencies in two ways. First, with the dismantling of regulation, the political rationale for maintaining multiple federal bank regulatory agencies was likely to be weakened, possibly even fueling a movement to eliminate one or more regulators. Second, calls for substantive regulatory reform tended to be accompanied by suggestions for agency restructuring as well (as one commentator has noted, these kinds of proposals have tended to accompany every recent change of political administration![19]) Finally, the example provided by British regulatory restructuring gave new life to plans for the rationalization and simplification of US financial regulatory structure.

For reasons that are explored more fully in the next chapter, proposals for radical restructuring of financial regulatory agencies tend to face particularly severe obstacles in the US. Nevertheless, politicians occasionally have rewarded or punished individual agencies by reallocating regulatory responsibilities in ways that have augmented or diminished agency authority. (For example, following the thrift crisis of the 1980s, Congress restructured federal thrift regulation to reduce the power and autonomy of the former thrift regulatory agencies.) Thus, both the Federal Reserve and the Comptroller of the Currency must always take seriously the possibility that Congress may decide to shift regulatory responsibilities in ways that may disempower an existing agency. The Federal Reserve has been threatened periodically with changes in its status as an independent (non-political) agency and removal of its regulatory authority over state-chartered member banks. Likewise, the Comptroller has been forced to defend the dual banking system and the national chartering option. Maximizing the number and the clout of their constituents may help both agencies to deflect political attack. And, to the extent that deregulation and industry consolidation are shrinking the number of regulated institutions, competition for the remaining players is growing fiercer.

Perhaps the strongest evidence that the federal banking agencies are capable of competition is the fact that they are competing. Moreover, this competition offered banks many of the benefits of deregulation that for most of the 1990s were not forthcoming from Congress. As will be shown, banks' entry into the long-forbidden fields of securities and insurance occurred, at least initially, as a result of the ongoing rivalry among bank regulators, especially the Federal Reserve and the Comptroller. First, however, the influence on the competitive process of two other players must be considered.

The roles of Congress and the courts

There are two other potential roadblocks to effective regulatory competition in US financial markets. First, Congress may legislate against competition. The legislature may simply override federal agency innovation, as it did in 1982, when it removed the authority of the Federal Reserve to use its discretion under the Bank Holding Company Act to define most insurance activities as 'closely related to banking', and therefore permissible for bank holding company affiliates. Alternatively, the legislature can impose a uniform national standard that preempts state experimentation, as occurred in 1991, when Congress amended federal deposit insurance legislation to limit the permissible non-banking powers of state-chartered insured banks to those already available to national banks.

This last restriction put a halt to the efforts by several states to compete for bank charters by allowing their banks to enter the insurance business. Interestingly, however, Congress did not interfere when, just a few years later, the Comptroller of the Currency began to expand the insurance powers of national banks. These actions by the Comptroller sparked a rivalry with the Federal Reserve that, as will be discussed, culminated in the Citicorp/Travelers combination. Thus, congressional inaction that leaves agencies free to innovate appears to be a precondition to effective regulatory competition.

Second, the courts may interfere with regulatory competition by invalidating agency interpretations of statutes that either expand the agency's jurisdiction or deregulate for the benefit of the agency's constituents. As mentioned earlier in this chapter, in the mid-1980s, the Supreme Court frustrated the Federal Reserve's attempt to expand its regulatory jurisdiction under the Bank Holding Company Act to reach non-bank banks owned by commercial firms. More frequently, however, the Supreme Court has been willing to defer to a regulatory agency's interpretation of its own statutes, especially when the effect of that deference has been to foster regulatory competition.

As a legal matter, the doctrine of judicial deference reflects the courts' acknowledgment of the legislature's decision to leave many details of administration of complex regulatory programs in the hands of expert agency employees. In some cases, Congress deliberately delegated questions of interpretation of statutory terms to the regulators by using sweeping statutory phrases such as 'closely related to banking' that required application to specific cases. In other instances, when statutory language admits of multiple readings, judges believe that the agency is better positioned than the courts to determine its meaning. Of course, if statutory language is clear and admits of only one reading, as the Supreme Court decided in the matter of the non-bank banks, courts will not defer to creative agency interpretation.

Usually, however, the judiciary will accept the agency's judgment so long as it is reasonable.

The practical consequence of judicial deference to reasonable agency interpretations of financial statutes has been that, in virtually every instance in which regulatory interpretation has facilitated financial innovation and deregulation, the courts have declined to interfere.[20] (In contrast, in the non-bank bank case, where the Federal Reserve was attempting to expand its jurisdiction to halt innovation, the Supreme Court did not defer to agency expertise.) This result may not have been accidental. Allowing regulatory competition to proceed has permitted considerable financial modernization in spite of congressional inaction.

Regulatory competition in action

With this background, it is time to consider the events that culminated in the dramatic Citicorp/Travelers decision in 1998. This decision was made possible by a series of earlier regulatory innovations that had allowed banks to gain a foothold in two long-forbidden businesses, corporate securities underwriting and insurance. At the time, bank entry into these non-bank financial businesses was restricted by three federal statutes. The Glass-Steagall Act barred banks from engaging in corporate securities underwriting either directly or through affiliates. The Bank Holding Company Act limited the permissible activities of non-bank affiliates to those 'closely related to banking', which expressly excluded most insurance activities. Finally, the National Bank Act, which governed the legal powers of nationally chartered banks, restricted national banks to certain specified deposit and lending activities and to other businesses that were incidental to the banking business.

State banking law was also relevant, since states had authority to determine the menu of powers available to their own banks. Prior to the 1990s, state innovation in response to charter competition was responsible for many of the gains made by banks seeking to enter the insurance business. Not every state chose to compete; some states actually tightened restrictions on bank insurance activities in the 1970s and 1980s, adopting anti-affiliation statutes that subsequently became the subject of a major legal contest that ultimately wound up in the Supreme Court.[21] Nevertheless, several key states did take the initiative in expanding their banks' insurance powers at a time when free bank entry into the insurance business was restricted by national and many state laws. A notable example was South Dakota, which adopted special legislation in 1983 permitting its state-chartered banks to engage in any insurance activity. At the time, it was assumed that this legislation was adopted at the behest of Citicorp, which had pledged to invest $2.5 million in a South Dakota bank subsidiary in order to take advantage of the new powers.

Nevertheless, this classic charter competition was halted by the intervention of the Federal Reserve and Congress. Although ordinarily the Federal Reserve claimed no power to regulate the activities of subsidiary banks (as opposed to subsidiary non-banks) of holding companies like Citicorp, in this case the Federal Reserve made an exception, arguing that Citicorp's proposed South Dakota bank, which had no plans to offer services, banking or otherwise, to people actually resident in South Dakota, was not really a bank at all but a non-bank affiliate. As such, it was governed by the Bank Holding Company Act, which had been amended by Congress in 1982 to provide that bank holding companies may not own general insurance firms.[22]

Other states, notably Delaware and California, were more successful in crafting laws that liberalized their banks' insurance powers without attracting the ire of the Federal Reserve, and these states were able to persuade large banking organizations to charter subsidiary banks in their jurisdictions. Nevertheless, in 1991, Congress put a stop to this regulatory competition, amending the Federal Deposit Insurance Act to equalize the permissible powers of national banks and insured state-chartered banks. Congress specifically took aim at insurance underwriting, forbidding insured state-chartered banks from exercising such powers even if they became legal under the laws of their state of incorporation.[23]

Although this instance of congressional intervention frustrated classic bank charter competition, it did not spell the end of regulatory innovation. Banks, particularly large banks, were still looking for ways to diversify into new businesses. Because Congress would not act, they turned to their regulators for assistance, and these regulators were willing to oblige. Unlike earlier charter competition, however, the next phase of regulatory competition erupted principally between the Comptroller of the Currency and the Federal Reserve, which agencies, as previously described, were engaged in a struggle to emerge as the premier regulators of the largest US banking organizations.

Interestingly, this particular competition more closely reflected the classic model of efficient regulatory competition than had previous regulatory rivalries among banking agencies. As the classic model would predict, the new regulatory competition took the form of agency innovations that assisted banks in breaching the legal barriers between banking and other financial businesses. Thus, regulatory competition produced deregulation. Moreover, this time, Congress did not put a stop to the competition. In fact, the rapid pace of regulatory competition may have made congressional interference impossible.

What form did this new regulatory competition take? As early as the 1980s, perhaps in response to the challenge posed by state chartering authorities, the Comptroller of the Currency had begun to look for ways to allow national banks to enter the insurance business, an effort that continued even after Congress moved in 1991 to curb the states' authority to liberalize their own banks' insurance powers. Unlike state bank chartering authorities in South Dakota and Delaware, who could count on the assistance of sympathetic state legislators to reform their banking laws, the Comptroller of the Currency could not expect Congress to rewrite the National Bank Act to allow national banks to become insurance firms. Instead, the Comptroller of the Currency had to find a way to interpret existing national bank laws to permit diversification. For example, the Comptroller ruled that the sale of annuities by national banks was not an insurance activity but a banking function and therefore perfectly legal for national banks. The Comptroller also construed an obscure 1916 provision of the National Bank Act that allowed national banks located in small towns to act as insurance agents to permit national banks to use small town branches as headquarters from which to sell all forms of insurance on a nationwide basis. Both of these interpretations of national banking laws ultimately were upheld by reviewing federal courts.[24]

One national bank that chose to take advantage of the newly authorized power to act as an insurance agent was Barnett, a large Florida bank. Florida was a state that strictly prohibited bank entry into the insurance business, and state officials argued that, since Congress had decades earlier made the choice to leave regulation of the insurance business to the states, Florida had the power to block national banks and their affiliates from selling insurance within its jurisdiction. The Supreme Court ultimately disagreed, finding that the National Bank Act (as interpreted by the Comptroller) preempted state insurance law.[25]

Since the national bank charter now conveyed the power to engage in at least two insurance activities – selling annuities and acting as agent for the sale of all forms of insurance through small town branches – the value of the national charter increased. Many states responded just as regulatory competition theory would predict, liberalizing their own laws to give state-chartered banks the same opportunities as national banks.[26] The Federal Reserve, however, was limited in its ability to respond to the Comptroller's competitive challenge, since, in 1982, Congress had spoken, amending the Bank Holding Company Act expressly to bar the Federal Reserve from expanding the insurance powers of bank holding companies. Bank holding companies did have the same power to sell insurance from small town offices as national banks, enabling the Federal Reserve to maintain parity with the Comptroller in the area of insurance agency. The sale of annuities, however, presented more of a problem, although the Federal Reserve was able to approve certain joint sales arrangements involving bank and bank holding company employees.[27] On the other hand, the Federal Reserve had greater flexibility to authorize bank holding companies to engage in insurance activities outside of the US, including certain forms of insurance underwriting, an activity still forbidden to national banks.[28]

Moreover, the Federal Reserve was able to offer bank holding companies greater securities powers than those available to national banks. Relying on a distinction drawn in the Glass-Steagall Act between banks, which were prohibited from engaging directly in any corporate securities underwriting, and affiliates of banks, which were prohibited only from engaging 'principally' in the underwriting business, the Federal Reserve had authorized bank holding companies to establish securities affiliates to engage in limited amounts of corporate securities underwriting. Originally, these affiliates were allowed to derive up to 5 percent of their revenues from 'ineligible' securities activities – that is, corporate securities underwriting and other securities activities that were illegal for banks under Glass-Steagall. The remaining 95 percent of the securities affiliates' revenues would come from so-called 'eligible' bank securities activities, such as dealing in government securities (expressly permitted by Glass-Steagall for all banks), securities brokerage (which the Federal Reserve had previously determined did not violate Glass-Steagall) and investment advice (which the Federal Reserve had previously determined was a banking function).[29]

As a result, so long as the bank holding company had sufficient eligible securities revenues to meet this ratio, it could enter the previously forbidden business of underwriting corporate equity and debt. The Federal Reserve obliged the banking industry by quickly raising the revenue ceiling for ineligible securities underwriting first to 10 percent and subsequently to 25 percent. This enabled several banking organizations with large government securities operations to engage in enough corporate securities underwriting to ascend quickly to the top brackets of the US underwriting business.

Interestingly, Federal Reserve Chairman Paul Volcker dissented from the Federal Reserve's decision authorizing securities affiliates, fearing that the interpretation would make possible affiliations of banks with some of the principal underwriting firms or investment houses in the US. Such a drastic change in the law, in his opinion, required congressional action.[30] Despite this warning, however, Congress did not act either to ratify or reverse the Federal Reserve's decision, and the courts upheld the agency's reading of Glass-Steagall.[31]

As a result of this interpretation, the bank holding company structure increased in value for banking organizations looking to enter the securities business. Both national and state banks could engage directly in a limited number of securities functions not prohibited by Glass-Steagall, but the potentially lucrative business of corporate securities underwriting was accessible only with the Federal Reserve's blessing. Thus, even after 1994, when congressional repeal of legal restrictions on interstate branching freed large banks from the necessity of forming holding companies in order to diversify geographically, the opportunity to own a securities affiliate persuaded most large banks to retain their holding companies.

In response, the Comptroller of the Currency mounted a new competitive challenge to the Federal Reserve by offering a way in which banking organizations potentially could consolidate their holding company operations within a unified national bank without giving up their securities powers. The Comptroller's new 'operating subsidiary' rule allowed national banks to establish subsidiaries to engage in activities that were not legally permissible for banks so long as the activities were determined by the Comptroller to be part of the 'business of banking'. The implications of this rule became clear in 1997 when the Comptroller permitted Zions First National Bank to expand the business of its operating subsidiary to include underwriting municipal revenue bonds.[32] Zions' subsidiary already engaged in brokerage and investment advisory activities, businesses that were permissible for banks under Glass-Steagall. Underwriting municipal revenue bonds, however, had previously been considered an ineligible bank securities activity that could be performed only by a bank holding company securities affiliate.

In the view of the Comptroller, so long as Zions located its underwriting business in a separate corporate entity from the bank itself, the Comptroller could take advantage of the Federal Reserve's own reading of Glass-Steagall, which allowed banks to affiliate with securities firms so long as they were not 'engaged principally' in securities underwriting. Nevertheless, because Zion's securities firm was a direct subsidiary of the bank rather than a subsidiary of a bank holding company, the Comptroller, and not the Federal Reserve, would regulate it. In theory, the operating subsidiary rule would allow a bank holding company to transfer all of its non-banking businesses, including its securities activities, to direct subsidiaries of the bank, making the holding company (and the Federal Reserve) redundant. The only precondition was that the Comptroller had to rule that the non-banking activities were part of the business of banking. Since the Federal Reserve had already decided that these activities were closely related to banking, however, this finding would be easy for the Comptroller to make.

This regulatory competition between the Comptroller and the Federal Reserve was occurring in the shadow of the debate in Congress over financial modernization which was going on through much of the 1990s. Congressman Jim Leach, chairman of the House Banking Committee, had taken the lead in promoting financial reform legislation that would allow banks to diversify. His original model for financial reform was the Bank Holding Company Act: under his plan, banks would be free to enter the insurance and securities businesses, but only through holding company affiliates separated from the bank and regulated by the Federal Reserve. As might be expected, this structure displeased the Comptroller of the Currency. The US Treasury Department opposed the original Leach bill and encouraged its constituents, especially large national banks, to lobby against it. Thus, as late as 1998, Citicorp was a vocal opponent of congressional banking reform.

Originally, banks had several reasons to oppose congressional reform of the banking laws. Although a consensus had been reached among at least large banks and securities firms in favor of repeal of the Glass-Steagall Act, until the late 1990s, politically powerful representatives of the insurance industry continued to oppose bank entry into the insurance business. In 1995, for example, congressional supporters of the insurance industry attempted to link Glass-Steagall repeal to new legislation that would have reaffirmed state autonomy over insurance regulation and barred the Comptroller of the Currency from expanding the insurance powers of national banks. Since banks wanted entry into both securities and insurance, this linkage was unacceptable, leading many banks to withdraw their support for Glass-Steagall reform legislation.

Eventually, regulatory competition broke the stalemate. The Comptroller of the Currency promised to continue to expand national bank insurance powers in the absence of congressional action. State legislatures responded to this competitive challenge by repealing their prohibitions on bank entry into the insurance business in order to ensure their own banks parity with national banks. As a result, support in Congress for new restrictions on bank insurance powers waned and, by the late 1990s, even the insurance industry was no longer united in its opposition to bank participation in the insurance business.

At that point, one might have expected financial modernization legislation to win easy passage in Congress, but reform efforts failed again in 1998. This time, the most significant roadblock may have been the ongoing regulatory competition between the Federal Reserve and the Comptroller. The Federal Reserve strongly supported the original Leach blueprint for reform because it mandated that banks diversify through the holding company structure. The Comptroller favored an approach that would allow banks direct entry into insurance and securities.

As the last chapter described, the debate over the appropriate organizational structure for bank diversification did raise serious issues concerning the deposit insurance subsidy and the ability of banks to export that subsidy to non-bank markets. Nevertheless, many observers believed that, so long as Congress required that the new activities be located in a separately incorporated entity from the bank, either an affiliate of a holding company or an operating subsidiary of a bank, this danger could be addressed by rules prohibiting funds transfers from the subsidized bank to the unsubsidized entity. Thus, by 1998, disagreements about bank structure appeared to reflect primarily a private turf war between two federal agencies vying for jurisdiction over the diversified financial services firm of the future.

Against this backdrop, Travelers and Citicorp announced their intentions to combine, requiring the Federal Reserve either to approve or to reject their proposal. The agency's response says much about the legal and political environment in which the US financial industry operates. In addition, it provides a good illustration of the link between regulatory competition and innovation in US financial law. In the US financial system, innovation is not simply a phenomenon of private markets designed to challenge or evade an otherwise static regulatory regime. Frequently, innovation occurs as a direct consequence of competition among regulators seeking to maintain or extend their political authority.

The Travelers decision[33]

One of the most interesting aspects of the Citicorp/Travelers combination was the structure of the deal. Travelers applied under the

Bank Holding Company Act to become a bank holding company by acquiring Citicorp (although the combined organization planned to use the name Citigroup). As will be discussed, the decision to make Travelers a bank holding company had sound legal motivations. Initially, however, students of US banking law may wonder why that decision did not itself doom the application to failure. How could the Federal Reserve allow Travelers to become a bank holding company when Travelers was already a diversified securities and insurance conglomerate?

Interestingly, Travelers' securities operations did not represent much of a legal barrier to approval given the Federal Reserve's own expansive reading of the statutes limiting bank securities powers. Travelers owned two securities companies, Salomon Smith Barney and Robinson-Humphrey, and by acquiring Citicorp would also control Citicorp's Section 20 securities affiliate, Citicorp Securities Inc. These firms were engaged in a broad spectrum of securities activities, some of which (such as government securities dealing) were permissible for banks and others of which (such as corporate securities underwriting) were not. Nevertheless, although Salomon Smith Barney by itself was one of the largest securities firms in the US and was empowered to engage in any securities activity, the Federal Reserve concluded that it derived less than 25 percent of its revenues from corporate securities underwriting and dealing. Thus, under the Federal Reserve's own Section 20 decisions, its affiliation with a bank would not violate the Glass-Steagall Act.

Of course, Salomon Smith Barney was still one of the principal investment houses in the US, and its affiliation with Citibank created the specter of financial conglomeration that Chairman Volcker had warned years before should not take place without full political debate and action by Congress. In 1998, however, the Federal Reserve apparently was no longer concerned about financial conglomeration. Likewise, in US financial markets, the combination of Citibank and Salomon Smith Barney evoked neither public shock nor outrage. To the contrary, once the Federal Reserve had raised the ceiling for ineligible securities revenues for Section 20 affiliates as high as 25 percent of total revenues, the possibility that banks would affiliate with major securities firms became real. The marriage of two such well-known retail financial institutions as Citibank and Salomon Smith Barney was certainly front page news, but it was not considered an entirely unexpected development.

Of perhaps more note was how the Federal Reserve dealt with Travelers' substantial business activities (projected to represent roughly

15 percent of the combined firm's total assets) that were not legal for bank holding companies under either relevant statutes or past Federal Reserve interpretations. These businesses included certain equity investments maintained in connection with market-making activities, mutual fund distribution and, of course, insurance underwriting, which, as the Bank Holding Company Act specifically provided, was not considered closely related to banking. So how could Travelers become a bank holding company yet remain in these businesses? In this case, the Federal Reserve took advantage of a provision of the Bank Holding Company Act that gave newly formed bank holding companies two years (with up to three one-year extensions) to divest their non-bank activities. Since Travelers had applied to become a new bank holding company, it could take advantage of this grace period gradually to conform its activities to the requirements of the Act.

Of course, if Congress passed financial modernization legislation along the lines of Congressman Leach's proposal within this time frame, divestiture would be unnecessary – which probably was the assumption under which both the Federal Reserve and Travelers were operating. Nevertheless, the Federal Reserve's decision made clear that the agency did not consider the required divestitures, even if they did become necessary, to be particularly onerous. To the contrary, the Federal Reserve noted that, in becoming a bank holding company, Travelers was not making any radical alteration in the nature of its business.

This may seem counterintuitive, given the long history of separation between banking and insurance. Nevertheless, in its ruling, the Federal Reserve signaled its intention of encouraging the integration of these two businesses that had for so long been separated in the US. In perhaps the most controversial part of its decision, the Federal Reserve agreed to allow Citigroup to cross-market banking, securities and insurance products to customers, including product lines that, under the terms of the Federal Reserve's decision, might have to be divested after the expiration of the two- (or five-) year grace period. This decision raised eyebrows for two reasons. First, in the past, the Federal Reserve had often prohibited cross-marketing of banking and insurance products even by firms, usually non-US banking organizations, that had been given special permission to retain their insurance businesses in the US. Second, the justifications cited by the Federal Reserve to permit the cross-marketing of banking and insurance products, such as the convenience of one-stop shopping for Citigroup's customers and the resulting increase in value of Travelers' insurance business, had implications that reached far beyond this particular decision: they were affirmative arguments for permitting unlimited bank/insurance affiliations.

Although the Federal Reserve did suggest that enhancing the value of Travelers' insurance subsidiaries would make them easier to divest, most observers believed that the Federal Reserve, and Travelers, fully anticipated that Congress would act to make divestiture unnecessary. In fact, by allowing the de facto integration of Citigroup's banking and insurance businesses even temporarily, the Federal Reserve was increasing pressure on Congress to act. Congress might be persuaded to amend the law to ratify the transaction simply to avoid the dislocation, and potential consumer confusion and dissatisfaction, that might occur were divestiture to be required.

Moreover, the Federal Reserve's initiative made congressional action less risky. The Citicorp/Travelers decision was the ultimate regulatory experiment. Citigroup would operate as an integrated financial supermarket for several years. If the results were successful, the experiment could be extended and codified by Congress with little danger of adverse political fallout.

In the meantime, the Federal Reserve had improved its own competitive position. The Citicorp/Travelers decision established the agency as the leader in regulatory innovation, giving banks renewed reason to retain the holding company organization. Moreover, the Federal Reserve expanded its jurisdiction by welcoming within its fold a leading member of a new and powerful constituency, the insurance industry.

Regulatory competition and congressional reform

What did the Federal Reserve accomplish by its decision on the Travelers application? First, it seized the initiative in its competition with the Comptroller of the Currency. Although the Federal Reserve had fewer opportunities than the Comptroller to use creative statutory interpretation to expand bank insurance powers, it did demonstrate that the holding company structure still offered valuable opportunities for the large, diversification-minded financial company.

Second, the Federal Reserve may have been trying to improve the odds that, in any future financial reform legislation, it would emerge as the principal regulator of newly diversified financial institutions. By facilitating a transaction that followed the blueprint of the Leach reform bill, the agency may have hoped to encourage the bill's chances of passage, betting that Congress would be more likely to ratify past market developments than to experiment with an entirely new format for financial reform. In this effort, the Federal Reserve was partially successful. In 1999, Congress did adopt financial modernization legislation that followed the original Leach bill in permitting the formation of diversified financial holding companies for bank, securities and insurance affiliates subject to Federal Reserve regulation. Nevertheless, Congress also endorsed the Comptroller of the Currency's national bank operating subsidiary (now called a financial subsidiary) as an alternative vehicle for bank diversification into new financial businesses (although significantly, not for insurance underwriting), and even allowed national banks to engage directly in underwriting municipal revenue bonds.

Finally, by allowing Travelers to become a bank holding company, the Federal Reserve gained an influential new constituent. Heretofore, the Federal Reserve and Comptroller of the Currency were competing for a dwindling group of constituent banks. Now, insurance/banking combinations potentially would put insurance companies within the reach of some bank regulator; which one would depend on how the firms chose to structure their combination.

Thus, the decision of a major insurer like Travelers to come within the regulatory authority of the Federal Reserve was an important victory for the agency in a new phase of regulatory competition. As barriers to financial diversification disappeared, it was inevitable that the traditional powers-based competition that had occupied the banking agencies in the 1980s and 1990s would diminish in importance. In 1999, Congress again tried to end interagency rivalry by roughly equalizing the diversification potential of holding companies and national banks and even requiring the Federal Reserve and the Secretary of the Treasury to act jointly on any future expansions of bank powers. Yet, by allowing diversification minded financial firms to opt between two separate and competing organizational forms and two separate and competing regulators, Congress ensured that regulatory competition would continue as each agency bid for constituents by demonstrating why it was the better regulator.

In this competition, Congress did give the Federal Reserve an edge. Banks looking to enter the insurance underwriting business were required to follow the Travelers/Citicorp blueprint and form a holding company.[34] Thus, assuming that congressional reform accelerates the pace of financial conglomeration, particularly between banks and insurance underwriters, the Federal Reserve has the opportunity to emerge as the lead regulator, if not of all diversified banks, at least of the future US megabank.

Conclusion

To many observers, the Federal Reserve's apparent willingness to flout its own statutes, daring Congress to act, may seem somewhat cavalier, as well as contrary to the conventional view of regulatory bureaucrats as conservative, motivated principally by the desire to shield their regulation from market change that threatens the status quo. Although public choice theorists might attribute the Federal Reserve's actions to the pressure exerted by constituent banks on their regulatory agency, the Federal Reserve's motives were more complex than mere regulatory 'capture'. Citicorp, the bank holding company, was the agency's constituent, but Travelers, the insurance company, was not (yet). Moreover, a combination of equals such as Citicorp and Travelers was beyond the reach of the majority of the Federal Reserve's bank constituents. Given the publicity that the combination received, one might have expected more public outrage had the Federal Reserve's decision been rooted solely in the desire to please a single bank.

In fact, however, the Federal Reserve's decision did not elicit a particularly negative response. This may be because the agency's action was consistent with an accepted tradition of regulatory competition in the financial regime. Agencies are expected to push the envelope in order to readjust regulatory handicaps. In most cases, regulatory innovation is welcomed by financial firms, policymakers and scholars who concede the difficulty of achieving efficient regulatory rehandicapping through the legislative process. Moreover, financial market participants are likely to perceive regulatory innovation as fair because they know that regulators, like financial players, are forced to compete. Ideally, competition keeps the regulators honest, preventing them from exerting monopoly power over their constituents. Competition also permits experimentation with alternative models of regulation as regulatory regimes vie for acceptance in the marketplace. The result, again ideally, is a level playing field.

In practice, regulatory competition may not always produce perfect results. In the short run, it may appear to exacerbate market inequities. For example, since Citigroup was the sole beneficiary of the Federal Reserve's innovative decision permitting bank/insurance combinations, rival financial players might have complained that Citigroup had gained a competitive advantage in both banking and insurance markets. Nevertheless, this particular kind of inequity rarely seems to bother financial market participants in the US. It may be that the players rationalize any short-term advantage as the innovating firm's reward for incurring the substantial startup costs involved in pioneering a new legal structure. It may also be that financial innovations are so easy to copy (with the help of friendly regulators) that one firm is unlikely to be able to exploit its advantage for long. When the Federal Reserve authorized the first bank holding company securities affiliates to engage in securities underwriting, only a handful of banks benefited. Very quickly, however, most major bank holding companies, as well as non-US banks, were able to take advantage of the opportunity to diversify.

Moreover, in the long run, regulatory innovation may benefit all players by jump-starting the process of regulatory rehandicapping. Through most of the 1990s, despite consensus as to the need for modernization of financial regulation, Congress was unable to resolve disagreements over details of reform legislation. The bank regulators acted instead, achieving considerable deregulation through regulatory decision-making. Of course, regulatory competition itself probably contributed to congressional gridlock as rival regulators battled for advantage through the legislative process. At least in 1998, rivalry between the Comptroller of the Currency and the Federal Reserve may have played a part in delaying passage of reform legislation for a year.

Nevertheless, from the perspective of players in US financial markets, the inability of Congress to take the initiative in restructuring financial regulation may not have been so bad after all. Regulatory innovation may be more palatable than legislative innovation because it occurs on a smaller scale and can be reversed if it proves inimical to efficient markets. To the extent that legislative change ratifies regulatory innovations that have already been tried and tested in the marketplace, legislation is more likely to achieve and retain legitimacy. The Citigroup experiment, like previous regulatory innovations, may have been necessary to convince both Congress and the public that financial conglomeration in the US is workable. In sum, regulatory competition may be the ultimate reflection of US financial markets' preference for competitive rather than government solutions to the problems that arise on the level playing field.

5
Regulatory Conflict and Competitive Equality

> Two ideals define the goals of a level playing field: first, one set of rules should govern competition between depositories and securities firms in any product or service market in which they compete; and second, the appropriate enforcement agencies should enforce those rules equally.[1]

> Often the conflict [among regulatory agencies] in the airing of policy results in a better approach because it blunts zealousness.[2]

Regulatory competition is an important part of US regulatory mythology, and, as suggested in Chapter 4, occasionally it works in practice as theory would predict, generating beneficial innovation and deregulation. Most players in US financial markets probably would concur that the deregulatory process that culminated in the approval of the Citicorp/Travelers combination represented regulatory competition at its best. Nevertheless, tributes to regulatory competition may overlook a troubling aspect of the competitive process that was mentioned in Chapter 4 but was not fully explored. Certainly, regulatory competition may encourage the innovation that is a hallmark of US financial markets. At the same time, however, regulatory competition does not necessarily result in equal regulatory treatment of competing financial players. To the contrary, in the short run, and perhaps even in the long run, regulatory competition may exacerbate inequities in the regulatory scheme.

As described in previous chapters, an important goal of US financial regulation is to ensure that all financial players enjoy equal starts on a level playing field. In theory, this competitive equality may be achieved through regulatory competition, since competition, if successful, should eventually result in a form of equilibrium whereby no player will be made better off by defecting to another regulatory regime. In the process of reaching that equilibrium, however, individual players may experience different and unequal regulatory treatment that produces significant competitive inequalities. In fact, competitive inequality may be a predicate for effective regulatory competition, igniting the bargaining process that is supposed to result in the survival of the most efficient regulation.

In contrast, coordination and cooperation among different regulatory agencies, although helpful to ensure like treatment of similarly situated regulated entities, is inimical to competition, since collusion may permit the formation of regulatory oligopolies that will act in concert to prevent regulated firms from opting among competing regulatory regimes. This exit option is essential to efficient regulatory competition because it keeps regulators honest and focused on their constituents' rather than their own interests. Thus, to employ a political analogy, regulatory agencies ideally should function as autonomous and even hostile nation states, focused solely on improving their constituents' strategic positions.

This state of affairs virtually ensures competitive inequalities among regulatory regimes. Perhaps regulated firms do not care much, since, in theory, they can always defect to a better regulator (or at least make a sufficiently credible threat of exit that their regulator heeds their complaint that the playing field is not level). In practice, however, exit may not be as easy as regulated firms might desire. First, individual firms must incur substantial transactions costs to identify the best regulatory regime. As all financial players are aware, structuring financial transactions in the US is a complex, lawyer-intensive process. Parties must assess the regulatory costs and benefits of a myriad of alternative structures.

Second, changing regulators involves additional costs. The rejected regulator may try to delay or even to block exit. (For example, a financial firm that is the subject of an ongoing investigation or enforcement action by one regulator cannot escape by simply switching to a different regulator.) Internal managerial or structural considerations may complicate the move. Although it is theoretically possible for the average US banking organization to dispense with its holding company and to consolidate its operations within a unitary national bank, thereby escaping the Federal Reserve's holding company regulation, a reorganization of this magnitude may prove daunting to managers who fear that customers, employees and capital suppliers will be confused by the change and react negatively. Therefore, it is possible that financial firms will tolerate considerable inequity in regulatory treatment before they exercise their option to exit.

Even if financial firms place so great a value on regulatory competition that they are willing to accept a little unequal regulatory treatment, other players in US financial markets may be less tolerant. Politicians tend to be far less enamored of regulatory competition than regulated industries because they realize that the public price of supporting regulatory competition is high. At the national level, Congress must fund multiple financial regulatory agencies, each with its own staff and infrastructure, to perform virtually identical supervisory functions. Even if an agency is self-funding, like the Federal Reserve, Congress must still commit resources to regulatory oversight and review. And lawmaking in the financial area is complicated by the need to solicit the views of each individual regulatory agency and, occasionally, to mediate among warring regulators. Recently, congressional committees considering financial modernization legislation heard, repeatedly, from the Federal Reserve, the Comptroller of the Currency, the Federal Deposit Insurance Corporation, the Securities and Exchange Commission and the Office of Thrift Supervision, as well as state financial supervisors.

Further, as a philosophical matter, unequal regulatory treatment is hard to justify to a public that believes that equal justice under the law is the hallmark of the US legal system. Even if the regulated entities are not complaining, it is difficult for observers to understand why the same laws are being applied entirely differently by different regulatory agencies. The US General Accounting Office made this point in a 1996 report that identified significant discrepancies in how the four federal bank regulatory agencies interpret, implement and enforce the identical federal banking laws. The General Accounting Office also noted that this division of regulatory responsibility had no counterpart in the industrialized world. If the complexity and costs associated with maintaining regulatory competition outweigh its benefits, then the US financial regime's love affair with regulatory competition ultimately may threaten the position of US financial markets in global competition.[3]

Finally, regulatory competition may now be becoming the victim of its own success. There are indications that the integration of financial markets and firms in the US, itself the result of competitive innovation and deregulation, is diminishing the effectiveness of regulatory competition. Regulatory competition may have facilitated the creation of modern financial behemoths like Citigroup even without formal congressional action, but as financial firms consolidate and diminish in number, the market for regulated firms is becoming less competitive. Simply put, in an oligopolistic financial market, oligopolistic regulation may be a more efficient approach.

Thus, how to reconcile the occasionally conflicting goals of regulatory competition and competitive equality is a question that is being asked more and more in US financial circles. This question was at the heart of the debate over 'functional' regulation versus 'entity' regulation that occupied financial reformers in the US in the late 1990s. At the time, the US was not alone in considering changes to its financial supervisory approach. By the end of the century, deregulation, financial industry consolidation, globalization and the increasing complexity of financial products had put pressure on policymakers everywhere to reform their financial regulatory regimes to achieve greater equality of regulatory treatment and consistency of regulatory enforcement. In most cases, this reform movement resulted in experimentation with more integrated financial supervisory structures. In the US, however, policymakers were beginning with a regulatory scheme that was far more fractured than its counterparts in the rest of the world. Moreover, US policymakers were faced with the perhaps impossible task of crafting a new regulatory structure that satisfied the desire for more equal regulatory treatment without sacrificing the benefits of regulatory competition.

Competition and entity regulation

Traditionally, the structure of US financial regulation has mirrored the structure of US financial markets. Markets were fractured, and so was regulation. An individual financial firm's choice of organizational form determined both its powers and its regulators. Thus, the institutional divide between banking firms, securities firms and insurance firms was reflected in financial regulatory jurisdiction. Firms that chose to be licensed as banks were supervised by one or more bank regulators. (As described in Chapter 4, once a firm decided to become a bank, it enjoyed still more choices as to chartering authority and principal federal bank regulator.) Firms that chose to be securities brokers or dealers were supervised by the national Securities and Exchange Commission. Firms that chose to be insurance companies were supervised by state insurance commissioners.

Initially, it may seem unclear whether this traditional regulatory divide is best characterized as 'entity' regulation or 'functional' regulation, since, until perhaps the 1980s, entity and function were indistinguishable. For example, entities regulated as banks, and only entities regulated as banks, were permitted to perform banking functions such as deposit-taking. Nevertheless, the language of much of traditional financial law, including the famous Glass-Steagall Act, was largely entity-based. Glass-Steagall's prohibition on corporate securities underwriting by banks and bank affiliates did not apply to every firm engaged in deposit-taking or lending or some other function traditionally associated with the business of banking. Rather, it covered institutions that were chartered as national banks or as state banks that joined the Federal Reserve system. This left out financial firms that performed one or more banking functions but did not fit within either of these categories – for example, banks that had state charters but that had not chosen to become Federal Reserve member banks.[4]

Congress may not have intended to create this loophole when it adopted Glass-Steagall in 1933, but may have anticipated that virtually every entity engaged in the banking business would come within one of the two categories. The same federal legislation that contained Glass-Steagall also established the federal deposit insurance program and, as originally crafted, the insurance program required all insured banks to join the Federal Reserve system. Had this occurred, then all insured banks eventually would have been subject to Glass-Steagall's prohibition on corporate securities underwriting. But the requirement for mandatory Federal Reserve membership was ultimately removed from the deposit insurance plan after many state-chartered banks objected. And, in any event, Congress never made federal deposit insurance mandatory for all state-chartered deposit-taking entities (although today most state bank chartering laws do require their banks to qualify for federal deposit insurance).

These gaps in the national bank regulatory scheme may appear odd to modern observers, but they may have a rational historical explanation. In 1933, many legal experts doubted whether Congress had the constitutional authority to regulate state-chartered businesses. Therefore, national legislators felt constrained to apply new laws like the Glass-Steagall Act only to banks that had voluntarily submitted themselves to federal banking supervision either by requesting a national charter or by seeking membership in the Federal Reserve system.[5] Regardless of congressional motive, however, Glass-Steagall's restrictions on bank securities activities provide a good example of entity-based financial regulation.

Another provision of Glass-Steagall did read more like functional regulation. Glass-Steagall also barred firms engaged in corporate securities underwriting from taking deposits. Nevertheless, this same section required all firms engaged in taking deposits to obtain a bank license or to submit to examination by a bank regulator. Further, only deposit-taking entities that were licensed as banks were eligible to join the federal deposit insurance program. Although some unlicensed and uninsured deposit-taking institutions did remain in business after 1933, the practical effect of these two provisions was to encourage firms that wanted to accept deposits from the public to apply for some form of bank charter.

Entity-based regulation also characterized the new federal securities laws, particularly the Securities Exchange Act of 1934. Securities brokers (firms that executed customers' orders for the purchase and sale of securities) and securities dealers (firms that traded securities for their own accounts) were required to register with the Securities and Exchange Commission, and securities regulation followed registration. Certain entities, such as banks, were specifically exempted from the registration requirements.[6] So again, entity status determined choice of regulatory regime.

This preference for entity regulation was less pronounced in later financial market legislation, such as the commodities laws, that gave a new national regulatory agency, the Commodity Futures Trading Commission, supervisory authority over all commodities futures contracts and, unlike the securities laws, did not expressly exempt banks from regulation. Nevertheless, in several key areas, even commodities regulation was interpreted in ways that allowed bank entities to avoid its jurisdiction.[7] The practical consequence was that, in the US, different financial entities historically were governed by their own regulatory regimes administered by their own regulatory agencies regardless of similarities of law and function. This entity-based division of regulatory authority was most obvious in the case of the most heavily regulated financial entity, the US bank. Until recently, bank regulators retained virtually exclusive oversight authority over banks even as banks began to diversify into businesses like securities and insurance that, when performed by any other entity, came within the jurisdiction of specialized securities and insurance regulators.

The tradition of entity regulation helps to explain the importance of the financial holding company, particularly to the banking industry. Bank managers could avoid entity-based bank regulation by shifting assets to separately incorporated non-bank affiliates owned by a parent holding company that also owned the regulated bank. These non-bank affiliates were not chartered as banks and therefore were not subject to the bank regulatory regime, particularly chartering law restrictions on permissible bank powers. As mentioned in Chapter 1, banks in the 1920s established their notorious securities affiliates in part to avoid any questions about the scope under their chartering laws of their authority to engage in securities activities.

Eventually, Congress did regulate the non-bank affiliates of banks. In 1933, Glass-Steagall forced banks to divest affiliates that were engaged principally in corporate securities underwriting and dealing. And, in 1956, the Bank Holding Company Act limited the power of banks to affiliate with commercial firms. Nevertheless, even after this regulation, non-bank affiliates were still considered separate legal entities from their sister banks, subject to separate regulatory regimes. The Securities Exchange Act of 1934 originally exempted bank entities from its broker regulation, but not their non-bank affiliates. Although the Bank Holding Company Act extended federal bank regulation to non-bank affiliates, Congress created a new regulatory regime, separate from national bank regulation, to govern them. Supervisory authority was given not to the Comptroller of the Currency, the chief national bank regulator, but to the Federal Reserve.

Chapter 4 described how, within the bank regulatory regime, charter competition and rivalries among banking agencies (the Comptroller and the Federal Reserve) encouraged regulatory innovation. In the financial industry as a whole, did entity regulation engender its own form of regulatory competition? At least some of the preconditions for regulatory competition were in place. Financial firms had some degree of choice as to regulator. When the Glass-Steagall Act required financial institutions to become either banks or securities firms, these institutions were opting between two very different regulatory regimes, bank regulation and securities regulation, administered by entirely separate regulatory agencies. Non-US universal banks seeking entry into US markets faced a similar decision; their choice of entity through which to do business in the US determined the regulatory scheme to which they became subject.

Moreover, at least in theory, financial firms could change their regulator by altering their entity status. As a practical matter, such a change meant abandoning an existing franchise, making this kind of transformation costly. Nevertheless, from time to time during the last few decades, several large wholesale banks have threatened to relinquish their banking licenses to become securities firms. And, in 1998, to complete its acquisition of Citicorp, Travelers, a major insurance company, promised to divest its insurance underwriting business if that move become necessary in order for the combined Citigroup to remain a bank holding company.[8]

Whether or not the threat of exit was credible, financial regulators did take seriously their constituents' demands for greater competitive flexibility. In the end, wholesale banks did not have to carry out their threat of relinquishing their bank licenses in order to enter the securities business. As described in previous chapters, long before congressional financial reform was possible, the Federal Reserve offered bank holding companies a way to engage in the securities business within the bank regulatory framework. Of course, this particular regulatory innovation probably was precipitated by the competitive threat posed to the Federal Reserve by rival bank regulators, such as the Comptroller of the Currency. Nevertheless, as the following stories suggest, without entity regulation, this kind of regulatory innovation might not have taken place at all.

Entity regulation from Carter Glass to Rule 3b–9

In less than thirteen months in 1933–34, Congress adopted three landmark statutes affecting the financial industry – the Glass-Steagall Act, the Securities Act of 1933 and the Securities Exchange Act of 1934. These statutes shared a common purpose: all three were designed to reform Wall Street to avert another stock market crash and banking crisis. All three were debated by a virtually identical national legislature and signed by the same president. And all three were enacted in the wake of highly publicized revelations of alleged stock market abuses by financial firms in the 1920s that were emerging daily from the hearings on stock market practices (known as the Pecora hearings) conducted by Senate Banking Committee simultaneously with congressional debate on financial reform legislation.[9]

Despite their common origins, however, the statutes that created the modern US bank and securities regulatory regimes shared surprisingly little common ground. In some respects, the regimes were so autonomous that students of US financial regulation might conclude that each was created in a vacuum. This conclusion is actually supported by the legislative history: for example, in February 1934, during congressional hearings on the proposed Securities Exchange Act of 1934, no one was able to recall what the Glass-Steagall Act had provided with respect to the power of banks to act as securities brokers, yet Glass-Steagall had been enacted by Congress just eight months previously. Since this question had bearing on the issue of whether banks would or would not be affected by certain contemplated provisions of the Exchange Act (such as rules governing borrowing by securities brokers), legislators might have been expected to want to know the answer. Yet, after brief, confusing and ultimately inconclusive discussion, policymakers simply moved on to another issue.[10]

Obviously this makes for murky legislative history, a problem that has plagued judicial interpretation of this (and other) provisions of 1930s financial legislation.[11] But were the legislators simply being sloppy, or was the failure to integrate the two regulatory schemes deliberate? Although this latter suggestion may sound strange, there is evidence that, in the 1930s, Congress was intent on constructing walls not just between banking markets and securities markets, but also between bank regulation and securities regulation.

A story told by James Landis, one of the architects of federal securities regulation, supports this reading of congressional intent. Among the members of the congressional conference committee that crafted the final version of the Securities Act of 1933 was Senator Carter Glass, of Glass-Steagall fame. Senator Glass was considered the Senate's leading expert on banking matters and he had drafted Glass-Steagall's provisions separating commercial and investment banking. According to Professor Landis, at a meeting of the conference committee, Senator Glass scanned the draft Securities Act and, finding some reference to banks, broke into a tirade that he was the proponent of legislation dealing with banks and their relationship to the sale of securities and that he wanted no interference with his handling of these issues. After it was pointed out to him that there was no conflict between the two regulatory schemes, he growled, thumbed through the securities bill looking for any further references to banks, found none and shortly thereafter left the committee room, never to reappear![12]

Senator Glass had no reason to worry. Both the Securities Act of 1933 and the Securities Exchange Act of 1934 carefully exempted banks from coverage. Stocks and bonds issued by banks were not subject to the registration and disclosure requirements applicable to securities issues by most other business firms.[13] And banks were exempted from securities registration and regulation as brokers or dealers.[14] The explanation for these exemptions cannot be that policymakers were confused about what banks could or could not do after Glass-Steagall. Certainly, Congress knew that banks, like other firms, would be issuing public debt and equity in order to raise capital. Instead, legislators apparently deferred to Senator Glass' wishes to leave virtually every aspect of regulation of bank entities to the bank regulators.[15]

To be fair to Senator Glass, he was equally determined to keep bank regulators out of the securities markets. Although the securities laws delegated regulatory authority over securities markets to a special securities regulator, a function now performed by the Securities and Exchange Commission, the Securities Exchange Act of 1934 originally gave the Federal Reserve power to regulate margin lending (loans collateralized by marketable securities) and brokers' loans.[16] Although this authority was considered by many to be necessary to allow the Federal Reserve to control the flow of credit into the securities markets (a major concern of 1930s policymakers, who believed that too much credit from too many sources had fueled securities speculation in the 1920s), Senator Glass disagreed, arguing that bank regulators should not be exercising authority over securities markets. Besides, he complained, no member of the Federal Reserve Board 'knows anything on earth about stock market transactions' and 'they ought not to be allowed to know anything about it'.[17]

Why did Senator Glass (and other policymakers) prefer entity regulation of financial markets? Senator Glass' comments suggest one possible reason. Bank regulators can become expert in banking and securities regulators can become expert in securities. Nevertheless, functional regulation, based on the nature of the transaction rather than the entity, appears to satisfy the need for regulatory expertise far better than entity regulation. For example, stock issued by banks cannot be so very different from stock issued by other companies as to require that bank regulators, rather than securities regulators, develop and oversee the basic public disclosure scheme. To the contrary, the Securities and Exchange Commission's experience with administering disclosure requirements should make it the better regulator.

Possibly, Congress may not have wanted banks to be subject to disclosure rules at all, perhaps fearing that public revelation of negative information about banks would cause depositors to panic and join bank runs, resulting in bank failure. Yet Congress did not exempt banks from all disclosure obligations. Rather, Congress apparently intended that the bank regulators would develop securities disclosure rules for their regulated entities that paralleled the securities law's requirements.[18] Thus, Congress fully anticipated that different regulators would administer like disclosure schemes, a result that appears at odds with the requirements of both regulatory expertise and regulatory economy.[19]

So what was accomplished by exempting banks from the jurisdiction of the securities regulators? Ironically, the significance of entity regulation became clear decades later when the question of whether banks could act as securities brokers was asked again. In 1934, legislators had not been able to answer this question conclusively, but the national bank regulators quickly put the issue to rest by reading Glass-Steagall to provide that banks could no longer engage in the securities brokerage business for profit. As a result, for decades, banks could execute securities trades as an accommodation for their trust accounts, but they did not compete for trade execution business with independent securities brokers.

In the early 1980s, however, the Comptroller of the Currency began to read Glass-Steagall more broadly to permit banks to establish securities brokerage operations that could solicit new customers and make a profit on their trades.[20] As banks began to compete directly with non-bank brokerage firms, the long-standing exemption of banks from the securities law's broker registration requirement was cited by rival securities firms as providing banks with an unfair starting advantage in the brokerage business.

In 1985, the Securities and Exchange Commission responded by adopting a new rule, Rule 3b-9, that extended its regulation of broker-dealers to cover any bank that engaged in securities brokerage for profit. In effect, the Commission was reading its statute as functional regulation: in its view, any entity that performed brokerage functions should be regulated as a broker. Nevertheless, a federal appellate court rejected this interpretation, citing the Securities Exchange Act's unambiguous exemption of banks from its definitions of broker and dealer as proof that Congress had created an entity-based regulatory scheme.[21] A change in bank function had no significance for regulatory jurisdiction. Bank regulators, not securities regulators, would continue to regulate all of the activities of banking entities.

The theoretical significance of this reaffirmation of entity regulation was more important than its impact on financial markets. The Securities Exchange Act exempted banks, but not bank affiliates, from its regulation of broker-dealers. If a banking organization located its brokerage business in an affiliate rather than in the bank itself, the Securities and Exchange Commission had the authority to require the brokerage entity to register as a broker-dealer. Although avoiding registration originally may have provided a reason for banking organizations to keep their new brokerage businesses within the bank, banking organizations that also wanted to engage in securities underwriting and dealing pursuant to the Federal Reserve's Section 20 rulings were required to set up separate securities affiliates subject to broker-dealer regulation.

Moreover, in 1999, the Securities and Exchange Commission finally was successful in persuading Congress to rewrite the Securities Exchange Act to narrow the bank exemption. So, as a practical matter, the Securities and Exchange Commission eventually did gain regulatory authority over most bank securities activities.

Theoretically, however, it is interesting to speculate what might have happened had Congress done in 1933 what the Securities and Exchange Commission tried to do in 1985. Suppose that Congress had adopted a regime of functional regulation, whereby the nature of the financial business rather than the identity of the entity determined the applicable regulator. In that case, when banks asked to re-enter the brokerage business, they would have needed the acquiescence of both bank and securities regulators. Would bank regulators have had an incentive to say yes when they would have been forced to cede regulatory authority to a rival regulator? And would the Securities and Exchange Commission have had an incentive to say yes when bank entry into brokerage posed a serious competitive threat to its existing constituents?

An answer is suggested by the experience of national banks that, with the help of the Comptroller of the Currency, re-entered the insurance agency business in the 1990s. Insurance agents were licensed and regulated by the states, and, at first, some state insurance commissioners moved to block bank entry into the insurance business by denying licenses to banks and bank affiliates. Eventually, the Supreme Court resolved this conflict in favor of the banks, holding that national banking law that permitted banks to act as insurance agents preempted state law that prohibited bank–insurance affiliations.[22] This story suggests that, when regulatory jurisdiction overlaps, regulators occasionally may try to protect the competitive interests of their existing constituents by frustrating innovations by rival regulators that allow new entrants into financial markets. In the case of bank insurance agency as well as bank brokerage, entity regulation ensured that bank regulators could permit banks to diversify without interference by a rival agency.

To the extent that this kind of regulatory innovation enhances the competitiveness of financial markets, a regulatory structure that fosters regulatory competition is likely to be viewed as desirable by financial players. This may explain the continued appeal of entity regulation to many financial industry participants. Entity regulation has been defended as promoting 'creative conflict', blunting regulatory zealousness and reflecting the US preference for political checks and balances.[23] Supporters of entity regulation include not just representatives of the banking industry who have benefited from their regulators' recent willingness to innovate. Representatives of the securities industry have benefited as well. For example, had a regime of functional regulation allowed bank regulators to classify the money market mutual funds created by securities firms as deposits, would the banking agencies have been tempted to use their regulatory authority to protect their bank constituents from the competitive challenge?[24]

Competitive equality and entity regulation

Although creative conflict among financial regulators may lead to desirable regulatory innovation, two problems remain. First, entity regulation has not been able to avoid all regulatory overlap, which may frustrate efficient competition. This problem has been exacerbated by recent deregulation that has permitted greater cross-industry diversification by banks and other financial firms. Although bank regulators continue to exercise supervisory authority over activities performed by bank entities, other regulators have claimed jurisdiction as well. For example, state insurance regulators were unable to bar national banks from the insurance business, yet states retained authority to license and regulate the conduct of bank-affiliated insurance agents so long as state regulation did not significantly interfere with the bank's exercise of insurance powers.[25] As a result, a national bank acting as an insurance agent may have to obtain two licenses and comply with two regulatory schemes.

Likewise, because bank affiliates were not exempted from broker-dealer registration under the securities laws, the bank holding company securities affiliates that were organized to take advantage of creative reinterpretation of the Glass-Steagall Act were at once regulated by the Federal Reserve and the Securities and Exchange Commission. As national banks entered the securities business through operating subsidiaries, they also became subject to dual regulation by banking and securities agencies. This regulatory overlap, in addition to potentially subjecting regulated firms to duplicative or inconsistent regulatory requirements, may also prevent regulatory innovation to the extent that one regulator may block experimentation by the other. In this case, creative conflict will not ignite beneficial regulatory competition that ultimately allows the best solution to prevail, but instead will result in a regulatory stalemate that may be resolved only through judicial or legislative intervention.

Second, even if regulatory overlap can be avoided in an entity-based regulatory regime, there still may be obstacles to efficient regulatory competition. The competitive process may be affected by external factors that influence how regulatory burdens are allocated among different financial entities. One such factor, discussed in Chapter 3, is the deposit insurance subsidy. So long as this subsidy is believed to provide banks with a starting advantage over rival financial firms, even bank regulators may feel constrained to impose special requirements on banks engaged in activities such insurance or securities that are not imposed on non-banks engaged in the same activities. The resulting balance of burdens and benefits may be accepted by most market players as fair insofar as the special bank subsidy justifies special regulatory burdens, although this view recently has been challenged by the banking industry. Nevertheless, any resulting differences in regulatory treatment will not ignite regulatory competition because they address problems that are unique to banks. The result may be the evolution of two entirely separate and non-competing regulatory regimes.

In the past, the Securities and Exchange Commission cited this potential problem with entity regulation as an argument for functional regulation – and for giving the Commission, rather than the bank regulators, authority over bank securities activities. On the one hand, securities regulators complained that the regulatory approach favored by bank regulators is not appropriate for firms in the securities business: 'Securities firms need to engage in risk-taking and entrepreneurial activities without taking on restrictive bank-style regulation that focuses on bank safety and soundness'.[26] On the other hand, securities regulators charged that bank regulators, although attentive to bank safety and soundness, are not sufficiently rigorous in policing marketing practices that may injure consumers or competitors.

Whether or not these particular accusations are justified,[27] entity regulation does run the danger of sacrificing competitive equality without necessarily encouraging beneficial regulatory competition that fosters innovation and ultimately smooths out inequities in regulatory treatment. This problem is exacerbated by financial industry consolidation, which makes entity identification more difficult and ensures regulatory overlap. The modern financial firm may be at once bank, broker-dealer and insurance company. Who should regulate it? Traditional entity regulation may not provide a satisfactory answer.

Competitive equality and functional regulation

In integrated financial markets, is functional regulation a more efficient approach? In a functional regulatory regime, similar diversified financial firms are not subject to entirely different regulatory burdens depending upon whether they call themselves bank or securities firm or insurance company. Rather, bank regulators regulate their banking functions, securities regulators regulate their securities functions and so on. As a result, banking operations will not necessarily be regulated in the same manner as securities operations, and bank regulators will not be applying bank regulatory techniques to securities activities.

To the extent that functional regulation promises that all firms performing the same functions or selling the same products will receive identical regulatory treatment, functional regulation appears more likely than entity regulation to achieve competitive equality. Functional regulation may also avoid the problem of regulatory overlap, since, for example, all securities brokers, whether owned by a bank or by an insurance company or some other entity, are supervised by a single securities regulator. Regulatory overlap might still occur if a financial firm chose to integrate its different financial activities into a unitary corporate entity. Thus, functional regulation may encourage the use of a holding company structure, or at least separate subsidiaries, for different financial activities. (In contrast, entity regulation encourages, or at least tolerates, the use of more integrated organizational structures.)

As a practical matter, the integration of financial firms and markets in the US during the 1990s was moving the financial regulatory structure closer to functional regulation. When financial firms such as Citicorp and Travelers that had operated in different markets (subject to different regulators) combined, they did not escape their former regulators. Instead, the same regulators continued to have responsibility for different business units of the newly combined entity. Moreover, to the extent that market integration was occurring through legislative reform, Congress appeared to favor the functional model of regulation. 1999 financial modernization legislation endorsed the principal of functional regulation, assigning specialized regulatory agencies oversight responsibility for different business units within diversified financial holding companies.

Why, in the late 1990s, did functional regulation appeal to policymakers when entity regulation prevailed six decades earlier? Functional regulation represents a political compromise that may satisfy competing regulatory agencies that fear that financial market integration will diminish their power. For example, if financial market consolidation results in the survival of a few large unitary banks that engage in securities and insurance activities as well as banking, then entity regulation would be likely to increase the regulatory responsibilities and powers of bank regulators, who would oversee the combined entity, and decrease the regulatory responsibilities and powers of securities and insurance regulators. Functional regulation ensures a place at the table for every regulator, who will continue to have some supervisory role regardless of whether the dominant financial firm of the future is a bank or some other entity.

Nevertheless, functional regulation has certain limitations that may diminish its effectiveness and legitimacy in financial markets. First, diversified financial firms are bigger than the sum of their parts. Although it may be feasible to have different financial regulators supervising one or more subsidiaries, some umbrella regulator must be responsible for the entity as a whole. Despite its endorsement of functional regulation, Congress designated the Federal Reserve as principal consolidated supervisor of diversified financial companies that own one or more banks. (Diversified financial firms that do not own banks may choose the Securities and Exchange Commission as their umbrella regulator.) Although, in theory, the Federal Reserve is required to defer to securities or insurance regulatory supervision of the holding company's functionally regulated affiliates, an affiliate's problems may affect the entire organization, demanding the involvement of the umbrella regulator. Thus, imposing a layer of entity regulation on top of functional regulation runs the risk of re-introducing the regulatory overlap that plagued pure entity-based regulation.

Second, under a regime of functional regulation, competition among regulators disappears. One regulator is responsible for a particular financial market, and firms seeking entry into that market must meet the qualifications and follow the rules adopted by that regulator. Thus, functional regulation permits specialized regulators to develop regulatory monopolies that may retard regulatory innovation and modernization.

As a practical matter, of course, regulatory jurisdiction probably cannot be divided so neatly among financial supervisory agencies as to avoid all overlap. Hybrid financial instruments may be at once banking and securities and insurance products.[28] A single financial transaction may take place in more than one financial market. Or different financial regulators may claim the same product as their own. Thus, successful functional regulation requires the presence of some arbiter who will decide how regulatory responsibility for particular financial products should be allocated.

Recent financial modernization legislation addressed this problem by requiring consultation among functional regulators before new financial products are labeled banking or securities or insurance.

Disagreements will be resolved by independent judicial review that gives no special deference to either agency's expertise. Yet this process ensures that legal battles over product classification will be costly, yield unpredictable outcomes and delay the introduction of new products. Ironically, in the case of hybrid financial instruments, entity regulation may be vastly more efficient, allowing innovating firms to predict which agency will exercise supervisory authority.

Finally, even functional regulation may not necessarily result in competitive equality for all entities operating in the same product market. For example, consider regulation of securities brokerage. Functional regulation ensures that all securities brokers are subject to securities regulation but it does not ensure that regulation will be applied equally to all brokers. For example, should a securities broker who offers customers both mutual funds (a securities product) and bank certificates of deposit be subject to the same regulation as a broker who offers only mutual funds? Should a securities broker who works for a bank be subject to the same regulation as a broker who works for an independent securities firm? If securities regulators decide that a broker who cross-markets bank and securities products or is an employee of a bank must be subjected to qualitatively different regulatory standards than brokers who have no connections to banks, then this broker will not be treated exactly like all other brokers despite functional regulation.

As described in Chapter 6, this particular example of competitive inequality has already arisen as regulators have adopted special rules to govern the new financial 'supermarkets' – firms that are now marketing a variety of financial products to retail customers. Securities regulators are treating banks that sell securities products differently from other firms that sell the same securities products, suggesting that functional regulation will not result in equal regulatory treatment of all entities operating in the same market. At that point, however, the principal advantage of functional regulation disappears. In fact, the need for special regulatory treatment of banks is a good argument for a return to entity regulation. If banks are so special that bank-affiliated securities brokers require a special regulatory regime specifically tailored to them, then bank regulators, as opposed to securities regulators, may be best positioned to perfect this regime.

The superregulator model

One way to avoid the pitfalls of both entity and functional regulation is to opt for a unitary regulatory system, with a single agency exercising supervisory authority over all financial markets. As financial firms integrate, integrated regulation appears to make sense, allowing one regulator to be responsible for all diversified financial organizations. On a day-to-day basis, regulatory responsibilities might be allocated within the agency upon functional lines, but any resulting jurisdictional conflicts would be resolved internally, avoiding the regulatory overlap that seems to bedevil both entity and functional regulation of diversified financial firms.

Is integrated regulation the most efficient approach for modern financial markets? Even if so, it may not have much appeal in US markets. The most serious drawback may be the difficulty of deciding just who will be the superregulator. Existing agencies will resist any diminution of their power and autonomy. Moreover, each agency is likely to have allies in Congress who will fight to preserve that agency's authority. The resulting stalemate may explain why even modest attempts at agency consolidation have failed in the past. In 1999, Congress chose not to elect a superregulator for all diversified financial firms. Although the Federal Reserve became the umbrella regulator of most financial holding companies, every competing regulatory agency, from the Comptroller of the Currency and the Securities and Exchange Commission to state banking and insurance supervisors, retained some regulatory role.

Resistance to a superregulator may have philosophical as well as political roots. The notion of a superregulator is at odds with three important and interrelated norms that animate American politics and markets – preference for federalism, fear of big government and faith in the power of regulatory competition. A superregulator of necessity would be a national agency, posing an immediate challenge to state authority over financial institutions. Both the dual banking system, that allows the states to charter and regulate banks, and state autonomy over insurance regulation would be threatened.

Of course, there are reasons to suspect that, as financial market consolidation proceeds in the US, state power to regulate financial institutions will diminish. As small local financial firms become part of large national financial services companies, the regulatory role of the states will be supplanted by federal regulators. In the 1930s, state banks and their state regulators won a victory for the dual banking system when they successfully resisted attempts to force all insured state banks to join the Federal Reserve system. Since then, the growth of bank holding companies and the expansion of the federal deposit insurance program to include virtually all full service US banks have meant that most if not all banks are now subject to some federal regulation. As a result, although the states' control over the menu of powers available to their banks still remains significant (although somewhat less so as legal restrictions on bank diversification have disappeared), in most instances states will be forced to share regulatory responsibility with their federal counterparts.

State autonomy over insurance regulation also may be waning. The entry by national banks into the insurance business, described in Chapter 4, made the Comptroller of the Currency an insurance regulator. Likewise, the combination of Citicorp and Travelers gave the Federal Reserve oversight authority over a major insurance underwriter. Although, as of 1999, states retained some power to license and regulate insurance firms, as bank/insurance affiliations proliferate, state insurance regulators may be forced to cede more supervisory authority to federal bank regulators.

Will this trend eventually lead to the demise of state financial regulation in favor a centralized national regulator? Whether financial market players will ever accept the complete nationalization of financial regulation may depend on what kind of national regulator supplants state control. At least one national bank regulator, the Federal Reserve, was designed to have local roots. Each Federal Reserve bank is owned and managed by local interests, which, in theory, keeps the bank attuned to local needs. It is these local Reserve banks that are largely responsible for bank examination and regulatory enforcement. Moreover, local Reserve banks provide information about regional banking conditions to the Federal Reserve Board in Washington, which itself is designed to be independent of the political branches of the national government.

At least in theory, this decentralization and independence may make Federal Reserve regulation more palatable to local financial interests than a new national financial superregulator. On the other hand, as financial consolidation continues, there is likely to be pressure within the Federal Reserve system to centralize regulatory authority over the new megabanks in the national Federal Reserve Board rather leaving supervision and enforcement to the local Federal Reserve banks. Therefore, if the Federal Reserve emerges as lead regulator of the new integrated financial firm of the future, as a practical matter, Washington may be in control. This result, however, may be resisted by local financial interests and their political allies, who may insist that states retain some regulatory role.

Finally, any superregulator creates the risk of regulatory monopoly, destroying all possibility of regulatory competition. This may be the most serious objection to regulatory consolidation, making it unacceptable to most players in US financial markets. In the end, any gains in efficiency from having a single regulatory arbiter may be outweighed by the resulting loss of experimentation and innovation that most financial market participants believe is a product of competition among multiple regulatory agencies.

Of course, some form of competition would still be possible between a US superregulator and its counterparts abroad. In globalized markets, US firms theoretically have another exit option. They may threaten to move their operations outside of the US in order to pressure their regulator to adopt reforms. What is interesting, however, is how infrequently financial firms have exercised this option despite the high regulatory costs associated with operating in US markets. This suggests that US financial regulation has offered net benefits for financial firms, a theme touched upon in previous chapters. One of these benefits may have been the promise of regulatory competition to keep US financial regulators honest and focused on the interests of their constituents.

Globalization and regulatory competition

There may be another reason why the globalization of financial markets has not lessened demand for domestic regulatory competition. US financial regulators' fondness for regulatory competition in the US apparently does not extend outside its borders. In global markets, US regulators have been willing to consider greater uniformity of regulatory approach, signing onto efforts in the 1980s and 1990s to develop uniform international standards on such regulatory issues as capital adequacy, managing derivatives trading risks and supervising multinational financial conglomerates.[29] In theory, uniform international regulation should trump cross-border regulatory competition, removing the discretion of national regulators to reallocate regulatory handicaps in order to benefit their constituents. Why then have US financial players apparently been willing to tolerate in global markets what they have rejected in their own national markets?

One possible explanation is that US market players fear that cross-border regulatory competition will commence a 'race to the bottom' that US financial markets, still the most heavily regulated in the world, are sure to lose. For example, before uniform capital adequacy standards were accepted internationally, different national accounting practices allowed rival banks to measure capital differently. In Japan, for example, but not in the US, unrealized gains on securities portfolios could be included in capital. As a result, at least before the decline in the Nikkei index in the early 1990s, Japanese banks appeared to be better capitalized than their US counterparts. In the eyes of US financial players, this difference put US firms at a competitive disadvantage. Japanese banks were able to expand their market shares at the expense of relatively less well capitalized US banks.[30]

This suggests that US players had incentives to promote uniform global bank capital standards in order to level the playing field. Nevertheless, classic regulatory competition theory suggests that US banks (and their regulators) had alternatives that were probably less costly than negotiating international standards. For example, US banks might have pressured their own regulators to relax accounting standards in order to level the playing field. Or US financial players might have tolerated a short-term competitive disadvantage with confidence that, sooner or later, sophisticated investors would recognize that unrealized securities gains turn quickly to losses in volatile markets, causing apparently well-capitalized banks to become undercapitalized. Investors then would return to those banks that followed the conservative accounting practices favored by US regulators. Nevertheless, in this case, US players were not content to wait for the competitive process to reward the most efficient regulatory regime, preferring instead to achieve competitive equality through international regulatory cooperation.

Perhaps US players were certain that they could dominate the negotiation process, ensuring outcomes that would benefit US financial firms. US agenda-setting was theoretically possible in certain areas of regulation where US regulators had relatively greater experience or where they could make a credible threat to retaliate against dissenters, for example, by barring non-US financial firms from US markets. Nevertheless, experts have noted that, although US positions on financial regulatory issues have influenced the evolution of global standards, the US position has not always prevailed.[31] US financial policymakers have had to cede some ground in order to gain consensus on international regulatory standards, a difficult undertaking for regulators more accustomed to competition than to cooperation.

Perhaps US policymakers had no choice but to cooperate because they feared that regulatory competition was not possible in international financial markets. Globalized markets inevitably create regulatory overlap as institutions must take into account the regulation of both their home country and the countries in which they are doing business. Hence, exit may be meaningless: a US bank doing business in the UK must deal with both US and UK regulation even if it switches to a UK charter and does business as a foreign bank in the US. At the same time, regulatory failure in one market may have negative consequences for other, better regulated markets, as scandals at BCCI, Daiwa and Barings, and banking crises in Asia, Latin America and Russia, vividly demonstrated in the 1990s. Thus, both overregulation and underregulation may frustrate efficient global regulatory competition, leading both industry participants and their regulators to consider international supervisory standards.

There is another possible explanation for US financial players' apparent willingness to tolerate international cooperation on uniform regulatory standards. Observers have pointed out that, through the 1990s, the process by which global financial regulation has emerged has been ad hoc, driven by periodic financial crises rather than rational planning. International standards have emerged not from public negotiations among elected political leaders but from private meetings of loosely organized quasi-governmental groups, such as the Basle Committee on Banking Supervision or the International Organisation of Securities Commissions.[32] Participants have tended to have close ties to their domestic financial industries and relatively little political accountability. Standards have been fluid, undergoing constant experimentation and adjustment, and voluntary, requiring the acquiescence of national governments for their implementation. Rulemaking has relied upon industry self-regulation, for example, allowing private financial firms to develop their own internal measurement systems to calculate capital requirements for market risk.[33]

Critics point out that this process of lawmaking runs the danger of yielding rules that are incomplete, ambiguous and perhaps of questionable political legitimacy.[34] Nevertheless, these very flaws may increase the legitimacy of international rulemaking in the eyes of many US financial players. The informal and largely voluntary process of international standard setting is likely to reassure US participants who might resist the edicts of a formal international superregulatory authority even if it were dominated by US representatives.

Moreover, the particular regulatory issues that have occupied the process, such as capital regulation, managing derivatives trading risks and regulatory supervision of multinational financial firms, are of special concern to large US financial firms that compete globally. These firms tend to believe, rightly or wrongly, that the US regulatory approach to these issues is stricter than that of at least some other national regulatory schemes, putting US firms, with their relatively higher regulatory costs, at a competitive disadvantage. Achieving consensus on uniform international standards may ensure US firms equal starts with their non-US competitors.

Finally, the responsiveness of the process to private constituencies and its willingness to draw on market-based solutions give US financial players a say in the evolution of international financial standards. Rules derived from industry practice are likely to be viewed as fair because they have been tested in the competitive markets. Although the process described here may not be the most efficient way to achieve the competitive equality that is the ultimate goal of international regulatory standard setting, it may come close to replicating the 'creative conflict' that US players value in their own regulatory framework.

6
The Level Playing Field and Rules of Fair Play

Mr Edgar D. Brown of Pottsville, Pennsylvania entrusted $100 000 to a large US bank to be invested in 'safe' bonds. A representative of the bank's securities affiliate advised Mr Brown that the US government securities that he owned were 'all wrong' and reinvested his account in Viennese, German, Greek, Peruvian, Chilean, Rhenish, Hungarian and Irish governmental obligations as well as bonds issued by private US corporations. Mr Brown was also persuaded to borrow to finance additional investments. When the bonds declined in value, Mr Brown complained, and was told by his broker that it was his own fault for buying bonds: 'Why don't you let me sell you some stock?' Once reinvested in stock, Mr Brown's portfolio still lost money, and he eventually sold out, sacrificing most of his capital.[1]

NationsSecurities, the brokerage unit of a large US bank, conducted a highly successful marketing program for two closed-end bond funds called 'Term Trusts' that were designed to generate yields of approximately 1 – 1.5 percent above the yield on ten-year US treasury securities. Sales representatives were encouraged to solicit customers who had formerly invested in bank certificates of deposit, and the bank assisted by giving salesmen its maturing deposit lists. Customers, many of whom were elderly and had annual incomes below $50 000, were told that the Term Trusts were as safe as certificates of deposit but better because they paid more. Although the Term Trusts invested in some traditional government securities, in order to achieve their yield goals they relied on high leverage, using derivative securities such as dollar rolls and inverse floaters that made them very sensitive to interest rate changes. When interest rates rose, the Term Trusts' net asset and share values declined, prompting complaints from investors.[2]

These two incidents occurred over sixty-five years apart, but both have assumed symbolic importance in the evolution of US financial regulation. Mr Brown's investment adventures with National City Company, the securities affiliate of National City Bank (whose direct descendent is today's Citigroup), were recounted in early 1933 to a US Senate committee during congressional hearings on stock market practices in the 1920s, hearings that, according to Ferdinand Pecora, the committee's chief investigating counsel, revealed how the entry of commercial banks into the business of selling securities had 'corrupted the very heart of ... old fashioned banking ethics'.[3] This story and others like it often are credited with providing at least a rhetorical justification for the financial market regulation of the early 1930s, including the Glass-Steagall Act that barred banks from acting as securities brokers and the securities legislation of 1933 and 1934 that regulated the conduct of securities brokers in dealings with the public.

The tale of the Term Trusts, and the bank's role in their promotion, became the subject of a 1998 enforcement action brought by US securities and bank regulators against one of many banking organizations that, as a result of relaxed regulatory interpretation of Glass-Steagall in the 1980s, had returned to the retail securities markets for the first time since the 1920s. The regulatory enforcement action did not result in the removal of banks from the securities business, but it did ensure a continuing role for regulation in US financial markets even after the ultimate demise of Glass-Steagall. Despite deregulation, or perhaps because of it, US financial regulators are being called upon to fashion new rules of conduct to guarantee that basic standards of fair play prevail in competitive financial product markets.[4]

Regulatory rules of fair play are not new to US financial markets. Rules that discourage conflicts of interest and unfair marketing practices have always occupied an important position in the US financial regulatory scheme. Fair play is so central to financial markets that, according to the Supreme Court's 1971 decision in *Investment Company Institute* v. *Camp,* it provided the leading motive for Glass-Steagall's separation of commercial and investment banking. In an often quoted passage, the Supreme Court noted that there is an inherent conflict between the 'promotional interest' of the investment banker and the obligation of the commercial banker to render disinterested investment advice. The Court then repeated, perhaps somewhat prophetically, Senator Bulkley's argument, made on the Senate floor in 1932, that the banker who has nothing to sell to his depositors is much better qualified to advise disinterestedly ... than the banker who uses the list of depositors in his savings department to distribute circulars concerning the advantages of this, that, or the other investment on which the bank is to receive an originating profit or an underwriting profit or a distribution profit or a trading profit or any combination of such profits.[5]

Concern with ensuring fair play in US financial markets also explains the prevalence of regulation that governs how financial firms market their products to customers, such as the 'antitying' rules. Coercive tying arrangements that compel a buyer of one product to purchase a second product from the same supplier are regulated by the US antitrust laws, but banking firms traditionally have been subject to special antitying rules that sweep more broadly than antitrust regulation. Under the antitrust laws, tying arrangements are prohibited when they lessen competition, for example, by enabling a firm with monopoly power in one product market to extend that monopoly to a second product market, thereby injuring competitors.[6] Under banking law, however, tying has been prohibited even when the bank does not possess any monopoly power, on the theory that tying is always unfair to the bank's customers although the bank's competitors are not harmed.

Bank regulation even frowns on so-called 'voluntary' ties, where, without any coercion, loan applicants decide to purchase a second product (such as credit insurance) from the bank because they believe that they will thereby improve their chances of obtaining credit.[7] In this case, the lending bank may not have sufficient market power to enforce an explicit tie, since, if savvy borrowers just say no, there are plenty of other banks and non-banks that are ready and willing to make consumer loans. Nevertheless, the bank may be exploiting the average borrower's lack of knowledge and sophistication that produces a (mistaken) perception that, in lending markets, the customer's choices are limited. This is unfair play, and must be prevented.

Despite the significance of rules of fair play to US financial regulation, financial players recognize that these rules are costly, occasionally diminishing the competitiveness of US financial markets. Ordinarily, players in US financial markets trust the market more than the government to determine competitive outcomes. Regulation may be legitimate to ensure equal starts, but once regulatory handicaps are in place, ideally, regulatory interference should cease, permitting the players to bargain for the degree of risk and return that they desire. In fact, on the truly level playing field, competition is the best defense against conflict of interest and other consumer abuses. If financial firms violate the terms of their bargains or otherwise abuse consumers, they should suffer reputational damage, losing customers and ultimately being driven from the market. Regulatory interference with this salutary market discipline may actually prove counterproductive, removing incentives for customers to remain vigilant and prudent in their choice of financial services provider. It also may prevent some customers from voluntarily assuming the degree of risk that they desire in their financial transactions. Thus, both efficiency and fairness suggest a minimal role for regulation in structuring financial market transactions.

Why then are regulatory rules of fair play tolerated in US financial markets? Many would answer that these rules are necessary when inequality of bargaining power prevents some players from negotiating for their own protection from risk. In this instance, market discipline may not work efficiently to identify and reward 'good' financial services providers and penalize 'bad' ones. Moreover, when vulnerable players are exploited, the resulting public perception of unfairness may taint the game, leading many players to conclude that, in fact, the playing field is not level. Thus, inequality of bargaining power has emerged as the proxy for entitlement to regulatory protection in financial market transactions.[8]

Judging from the number and complexity of fairness rules that comprise US financial regulation, observers may conclude that inequality of bargaining power is the rule rather than the exception. Why, for example, is US financial regulation so concerned with the appearance as well as the reality of fair play? The answer may be the singular importance of the retail investor in US financial markets. As noted in previous chapters, the participation of individual investors contributed to the liquidity and competitiveness of securities markets in the 1920s. It may be just as essential to maintaining the vibrancy of modern financial markets.

Further, as a political matter, public confidence in the financial markets has been an important although perhaps unarticulated force in favor of deregulation. Although the average investor probably does not pay attention to the often esoteric debate over financial law reform, most US investors seem to believe that competitive financial markets are more likely to offer opportunities for individual participation than heavily regulated markets, a factor that has influenced political rhetoric and perhaps even political decision-making in favor of deregulation. Even the occasional financial market crisis, from the stock market crash of 1929 to the market 'break' of 1987, that might have been expected to call into question the efficiency of free markets has not resulted in public demand on the government to shut down markets – or to limit individual participation in markets.

This public preference for free markets is not just a late twentieth century phenomenon. As described in Chapter 1, it was apparent even during the 1930s when modern financial regulation was born. Contrary to conventional wisdom, populist rhetoric was often hostile to proposed government regulation of markets, such as the Glass-Steagall Act, despite public awareness of investment horror stories such as Mr Brown's. Populists feared that removing banks from securities markets would actually reverse the beneficial democratization of markets that had occurred in the 1920s when banks and other new entrants had facilitated participation in the stock market by new clients, typically small businesses and individuals, who had not been welcome at the older, elite investment houses such as Morgan.[9] Today, many individual investors might make a similar complaint were the government to propose significant limitations on online stock trading or other innovations that improve public access to the securities markets.

Nevertheless, if individual confidence in the financial markets has kept markets healthy and free from the threat of punitive regulation, the risk that individuals suddenly will decide that the investment game is rigged is a constant threat to markets that cannot afford to lose the good will, or the custom, of the small investor. As a result, maintaining investor confidence has influenced the business strategies of private financial firms. For example, in the past, banks may have resisted the trend, confidently predicted by financial analysts, toward the formation of multiservice financial 'supermarkets' because they took seriously their retail customers' complaint that bigger is not necessarily better when it comes to customer service. Even today, huge megabanks promote themselves as 'your friendly neighborhood institution'. Likewise, the securities brokerage industry has done much to demystify the stock market by reassuring individual investors that, whether through collective investment vehicles such as mutual funds or innovative trading devices such as online brokerage, the small saver has the same chance to profit in the market as large investors with superior information and management skills.

The need to maintain investor confidence in financial markets may also explain the willingness of players to accept regulation that is designed to redress inequality of bargaining power by enforcing rules of fair play. Mr Brown's story continues to haunt US financial markets, and the modern saga of the Term Trusts suggests that investor confidence may still be fragile despite the growing sophistication and market experience of both financial services providers and their customers. Critics may complain that, historically, serious customer abuses have been infrequent,[10] but they cannot deny these stories' rhetorical power or their potentially negative impact on investor behavior.

Fair play and market bifurcation

Recent deregulation of US financial markets has not dampened concern for fair play, but it has altered its focus. Policymakers face a dilemma in urging deregulation: if regulatory intervention is necessary to protect vulnerable investors like Mr Brown, then deregulation of financial markets can never be complete. Yet advocates of deregulation have argued persuasively that regulating the substance of financial transactions may distort market discipline and interfere with market efficiency. The solution to this dilemma is suggested by the NationsSecurities enforcement action. Regulation is still required to enforce rules of fair play in deregulated financial markets, but only in those markets in which inequality of bargaining power is a significant possibility. As a practical matter, that means that rules of fair play will be a factor primarily (although not exclusively) in retail markets.

The result, for regulatory purposes, is a new bifurcation of financial markets along customer, as opposed to producer, lines.[11] Whereas, once, US financial regulation enforced distinctions between commercial banks and investment banks, now, regulation is distinguishing between wholesale financial markets, where competition may proceed without regulatory interference, and retail financial markets, that remain highly regulated. In theory, bifurcation encourages the development of two separate playing fields subject to separate rules of play. Wholesale markets may be deregulated at the same time that regulation of retail markets is strengthened.

This approach is likely to appeal to financial policymakers (and scholars) because it appears to offer the best of both worlds, limiting regulation to those markets that need it the most while allowing wholesale markets to move more rapidly toward complete deregulation. It may also facilitate global financial integration by allowing at least wholesale financial markets in the US to look more like other national financial markets. Finally, it may reassure non-US firms that have been deterred by the high regulatory costs associated with doing business in the US. Non-US institutions seeking entry into US markets can choose their regulatory track, eschewing retail markets entirely if they want to avoid the high compliance costs associated with the rules of fair play. Ironically, US financial institutions may have greater difficulty adjusting to the new market bifurcation because US firms, especially banks, traditionally have straddled customer markets; being a 'full service' bank meant having a presence in both wholesale and retail markets. The regulatory bifurcation of markets may provide a compelling reason for US financial firms to specialize on customer lines, with many opting to become purely wholesale institutions.

Nevertheless, like past regulatory bifurcations of markets, this particular division of the playing field is probably unsustainable in the long run. Market bifurcation runs the danger of resulting in the inefficient production of regulation as retail markets are overregulated and wholesale markets are underregulated.[12] As in other cases of overregulation, players in retail markets who find themselves at a competitive disadvantage will look for ways to readjust their regulatory burden, either by evading regulation or by bringing pressure for regulatory reform. At that point, the logic of market bifurcation disappears.

This result may be inevitable, since market bifurcation is inconsistent with the ideal of a level playing field. By limiting competition and innovation, the rules of fair play impose special costs on one market, denying its participants the investment opportunities available in other markets. At the same time, financial firms operating in more heavily regulated markets have cause to complain of the special regulatory burden that they face in complying with special rules. These problems ultimately may threaten the legitimacy of rules of fair play, particularly the most recent generation of rules that have been crafted to govern the sales practices of newly integrated US financial 'supermarkets'.

Nevertheless, in this instance, the process of regulatory readjustment may be complicated by the absence of the competitive forces that tend to precipitate regulatory change in US financial markets. In developing the rules of fair play, the usually warring US financial regulatory agencies have shown an unusual willingness to cooperate. As a result, individual regulators may be more reluctant than usual to respond to their constituents' requests to level the playing field by lessening their regulatory burdens.

The rules of fair play

How does US financial regulation define fair play in retail financial markets? A partial answer is provided by the two stories that began this chapter. What is troubling about the NationsSecurities case, or the experience of Mr Brown? US financial lawyers would immediately identify violations of several longstanding rules of fair play that govern the conduct of financial market transactions in the US. For instance, in both stories, the financial firms apparently ignored the suitability of their investment recommendations to their customers' financial positions and investment objectives. Highly leveraged investments such as the Term Trusts probably were unsuitable for risk-averse elderly depositors living on fixed incomes. Likewise, high-risk bonds or even stocks may not have been right for Mr Brown. Even if the investments were suitable, Mr Brown's broker may have been guilty of the separate offense of churning, or overtrading his account, in order to produce brokerage commissions for the bank. Today, violations of one or both of these rules of fair play by a securities firm could result in legal penalties under US securities regulation.

In both stories, however, another element of unfairness was present. In the NationsSecurities matter, the problem was not simply that unsuitable high risk investments were marketed to unsophisticated investors. Financial regulators were also concerned about the way in which these investments were being marketed to bank depositors. The investors' status as depositors was important because, as depositors, they apparently assumed, mistakenly, that the Term Trusts offered by their bank, just like its certificates of deposit, were protected by federal deposit insurance. Even if sales personnel never made this claim, investors complained that the firm's marketing tactics created this false impression. Customers were approached to buy Term Trusts just as their insured bank certificates of deposit were maturing. Mass mailings of sales literature advertising securities products were made to retail customers in envelopes that were similar to those used by the bank to mail deposit account statements. The bank's lobby displayed posters reading 'Invest in Tomorrow Where You Bank Today' and 'Introducing the Investment Firm You Can Bank On'. Securities sales personnel were trained to avoid using securities 'lingo' because the typical bank customer would find bank terminology 'less alarming'. These marketing tactics, although not by themselves illegal, were viewed by the regulators as blurring the distinction between insured bank deposits and uninsured securities products like the Term Trusts, thereby misleading customers.[13]

The underlying regulatory assumption is that bank depositors are at a special disadvantage in diversified financial product markets because they are likely to confuse *insured* deposits with *uninsured* non-deposit investment products such as securities, mutual funds and insurance. Moreover, bank sales personnel, eager to expand their customer base, will be tempted to exploit this confusion to make a sale. Regulatory intervention to prevent any marketing practices that perpetuate this confusion is therefore legitimized by the need to ensure fair play.

This same concern – that banks may exploit the average retail depositor's lack of investment experience in order to persuade a vulnerable client to make unsuitable investments – is raised by Mr Brown's story and is expressly articulated in the excerpt from the Supreme Court's decision in *Investment Company Institute* v. *Camp* quoted earlier. Bank depositors are assumed to rely on their bankers for prudent impartial advice on money matters, and, because they trust their bankers, they are especially vulnerable to unfair sales pressures. In fact, for years, defenders of the Glass-Steagall Act, which kept banks out of securities markets, argued that, regardless of the original motives for the Act, its prohibitions were still needed in modern financial markets because banks with securities operations would naturally be tempted to confuse and abuse their retail customers.

Critics of Glass-Steagall typically responded that, even in the 1920s, evidence of actual abuse of retail bank customers (apart, perhaps, from Mr Brown) was thin.[14] They also issued a challenge to Glass-Steagall's defenders. If the danger of consumer abuse is the only remaining rationale for excluding banks from securities markets, they asked, could consumer protection be guaranteed by the creation of regulatory rules of conduct that would be more narrowly drawn than Glass-Steagall's ban on virtually all bank securities activities?

Beginning in the 1980s, this challenge was accepted by the bank regulators, who began to redefine Glass-Steagall to emphasize its consumer protection goals. This rereading of Glass-Steagall offered a philosophical justification for the narrow statutory construction that permitted banks to recommence many long-forbidden securities activities. In each case, however, deregulation was accompanied by the imposition of new regulatory rules of conduct designed to minimize dangers of conflict of interest and other unfair practices historically associated with bank participation in securities markets.

An example is provided by the terms of bank re-entry into the securities brokerage business. In 1986, the Federal Reserve allowed banking organizations to offer full service brokerage (investment advice plus trade execution) to clients through affiliates. Originally, however, bank brokerage affiliates could act only for wholesale customers (institutions and high net worth individuals) and had to operate under a different name and at a different location from the affiliated bank.[15] These conditions were intended to minimize the danger that customers might confuse insured bank products with uninsured securities products and to insulate the most vulnerable bank customers, retail depositors, from any unfair pressure from their banks to buy securities, thereby preventing a reoccurrence of the abuses that, thanks to Senator Bulkley and the Supreme Court's decision in *Investment Company Institute* v. *Camp*, have become inexorably linked in the public's mind to the notorious bank securities affiliates of the 1920s.

Just two years later, the Federal Reserve allowed bank brokerage units to solicit retail customers, but subject to additional disclosure rules and cross-marketing restrictions. This time, brokers had to disclose, in writing, that they were not banks and that the securities that they recommended were neither bank deposits nor federally insured. They also were forbidden to solicit bank depositors individually for their custom or to share confidential information concerning clients with affiliated companies.[16]

These particular conditions were further modified as the Federal Reserve permitted banks to push even deeper into the securities markets, but they illustrate how rules of fair play have been employed to facilitate deregulation of financial product markets. As Glass-Steagall's barriers gave way, new rules of fair play were crafted to address the danger that customers, especially individuals, would be confused and abused by banks eager to exploit their vulnerability to sell them securities products. Thus, rules of fair play were essential to the process by which Glass-Steagall reform was legitimized, helping to neutralize the most potent modern objection to financial deregulation.

Nevertheless, the evolution of these rules of fair play highlights a basic tension between the goals of deregulation and of consumer protection. The reinterpretation of Glass-Steagall that began in the 1980s was justified as a way to increase the competitiveness of financial markets by allowing banks to compete with securities firms. Yet, especially in retail markets, the rules of fair play actually increased the cost of product delivery by forcing banks to adopt special new organizational forms and marketing procedures to avoid the possibility of customer confusion.

Moreover, because players in wholesale financial markets were exempt from some or all of the new regulations, the rules of fair play exacerbated competitive inequalities between wholesale and retail markets. These inequalities already existed, thanks in part to the slow pace of financial reform in the US that (with one important exception) had allowed wholesale customers to capture most of the early benefits of deregulation. For decades, deregulation of US financial markets occurred principally through industry and regulatory innovation. Yet many innovative financial products designed by financial firms to evade regulatory limitations were restricted to wholesale markets because their complex structures made mass marketing difficult. (The exception was the money market mutual fund, a retail securities product designed to offer the liquidity and safety of deposits while avoiding deposit interest rate ceilings. Although deposit interest rate ceilings disappeared in the 1980s, the money market mutual fund remained a highly successful retail innovation.)

Likewise, large financial firms were, on balance, more likely than small retail oriented institutions to take advantage of opportunities to innovate. As noted, the return of banks to the securities business in the 1980s came about largely as a result of creative regulatory reinterpretation of statutes, yet the benefits accrued primarily to large banking organizations with the resources to undertake the lengthy regulatory approval process, to defend against legal challenges by competitors and to comply with the complex operating rules imposed upon successful applicants. Because both large and small banks in the US serve retail markets, some retail customers, especially those who lived in major financial centers, were able to share the advantages of their banks' entry into such securities businesses as retail brokerage. Nevertheless, it is likely that the benefits of deregulation were not evenly distributed, excluding many customers of small town and country banks that were not able to take advantage of new opportunities to diversify.

In theory, repeal of Glass-Steagall and other restrictive banking legislation should help to level the playing field by reducing the regulatory cost of diversification. Nevertheless, to the extent that deregulation is being accompanied by the imposition of new rules of fair play specifically targeted to retail markets, these inequities may be perpetuated. This raises the question whether the special regulatory burdens that the rules of fair play impose on retail markets are really justified by the special dangers that deregulation potentially creates in those markets.

Are retail markets overregulated?

As previously described, the new rules of fair play that are being prescribed for US financial markets presume that retail bank depositors are especially likely to be confused and abused in increasingly integrated financial product markets. Why is this the case? Many bank depositors may be inexperienced investors who are unfamiliar with the risks associated with stocks, bonds or mutual funds. When they are approached by their banks to buy these securities products, they may mistakenly assume that all products available from a bank are as safe as insured deposits. Thus, the presence of a bank or its depositors in the mix creates, from a regulatory standpoint, a unique opportunity for consumer abuse that requires a special response.

This explains why the demise of Glass-Steagall caused the proliferation of new rules of fair play that have required that financial firms selling new investment products to bank customers take affirmative steps to avoid exploitation of depositor confusion. One such rule that has been in place, in some form, since Glass-Steagall reform began in the 1980s is the requirement for special disclosure to alert bank customers to the differences between insured deposits and uninsured investment products. As banks have re-entered the retail securities markets, regulators have demanded that bank managers ensure that retail sales personnel inform customers that mutual funds and other securities products are not insured and are subject to investment risk, including risk of loss of principal. In some instances, sales personnel have been required to repeat this disclosure during every sales contact with a retail customer.[17] Interestingly, these disclosure rules were developed jointly by the bank regulatory agencies in a perhaps rare instance of interagency cooperation. In addition, securities regulators adopted remarkably similar disclosure rules governing all registered broker-dealers, including bank securities affiliates, that deal with bank customers.[18]

So the financial regulators were in agreement as to the desirability of this disclosure, and, at least initially, it appeared that no one could object very much. Ideally, disclosure would improve the transparency of retail product markets, allowing better assessment of risk by retail customers and preventing a repetition of the unfortunate investment experience of Mr Edgar Brown. In any event, disclosure would certainly do no harm, and the disclosure requirement did not seem to be particularly burdensome for financial firms and their employees.

Yet these simple disclosure rules proved surprisingly controversial. For banking organizations, implementation was not as easy as policy-makers anticipated. For example, how could bank managers hope to police compliance with the disclosure requirements by each individual securities salesperson during each client contact, particularly when many banks owned huge securities operations with multiple branch offices? Did managers have to monitor every sales call? Could they rely on customer complaints to identify isolated abuses? Or would aggrieved customers be more likely to complain to the bank's regulators (or to a congressional committee or a class action lawyer) rather than alerting bank managers to a problem? Since policymakers and regulators promised to take violations seriously and to punish offenders harshly, as demonstrated by the NationsSecurities enforcement action, failure of bank management to detect and prevent transgressions could impose major costs on the bank in the form of regulatory penalties, litigation expenses and negative publicity.

Moreover, how effective was the disclosure in providing retail customers with new and helpful investment information? Broadly defined, 'retail customer' might include everyone except institutional investors and perhaps very wealthy individuals. Yet many ordinary bank customers already owned stock and were familiar with the securities markets. Banks were eager to win these customers' brokerage business, but they feared that these customers might be distracted or even offended by repeat disclosure of information that they already knew (such as the fact that securities are subject to investment risk). On the other hand, disclosure alone, even if repeated, might not be enough to protect the truly inexperienced investor who did not know the difference between a deposit and a security and did not appreciate the nature of investment risk. Interestingly, in the NationsSecurities case, the firm's manuals apparently did instruct sales personnel to make the appropriate disclosures, but regulators concluded that this was not enough to prevent customer confusion.[19]

These objections to repeat disclosure were persuasive to the Federal Reserve, which in 1998 agreed to exempt bank holding company securities affiliates whose brokerage business was conducted off bank premises from the requirement of repeat disclosure during every sales contact so long as securities employees made the proper disclosures once, in writing.[20] Observers may surmise that the regulators may have welcomed this compromise almost as much as the banks. For regulators, monitoring individual firms' compliance with the repeat disclosure rule was as difficult, if not more difficult, than for bank holding company managers. Yet failure to detect violations could subject the regulators to the charge of lax supervision. Thus, both regulators and industry had reason to object to rules that created an impossible monitoring burden.

The resulting compromise, although sensible, highlights a fundamental problem with the regulatory rules of fair play. Rules regulating the details of individual financial transactions are likely to be costly for financial firms to obey and difficult for financial regulators to enforce.

At the same time, the benefits of these rules are particularly difficult to quantify, often involving subjective judgments about what is needed to maintain elusive investor confidence in the financial markets. Although the importance of maintaining investor confidence has allowed many of these rules of fair play to retain their legitimacy among financial market participants even when their net benefits cannot be objectively measured, some rules may prove so costly to implement and enforce that they become counterproductive. The resulting overregulation, if uncorrected, may prove as damaging to investor confidence as the absence of rules of fair play.

This problem may doom regulatory attempts to restrict the cross-marketing of bank and non-bank investment products to retail bank customers. The NationsSecurities enforcement action suggested that cross-marketing may blur distinctions between insured and uninsured investments, misleading retail bank customers. The regulators specifically disapproved of such practices as advertising investment services in deposit-taking bank facilities and targeting depositors without much investment experience to buy securities products. Nevertheless, policy-makers fashioning a regulatory cure to this 'blurring conduct' face a dilemma. The most efficient way to prevent the danger of customer confusion is to prohibit any cross-marketing of deposit and non-deposit investment products. Yet cross-marketing may be the only way to introduce neophyte customers to new investment markets.

Thus, avoiding cross-marketing may prevent another Term Trust story, but it also may deprive retail customers of investment opportunities that are available to more sophisticated market players. From the retail consumer's point of view, whether the benefits of restricting cross-marketing outweigh its costs is unclear, and different consumers would probably reach different conclusions. This makes the decision to regulate, or not to regulate, very difficult, which may account for the ambiguity surrounding recent regulatory attitudes toward cross-marketing.[21]

The price of overregulation

The difficulties that have arisen in balancing the costs and benefits of the new regulation governing retail sales of investment products may reflect a flaw in the assumption that, when inequality of bargaining power exists, rules of fair play are necessary even when they are inefficient. In the long run, any inefficiencies created by rules of fair play may simply exacerbate competitive inequalities between different financial players, resulting in a very unlevel playing field. To the extent that the selective application of the rules of fair play to retail markets is producing market bifurcation in the US, inequalities between markets are magnified, negatively affecting the starting positions of retail customers as well as the firms, usually banks, that serve them.

That rules of fair play may increase the cost of financial transactions has already been suggested with respect to cross-marketing. Cross-marketing may be an efficient way for financial firms to introduce unfamiliar products to retail investors; moreover, the resulting efficiencies are likely to benefit retail customers as well as financial firms. For example, joint advertising and sale of bank and securities products lower search costs for bank customers who otherwise would have to locate a securities broker on their own. To the extent that the bank can economize on its marketing costs, it may pass those savings on to retail customers. Finally, cross-marketing allows a bank to draw upon its knowledge of its customer's financial position and investment preferences to craft a package of financial products that meets the client's specific needs. Thus, the Term Trust story might have had a different ending. Cross-marketing could have been employed to make available to retail depositors a package of financial products that was suited to their needs as risk-averse small investors.

In sum, rules against cross-marketing may protect the retail customer from potential abuses, but they also may deprive the consumer of potential efficiencies. In this sense, the customer ultimately is paying for special regulatory protection whether or not she really needs or wants it. The same argument may be made with respect to the antitying rules that have long been part of bank consumer regulation. Like cross-marketing, tying may create the potential for consumer abuse but it may also enhance the efficiency of retail financial transactions, benefiting the consumer.

The rules prohibiting tying presume that, if bank employees require borrowers to purchase a second product, such as credit insurance, from the bank, then those customers are denied the opportunity to obtain better-priced insurance elsewhere. In fact, however, in many cases, the search costs that customers would incur in shopping for alternative quotes may exceed any price advantage. Insurance supplied by an independent firm may actually turn out to be more costly than the bank's because the supplier is not familiar with the borrower's credit history and must perform its own credit check. Negotiating costs may be higher because the lending bank may require some special term that may not be in the insurer's standard contract. In any event, borrowers may not have the skill accurately to evaluate the comparative cost of different insurance packages. In these cases, tying arrangements may be efficient for customer and bank alike.

Moreover, the most vulnerable customers are also the most likely to benefit. More experienced borrowers probably enjoy lower search costs when shopping for credit insurance. (For example, some may be able to shop for the lowest price insurance online.) Many may have sufficient market power to bargain for their own discounts. The benefits of cross-marketing of banking and securities products are more likely to accrue to inexperienced investors than to investors who already employ brokers or investment advisers.

Critics may point out that, without rules of fair play, financial firms would have no incentive to share with their retail customers any of the savings produced by the joint marketing and sale of financial products. For example, so long as tying is prohibited and bank borrowers are free to shop around for credit insurance, banks must persuade their borrowers that they are most efficient suppliers of insurance and must price the product accordingly. Yet if the bank tells its borrower 'Should you agree to purchase insurance from us, we will give you a discount on the entire financial package,' the bank may still be accused of coercion.[22] In fact, in the past, a bank's record of success in jointly selling credit and credit insurance was itself considered possible evidence of illegal voluntary tying, although it might actually reflect the superiority of the bank's products.[23]

Why then does financial regulation presume that, in most cases, tying, or cross-marketing, is harmful to consumers? The explanation may be the rhetorical power of stories like Mr Brown's, or the tale of the Term Trusts. If even one case of customer abuse can be documented, the potential damage to investor confidence may be immense, justifying regulation. Nevertheless, the impact of these stories on investor confidence may be exaggerated. For example, historically, complaints by retail consumers about unfair tying have been rare. A 1993 study of private litigation alleging bank ties found that most complaints arose not in the context of retail consumer transactions but in loan restructurings where a bank had sought to protect its position by imposing additional conditions on a defaulting borrower.[24] And as banks began to expand their sales of securities products in the 1990s, concern over the possibility of tying was expressed not by retail bank customers but by sophisticated corporate borrowers that feared pressure from their bank lenders to use the bank's new underwriting services.[25]

If retail markets are overregulated, then one might expect burdened financial players to respond by pressuring their regulators for relief or threatening to abandon overregulated markets. In the case of the rules of fair play, however, the process of regulatory rehandicapping may not proceed as efficiently as in other areas of overregulation. Many retail customers may not be sophisticated enough to recognize the costs of regulation. Even if they do, they may lack the political clout to pressure financial regulators for some adjustment of their regulatory burden.

Further, their threat of exit may be meaningless given the willingness of competing financial regulators to cooperate in crafting rules of fair play for retail markets. In the case of retail sales of non-deposit investment products, virtually identical rules govern the marketing practices of employees of banks, bank securities affiliates and even non-bank brokers operating on bank premises. The Term Trust story ended in a joint enforcement action against NationsBank, a national bank, and its securities subsidiary by the Securities and Exchange Commission, the National Association of Securities Dealers and the Comptroller of the Currency, each of which exacted penalties for the same marketing practices. To the extent that rules of fair play are developed jointly by financial regulatory agencies, or are formalized in congressional legislation, there is little opportunity for regulatory competition. Once defined as members of the protected class, retail customers may have no escape route.

Of course, retail customers are not the only players affected by overregulation. Firms that operate in retail markets bear the cost of complying with the rules of fair play, and are likely to recognize any resulting competitive inequity. One inequity is already apparent: because many of the new rules of fair play are concerned with preventing depositors from confusing bank and non-bank products, they apply only to financial firms whose customer base consists of depositors, primarily banks and bank affiliates. Independent securities firms may serve unsophisticated retail clients, but these firms are not subject to the special new rules unless they actually market their products on bank premises. So banks selling mutual funds to retail customers are likely to be subject to different and more costly regulatory requirements than non-banks selling the identical product.

As previously mentioned, banking organizations occasionally have been successful in obtaining relief from their regulators from some regulatory burdens imposed by the new rules of fair play, such as the requirement for repeat disclosure during every sales contact. In that case, however, bank holding companies were seeking a change in a rule adopted by their own regulator, the Federal Reserve. As regulatory coordination increases, resulting in joint rulemaking and enforcement of consumer regulation, individual agencies will have less and less room to innovate at the behest of their constituent firms.

Unlike their retail customers, banks seeking to lessen their regulatory burden have two other avenues of escape that may be more effective than lobbying their regulator. First, they may simply pass their regulatory costs onto consumers by increasing the price of retail products, hoping that their customers, unable or unwilling to shop around, will not complain. Second, they may decide to abandon retail markets in order to avoid costly regulation. In either case, retail customers will be denied the gains in efficiency and increased investment opportunities that financial deregulation has long been promising. If so, rules designed to level the playing field by equalizing the bargaining power of retail customers may turn out to harm rather than improve these players' starting positions.

Market bifurcation and underregulation

What about wholesale financial markets? Are these markets exempt from the rules of fair play and should they be? Recently, US policymakers appear to have concluded that, in most cases, the answer is yes. Participants in wholesale financial markets are able to bargain for the degree of protection that they desire far more effectively than the government can ensure that protection by regulation. Enforcing rules of fair play in wholesale markets is unnecessary and adds to the cost of operating in those markets.

In theory, both efficiency and fairness militate against providing regulatory protection to sophisticated wholesale customers. Regulatory protection may lead to undesirable moral hazard as sophisticated players abdicate their responsibility to remain vigilant in their own defense. Moreover, to the extent that regulatory rules of fair play provide any net subsidy to the consumer, sophisticated investors who can protect themselves are undeserving of government protection. (As will be described in Chapter 7, this later argument was employed with considerable success in the early 1990s by critics of bank failure policy who argued that, as a result of bank bailouts, such as the rescue of Continental Illinois, the deposit insurance guarantee was being extended, unfairly, to sophisticated uninsured investors.)

In practice, however, rules of fair play have occasionally been applied to wholesale markets. Even sophisticated wholesale investors sometimes complain of inequality of bargaining power. In the 1990s, a number of corporate derivatives users were able to convince the financial regulators that, in the derivatives markets, corporations may become unsuspecting victims of the more knowledgeable financial institutions that structure and sell derivatives products. In the name of ensuring fair play, the regulators were willing to intervene in private financial transactions even in wholesale markets. In fact, in response to one complaint, the regulators required the bank seller of derivative products to adopt sales procedures to minimize customer confusion that were reminiscent of the rules of fair play governing retail sales of non-deposit investment products. For example, the bank agreed to conduct its sales and provide information to customers in ways that ensured that customers fully understood the nature of the risks associated with investment in derivatives.[26]

This is not to say that the regulation of derivatives markets is, or is likely to become, as intense and transaction-specific as are the rules governing, for example, bank sales of retail mutual funds. US regulators generally have been more willing to rely upon self-policing by financial firms in wholesale markets than in retail markets. This may reflect a growing expertise gap between regulators and private financial market players in increasingly esoteric wholesale financial product markets, making self-regulation a necessity.[27] Players in wholesale markets may not always enjoy equal bargaining positions, but government regulators may be powerless to correct inequities.

Another factor may frustrate the complete bifurcation of US financial markets. Maintaining impermeable barriers between wholesale and retail markets is likely to prove impossible. Retail customers may venture into wholesale markets. And, in many cases, the distinction between wholesale and retail investors may be unclear. For example, although institutional investors are typically classified as wholesale customers, high net worth individuals may be treated as wholesale investors in some transactions[28] but not in others.[29] Moreover, in both wholesale and retail markets, different players are likely to have different levels of knowledge, investment experience and risk tolerance. Thus, in the long run, market bifurcation may prove too simple a solution to the problem of unequal bargaining power in financial markets.

Globalization and rules of fair play

The US financial regulatory system's preoccupation with ensuring fair play in financial markets may be a sign of the democratization of US markets. The assumption underlying the rules of fair play is that financial firms may exploit customer ignorance, confusion or lack of information to sell clients unsuitable or unnecessary financial products. This presumes that financial firms are ready and willing to market a variety of products to retail customers. Were securities markets closed to retail customers, for example, than investors like Mr Brown would not have to worry about making bad investments. They would have to leave their money in safe but low-yielding bank deposit accounts.

Likewise, if only lending banks offered credit insurance, then tying would not be a concern. Whether or not the bank's insurance was priced correctly, the borrower would have no alternative. Antitying rules presume that consumers may be able to find a more efficient supplier if they are allowed to shop around, which, in turn, presumes that there are plenty of other potential entrants in the credit insurance market.

Thus, the rules of fair play address problems that arise in competitive, inclusive and democratized financial product markets. This may offer some insight as to the future of rules of fair play in increasingly globalized financial markets. The trend toward global market integration is likely to mean that more investment opportunities are open to more and more customers. Retail consumers will have more options as to both financial service providers and as to financial products. Although US financial firms expect that they will bring their innovative products to non-US retail customers, non-US firms may find new customers for their own products in US retail markets.

Assuming that international financial product markets will become increasingly democratized, two questions arise with respect to the future of rules of fair play. First, will these rules inhibit market integration by discouraging participation in retail markets in the US? For example, both US and non-US firms may seek to economize on regulatory costs by avoiding US retail markets, instead preferring to sell products in wholesale markets or in retail markets outside of the US that are less heavily regulated. If so, then US retail customers will be denied the efficiencies of global financial competition.

Second, will market bifurcation, US-style, be an exportable regulatory strategy as other regulatory systems, concerned about maintaining consumer confidence, feel pressure to adopt their own rules of fair play? Some US rules seem culturally bound; for example, the rules seeking to prevent confusion between insured and uninsured bank products may be grounded in peculiarities of the US banking system and may not be necessary in regulatory systems in which, for example, the tradition of deposit insurance is not so deeply ingrained.

Nevertheless, the desire to improve the transparency of retail financial product markets cuts across national market boundaries, and growing individual participation in global financial markets may cause all national regulators to rely increasingly on rules of fair play.

Further, to the extent that market bifurcation allows wholesale markets to be deregulated more rapidly than retail markets, bifurcation may make adjustment to globalized markets somewhat easier for all national regulators who may be more willing to allow their wholesale markets to operate free from government control so long as they retain the discretion to regulate their retail markets. This would please wholesale financial institutions that are increasingly impatient with national financial regulation and that may already view themselves as global firms. And it may be inevitable as global financial transactions become increasingly difficult for national regulators to supervise effectively.

So will the global financial markets of the future be bifurcated, consisting of a largely borderless and self-regulating wholesale sector and a series of nationally regulated retail sectors? In addition to the limitations already identified, global bifurcation creates one new problem. Wholesale financial markets can never be completely stateless because their operations have an impact on national monetary policy and prosperity. In particular, the failure of a wholesale financial firm may require government intervention to prevent financial market disruption.

Traditionally, government response to institutional or market failure has varied from nation to nation. As in many areas of regulation, US policy has tended to differ from that of other financial systems and to be driven by goals that may appear to be ambiguous and perhaps even somewhat contradictory. This may be because US failure policy has been animated by two distinct and perhaps conflicting norms, the desire for fair play and the equally strong preference that the market, rather than the government, determines financial outcomes. As the next chapter describes, these norms have been uneasily reflected in a regulatory policy that has attempted to protect financial markets without protecting financial firms.

7
Failure on a Level Playing Field

The modern history of US government policy toward the failure of financial firms is marked by a series of milestones: the 1933 banking crisis is one, but several others loom as large. Among them are the failure of Penn Square Bank, the first $100 million bank to be liquidated, in 1982, the bailout of Continental Illinois, at the time the nation's seventh largest bank, in 1984 and the rescue of Long Term Capital Management, a hedge fund, in 1998.

With the exception of the 1933 banking crisis, these events are not remarkable for producing landmark legislative change or significant policy shifts in the way that the US treats the failure of its financial institutions. Rather, these events are milestones because each has served to remind the financial markets of the unresolved conflict that has always complicated US financial failure policy. The problem is one of legitimization: US financial players are, and always have been, ambivalent about their government's involvement in resolving financial failure. As a result, each time that public failure policy is required to be implemented because of the imminent demise of a major financial firm, the legitimacy of the government's action once again is at issue.

This may account for the anomaly that, although financial regulators in the US traditionally have played a relatively active role in resolving financial failure, they profess to abhor bailouts. This opinion is widely shared in US financial markets: preventing failure, in the view of most US financial market participants, subsidizes inefficient players, a result that is at once unfair and anticompetitive. On the level playing field, the competitive markets, not the government, should pick winners and losers. Financial failure, although not desirable for its own sake, serves the desirable function of enhancing market efficiency by eliminating inefficient competitors. This sentiment was neatly expressed in a 1967 article aptly titled 'The Case for Bank Failure'[1] and remains influential despite the dislocations subsequently experienced by US financial markets as a result of unusually high rates of failure in the bank and thrift industries during the 1980s. In fact, the conventional wisdom is that the financial firms that survived the 1980s emerged stronger than ever, with no thanks to the government's misguided efforts to prevent troubled firms from failing – including the controversial rescue of Continental Illinois in 1984.

Nevertheless, as the Continental rescue demonstrated, in markets where bailouts are an anathema, bailouts still occur. Despite the considerable negative fallout that followed the Continental bailout (and the less successful government effort to save the US thrift industry in the 1980s), in 1998, the government once again became involved in a rescue, in this case of the troubled non-bank hedge fund Long-Term Capital Management. Although Federal Reserve officials insisted that, this time, the government merely brokered a private bailout and did not contribute either public or deposit insurance monies[2] to the effort, the government's involvement produced the usual round of public criticism, hostile congressional hearings and regulatory self-examination.[3]

Why then do US financial regulators persist in intervening to resolve financial failure when they rarely receive any thanks from either financial market participants or the public? In the end, they may be forced to intervene because no one else will. In highly competitive US financial markets, there is no tradition of voluntary collective action by private players to rescue their ailing rivals. Even when the failure of one player creates systemic risks, weakening its financial counterparties and disrupting the smooth functioning of markets, private firms will not necessarily take the initiative to restore market order. Regulators are required to compel 'voluntary' collective action, or in some cases to act alone to preserve market stability.

The failure of voluntary collective action is fully consistent with US notions of fair play on a level playing field. US financial institutions are encouraged to compete, not to cooperate. The winners are naturally reluctant to bail out the losers. Moreover, because US financial regulation frowns on financial oligopoly and other agreements among players that restrict competition, no single firm or group of firms has the market power to compel fellow players to participate in a rescue. Only the regulators can hope to do that, and even they have had difficulty doing so. Finally, on a level playing field, weak players are not entitled to protection from failure. Failure is an inevitable byproduct of competition, permitting efficient players to replace inefficient ones.

This is a compelling argument for simply letting financial firms fail, a policy that has had considerable appeal, at least in theory, since the 1980s. Nevertheless, in practice, the regulatory agencies have never quite been willing to adopt this hands off approach. The problem is that, in real life, failure is messy. Failure may promote market efficiency by eliminating inefficient players, but the process of unwinding their financial transactions and selling off their financial assets is costly. Moreover, the process may itself disrupt markets, distorting asset pricing and interrupting normal market functions. As globalization links financial markets, this paralysis may spread from market to market.

Most governments view as the responsibility of their financial regulatory regime to protect their domestic financial markets from this kind of risk. Thus, at a minimum, the consequences of financial failure must be managed, and it has fallen to US financial regulators, especially bank regulators, to perform this function. Yet, to the extent that government intervention violates the fundamental maxim that, on a level playing field, the market, not the government, picks winners and losers, the problem of legitimization arises. Players perceive that the government is unfairly subsidizing particular competitors and complain of unfair regulatory burden. Moreover, in most cases, this regulatory subsidy cannot be defended by the need to ensure equal starting positions or to equalize the bargaining power of unsophisticated players. Rather, the government is deliberately shielding individual players from the consequences of past competition on a perfectly level playing field, in the name of protecting the playing field from future, often unquantifiable, risk.

This contradiction explains why US financial failure policy tends to follow a predictable, and unsatisfactory, course. First, a threatened financial crisis resulting from the failure of one or more financial firms forces a regulatory response. That response, whether or not it is successful in achieving its stated goal of averting the crisis, is followed by a lengthy period of public criticism and regulatory introspection. A consensus then emerges, embraced by regulator and non-regulator alike, that the government's role in failure resolution henceforth should be sharply curtailed and that inefficient financial firms that cannot successfully compete should be allowed to fail. Finally, a year or two later, another financial crisis is threatened and the entire process begins anew.

Deposit insurance and failure policy

Like so many other elements of US financial regulation, modern failure policy begins with the banking crisis of the early 1930s that threatened the survival of the US banking system and forced the declaration of a nationwide bank holiday in March 1933 to stem a massive withdrawal of funds from the banking industry. The banking crisis is often credited with initiating the modern active role of the national government in resolving problem banks. Nevertheless, the failure resolution mechanism put in place in 1933 was quite modest. In fact, it was inadequate to deal with a repetition of the kind of banking crisis that US financial markets had just experienced. There is evidence that policymakers knew this, but chose not to design a more comprehensive bank failure policy. This choice probably reflected policymakers' ambivalence about the legitimacy of government intervention to resolve bank failure, an ambivalence that continues to this day.

This ambivalence is reflected in the decision made in 1933 to link bank failure resolution to administration of the deposit insurance system. The federal deposit insurance scheme contemplated that participating banks would contribute to a fund by paying assessments calculated as a percentage of their deposit base. When a participating bank failed, the Federal Deposit Insurance Corporation (FDIC), a new government agency, would take charge of its disposition. The FDIC would perform two functions, paying off the failed bank's insured depositors out of the fund and then acting as receiver for the failed bank, liquidating its assets for the benefit of uninsured creditors. One of those creditors would be the deposit insurance fund itself, which would look to the proceeds of liquidation for reimbursement, in whole or in part, of sums paid out to insured depositors. This scheme was designed to offer two improvements over previous bank liquidations. First, insured depositors were guaranteed immediate access to their funds and did not have to await the uncertain outcome of a lengthy liquidation. Second, the FDIC would serve as the sole liquidator of all insured banks, which was expected to lead to a more orderly and efficient bank liquidation market and thereby improve recovery rates for uninsured creditors, including the fund itself.[4]

Initially, the decision to rely on the deposit insurance scheme to resolve bank failure whenever possible does not seem unusual. Now that deposit guarantee schemes have become part of financial regimes around the world, many financial regulators may hope that this method of resolution will be adequate to handle ordinary bank failure. Nevertheless, as US policymakers were fully aware in 1933, deposit insurance schemes alone cannot cope with extraordinary bank failure. In fact, the US deposit insurance scheme began operations with such a modest level of funding that, had US bank failure rates continued at their historical levels, even excluding the extraordinary period of the early 1930s, the insurance fund would have been rapidly exhausted. Nevertheless, although this funding problem was immediately identified by federal bank regulators, Congress still chose to keep the deposit insurance assessment rate low and declined to give the FDIC power to levy special taxes on banks to make up any future shortfall.[5]

Moreover, despite the obvious inadequacy of deposit insurance to deal with a systemic banking crisis, Congress did not put in place any alternative scheme to deal with bank failure. To the contrary, insured deposit payoffs and liquidation procedures apparently were intended to become the sole method of future government bank failure resolution. That this was a deliberate choice, rather than an oversight, on the part of Congress is suggested by the fact that policymakers declined to make permanent another approach to failure resolution that the government was using in the 1930s. In 1932, Congress had created a new temporary agency known as the Reconstruction Finance Corporation (RFC) to make loans and capital investments in the form of preferred stock in order to prevent troubled banks from closing. At year end 1934, the RFC held investments of approximately $821 million in over 5400 US banks, or roughly one-third of the banking industry. Moreover, it was the RFC that, as described in Chapter 3, helped many ailing banks to qualify for federal deposit insurance by supplying them with enough public capital to meet the minimum solvency requirement for admission to the insurance plan.[6]

When Congress created deposit insurance, it might have made the RFC's recapitalization program permanent or consolidated its powers within the newly formed FDIC, but it chose not to do so. Government recapitalization remained a temporary solution to the 1930s banking crisis. Although the RFC survived a lot longer than most policymakers probably expected, its authority to invest in troubled banks was terminated in 1947 and it was liquidated six years later. Its functions were not transferred to the FDIC or to any other agency. To the extent that the US government subsequently has recapitalized troubled banks (like Continental), the action was taken by the FDIC within the confines of the deposit insurance scheme and using deposit insurance monies (occasionally with the quiet assistance of advances made by Federal Reserve's discount window).

How the FDIC managed to accomplish this feat will be explained later, but it should not be surprising that the agency encountered problems of legitimization and implementation. As critics have repeatedly pointed out, the mission of deposit insurance is to pay off insured depositors and liquidate failed banks. Each time that the FDIC has tried to convert this neutral liquidation function into a more comprehensive bank failure policy, its actions have led to objections that the agency is exceeding both its statutory authority and its political legitimacy.

Nevertheless, the FDIC may have been forced to develop creative new approaches to bank failure resolution because of what Congress apparently did not anticipate in 1933, namely, that the FDIC ultimately would be called upon to resolve more costly bank failures than the deposit insurance system could handle comfortably. As originally designed, deposit insurance may have been intended to be a somewhat exclusive club. Members would face rigorous admission standards (including meeting the qualifications for Federal Reserve membership) and would pay for their own protection. And only members would receive that protection: significantly, the new deposit insurance scheme was not given the responsibility for reimbursing the large numbers of depositors in institutions that had become casualties of the 1930–33 banking crisis. Only solvent banks would qualify for membership. Banks that were too weak to qualify would either be resuscitated by the RFC's capital or be allowed to fail.

Yet, perhaps inevitably, deposit insurance was democratized. In 1933, deposit insurance administrators faced political pressure to admit all operating banks to the insurance scheme, even insolvent ones. Although the FDIC lobbied Congress to increase future admission standards, Congress refused, even dropping the requirement that all insured banks join the Federal Reserve.[7] As a result, virtually every bank that wanted deposit insurance could join the club. Today, all national banks and virtually all state-chartered banks are members. This democratization of deposit insurance converted the program from a quasi-private insurance scheme, whose administrators had discretion to expel risky banks that violated their standards, to a full guarantee. This put considerable strain on a program that, from the beginning, was considered by its own administrators to be inadequately funded.

Deposit insurance still might have been adequate as bank failure policy had the banking business remained as failure proof as policy-makers in the 1930s imagined that it would be. It may seem odd that policymakers who had just lived through the worst banking crisis in US history anticipated few bank failures in the future. Perhaps they believed that banks that had survived the crisis had emerged stronger and wiser. Or perhaps they expected that the subsidy created by deposit insurance would give banks such a competitive advantage over rival financial players as to make the banking business practically fool proof. And they had reason to be optimistic. By 1934, bank earnings were once again increasing. New legislation had enhanced the oversight powers of federal regulators in both banking and securities markets. Many observers believed that the downsizing of the banking industry as a result of recent failures had solved the problem of overbanking that was itself a major cause of bank failure.[8]

Further, deposit insurance was expected to eliminate the risk of bank runs, considered the major contributing factor to the banking crisis of the 1930s. Retail customers with relatively modest savings were assumed to be most likely to join bank runs; seeing a queue outside of their bank, or even outside of another bank, they would panic and, fearing the safety of their funds, would rush to withdraw their deposits. Liquidity crises were contagious, spreading from weak banks to otherwise healthy banks. This systemic risk led to the decision in March 1933 to declare a nationwide bank holiday in order to protect the remaining solvent banks against the danger of bank runs.

Deposit insurance has been an effective vaccine against bank runs, reassuring retail depositors that their funds are safe regardless of the risk of bank closure. Since deposit insurance was put in place, retail deposit runs, at least on insured banks, have been rare in US banking markets. Thus, perhaps policymakers of the 1930s had reason to hope that the problem of bank failure had been virtually eliminated.

Observers were still optimistic in the 1960s. As one scholar noted, bank failure could no longer be blamed on the unavailability of good assets or unforeseen depressions or anything other than bad management.[9] Moreover, if a few mismanaged banks did fail, the fallout would be minor. Insured depositors could count on quick reimbursement and therefore would not be prone to join panic runs that would threaten other banks. And, given the marketability of bank assets, liquidation could be accomplished rapidly without imposing significant transactions costs on uninsured creditors.[10] Thus, the procedure created in 1933 was still considered sufficient to handle bank failure.

Nevertheless, by the 1980s, three difficulties had emerged to undermine this optimism. First, markets were reminded that not only small retail depositors join bank runs. Even in the 1930s, although they did not stand in line outside of their banks, large depositors abandoned the banking system as rapidly as small depositors.[11] By the 1980s, as a result of the growth of international wholesale money markets as well as the development of new financing techniques that enabled more banks to reach those markets (such as deposit brokerage), uninsured deposits had become an increasingly important source of funding, especially for large banks but even for smaller banks. The typical uninsured depositor was an institutional investor, with no business ties or loyalty to its bank, that was ready and able to withdraw its funds very quickly at the first suspicion of trouble. As a result, electronic 'hot money' runs by wholesale investors came to pose a far greater threat to bank liquidity than retail deposit runs. In the case of Continental Illinois, for example, 70 percent of the bank's deposits were wholesale; their volatility greatly exacerbated Continental's financial problems, forcing the regulators to intervene.[12]

Second, by the 1980s, the banking business no longer seemed fool proof. Bad assets, or the unavailability of good assets, had emerged as a serious problem for surprising numbers of US banks. Banks located in particular regions, such as the southwest and the northeast, were especially affected. As those regions experienced economic downturns, banks based in those regions that were heavily invested in local real estate and local business loans suffered losses. The new contagion threatening the banking industry was spreading not from bank to bank, but from borrower to bank lender as entire loan portfolios became worthless. Simultaneously, the US thrift industry was collapsing, the victim of bad assets, particularly real estate loans and investments that had gone sour, and of rising interest rates.

Finally, liquidating all of these failed bank and thrift assets was proving difficult. Financial assets are theoretically marketable, but only if buyers are available. In secondary markets already glutted with real estate loans, liquidation became a slow and risky process. Assets were sold at a fraction of their appraised value, raising questions about the ability of liquidation to reallocate assets to their highest valued uses. Uninsured creditors, fearing delays and losses if they waited for the outcome of liquidation to recover their funds, had another reason to join electronic runs when failure of their bank was rumored. And the deposit insurance fund could not hope to recoup the monies that it had to expend to reimburse insured depositors.

Thus, the funding issue, dismissed in 1930s, came back decades later to haunt the deposit insurance program. As will be discussed, the first deposit insurance administrators were sufficiently concerned about future funding shortfalls that they began developing alternatives to liquidation of failed banks almost immediately. By the 1980s, however, as failure became more frequent and costly, these alternatives became increasingly controversial, raising questions about the legitimacy of bank failure policy itself.

Penn Square and the problem of resolution cost

Understanding US bank failure policy requires an appreciation of how and why the issue of cost drives failure policy. Because bank failure policy is implemented exclusively through a deposit insurance scheme that from its inception has been inadequately funded, administrators and policymakers are preoccupied with the problem of resolution cost. This problem is compounded by the insistence of policymakers, both in 1933 and today, that deposit insurance remain self-funding, relying solely on premiums collected from insured banks at an assessment rate set by statute. As mentioned, as early as 1934, some regulators worried that the assessment rate was too low. Yet no provision was made for alternative funding to cover future shortfalls.

Of course, today, just about everyone believes that the US government will stand behind the deposit insurance fund as it did in the early 1990s when the (then) independent thrift insurance fund experienced liquidity problems. Congress has even passed a resolution confirming that the deposit insurance obligation is backed by the full faith and credit of the national government. Nevertheless, the myth that deposit insurance is private, relying on self-generated resources for its operations, continues to shape both public opinion and the actions of deposit insurance administrators. The problems experienced by the thrift insurance fund were viewed by most people as imposing an enormous financial burden on the US taxpayer, never to be repeated, although the monies actually spent to recapitalize the fund were modest compared with US government expenditures on other programs. Justly or unjustly, deposit insurance administrators are subjected to intense political pressure not to spend more in any given year than they collect in premiums. This has forced the FDIC to attempt to economize on resolution expenses by looking for the least-cost solution to every bank failure.

One might suppose that frugality on the part of insurance administrators would make them less likely to indulge in creative bank failure resolution, but in fact the opposite is the case. The FDIC developed its controversial alternatives to liquidating failed banks in order to minimize the financial impact of failure on the insurance fund. The FDIC discovered early on that it could save money by paying a healthy bank to assume a failing bank's liabilities rather than shutting down the bank, reimbursing its insured depositors and conducting a fire sale of its assets. The economics of the transaction, which became known as a 'purchase and assumption', were driven by the special value traditionally attached to the bank franchise. Healthy banks (and, to the extent that their ownership of a bank was permitted by law, non-banks) often were willing to pay a premium to acquire a particularly lucrative deposit base or a valuable branch network.

The FDIC could offset this premium against the payment (in the form of cash or performing assets) that it would have to offer the healthy bank to persuade it to assume the failed bank's deposit liabilities. If the cost of arranging this purchase and assumption was less than the estimated cost of an insured deposit payoff and liquidation, the FDIC could save money, theoretically earning the praise of a grateful public as well as healthy insured banks that were footing the bill for deposit insurance and wanted insurance premiums to remain low.[13] As early as 1935, just a year after the deposit insurance scheme took effect, the FDIC was able to convince Congress that permitting it to utilize deposit insurance funds to arrange mergers of failed banks would be a cost effective use of its limited resources.

Thus, the deposit insurance program quickly took on new dimensions. The FDIC was no longer just a national bank liquidator but was playing an active role in resolving bank problems in a way that avoided liquidation. Although the FDIC was acting within its legislative authority, this expansion of its role in failure resolution eventually exposed pre-existing fault lines in US bank failure policy. One problem that will be discussed in more detail later is that, by resolving bank failure in a way that preserved the bank's franchise and protected the investments of its depositors, including, in many cases, uninsured depositors, the government was engaged in failure prevention, a policy that Congress had deliberately refused to endorse when it had the chance to do so in 1933. Moreover, failure prevention ran counter to prevailing notions of competitive fairness on the level playing field.

In addition, however, avoiding liquidation did not completely solve the problem of failure resolution cost. The purchase and assumption worked most effectively when bank failures were relatively infrequent and failed banks were relatively small, allowing healthy banks to absorb them without demanding much financial assistance. In the 1980s, failure rates began to increase significantly for the first time since the 1930s, and the typical failed bank was big (and bad). The larger the failed bank's liabilities, and the poorer the quality of its assets, the more money was required to persuade a healthy bank to take it over – if any willing bidder could be found at all. Yet the alternative, an insured deposit payoff and liquidation, promised to be an expensive proposition.

In 1982, this dilemma was starkly illustrated by the failure of Penn Square Bank, an institution that had gained national notoriety for its rapid asset growth, its aggressive and ultimately disastrous lending policies and its ability to persuade much larger and more sober institutions, including Continental Illinois, to join it on its wild ride to insolvency. When it failed, Penn Square had assets in excess of $100 million. Given its size and the doubtful quality of its assets, deposit payoff and liquidation threatened to put serious financial stress on the deposit insurance fund. Yet these same problems discouraged potential bidders. Since no buyer was willing to take its franchise, the bank had to be liquidated.

The liquidation of Penn Square sent a sobering message to banking markets and their regulators that had become accustomed to quiet and relatively easily dispositions of failed banks.[14] In the 1980s, the banks that were failing were bigger, and badder, than ever before in the history of deposit insurance. Moreover, more banks were failing, creating a buyer's market in failed banks and making purchase and assumption transactions even more costly to arrange. Yet paying off depositors in all these failed banks threatened to break the fund. By 1983, observers were estimating that thirteen US banks were already so large that the failure of any one of them would deplete the insurance fund.[15]

By virtue of the congressional decision made in 1933, the deposit insurance fund remained the only defense against bank failure. Given the stress on the fund during the 1980s, market players had reason to worry about maintaining public confidence in US banks. Investors, particularly non-US investors, might come to doubt both the safety of US banks and the willingness of the US government to stand behind the banking system. In 1982, the potential cost to US markets of a non-interventionist government bank failure policy was becoming clear, at least to regulators. Ironically, within two years, the cost of an interventionist policy also had become apparent.

Continental Illinois and failure prevention

The FDIC had an alternative to either liquidation or merger of failed banks. In 1950, the FDIC had been given the power to use deposit insurance funds to make loans to or purchase assets from a bank in order to prevent it from closing. Although it might appear that Congress was transferring the RFC's failure prevention mandate to the FDIC, Congress had terminated the RFC's power to invest in banks three years earlier. (Because the RFC still held stock in a number of banks, Congress was unable to liquidate the agency until 1953.) Moreover, the power given to the FDIC to prevent bank closing was limited to the narrow case when the ailing bank was essential to its community because, for example, no other bank was available to provide services to the public. In 1982, however, Congress did empower the FDIC to recapitalize troubled banks. This expansion of power, however, was again tied to the issue of cost: unless the bank in question was essential to its community, open bank assistance to prevent failure was permissible only when it was a more cost effective solution than liquidation.

In 1984, the FDIC used this authority to arrange what became the most controversial bank rescue in the agency's history, the recapitalization of Continental Illinois. Continental Illinois posed many of the same resolution problems as Penn Square had two years earlier: as the seventh largest US bank, Continental was too large to attract an obvious bidder for a purchase and assumption, but paying off its $3 billion of insured deposits would strain the resources of the insurance fund.

In addition, the failure of Continental created special risks that were not present in the case of Penn Square. Continental was a money center bank that operated in international financial markets. A large portion of its funding consisted of wholesale money, including uninsured deposits of $37 billion. Rumors of the bank's imminent demise, which had begun as soon as Continental's large exposure to failed Penn Square Bank became known, had already caused wholesale investors to flee, threatening the bank's liquidity and forcing it to borrow extensively from the Federal Reserve. As a major correspondent bank, Continental had significant financial ties to over 2000 US depository firms. Regulators estimated that sixty-six US banks had deposits in Continental in excess of their net worth, and a protracted liquidation might threaten their liquidity. Thus, a Continental failure, followed by liquidation, was expected to have ripple effects both in US banking markets and in international funding markets.

These risks led to the decision to recapitalize Continental.[16] In doing so, the government took several actions that, although not necessarily novel, ran counter to the accepted wisdom of how bank failure should be handled in the US. For example, Continental never technically 'failed'; the FDIC kept it afloat with a capital infusion that made the government a major equity stakeholder. Public recapitalization preserved the investments of both the bank's creditors and those of the bank holding company, which critics viewed as an unprecedented extension of the deposit insurance guarantee.[17] Finally, as the complex rescue package was negotiated, the Federal Reserve kept Continental alive through discount window loans to replace private funding that was no longer forthcoming from competitive money markets.

The bank regulators defended this resolution as fully consistent with their statutory mandate to minimize financial stress on the deposit insurance fund, arguing that either liquidation or sale of Continental would have been far more costly. Moreover, the recapitalization protected US financial markets, reassuring non-US investors that the US government, like most of its counterparts abroad, would not tolerate the failure of one of its major banks. This was important during a decade in which the viability of several large US banks was called into question. Arguably, the Continental rescue prevented a loss of confidence in the US banking system that might have put even healthy US firms at a serious disadvantage in international funding markets. In signaling its intention to provide the same support to its large banks that most investors believed would be provided by other governments to their own major banks, the US government was effectively leveling the international playing field on behalf of US institutions.

So why did so many players in US financial markets object to Continental's rescue? Despite its favorable outcome, government intervention ran counter to many of the basic norms that animated US financial markets. First, by preventing failure, the government was interfering with the results of competition, rewarding inefficiency at the expense of more efficient competitors. In the case of Continental, this unfairness was keenly felt because, rightly or wrongly, most financial market players concluded that bad management, especially the ill-advised decision to buy loans from Penn Square, rather than bad luck was at the root of the Continental failure.

Second, by preventing failure, the government signaled its intention to convert US bank failure policy into a 'too big to fail' policy. According to bank regulators, Continental was rescued because letting it fail would have been too costly. The lesson was that large money center banks whose liquidation would break the insurance fund or impose other costs on US financial markets would be saved. Small banks that could be liquidated with minimal adverse consequences would not. This difference would be appreciated by uninsured depositors; rather than risking even a remote chance of bank failure and liquidation, they would invest exclusively in banks that were too big to fail whether or not these banks were efficient competitors. As a result, in wholesale funding markets, government bank failure policy gave large banks a starting advantage over small banks as well as non-bank financial firms.

Finally, failure prevention shielded sophisticated investors from the consequences of their own monitoring failure. In the recapitalization of Continental, the FDIC was careful to dilute the interests of existing shareholders, and incumbent management was replaced. Nevertheless, all creditors were protected. As a result, deposit insurance funds were being used to subsidize uninsured investors as well as insured depositors. Subsidization of insured depositors might be justified by the requirements of fair play, since small retail depositors probably would not have sufficient knowledge or bargaining power to protect themselves from risk, but this was certainly not true of sophisticated uninsured creditors, who could and should bargain for their own protection. So long as failure prevention shielded uninsured creditors from risk of loss, they would have no incentive to monitor and discipline bank management. Inefficient management would survive and even prosper. The competitive process would not work efficiently to weed out bad players.

This same problem had often arisen in purchase and assumption transactions, since many buyers of failed bank franchises chose to assume both insured and uninsured deposits. At least prior to the 1980s, however, this subsidization may have gone unnoticed, since uninsured depositors had little to fear even in a liquidation. The FDIC's liquidation record was so exemplary that very few depositors, insured or uninsured, experienced significant losses.[18] By the 1980s, however, liquidation had become more risky and involved more delays. If their accounts were taken over by a healthy bank, uninsured depositors experienced no change in position. As a result, in any failure resolution technique that did not involve liquidation, uninsured depositors were likely to enjoy a de facto deposit insurance subsidy that would relieve them of the obligation to protect themselves by monitoring their bank's financial condition. The only way to restore fairness and efficiency in wholesale funding markets was to return to the original deposit insurance plan, liquidating all failed banks and paying off only insured depositors.[19]

What about the cost of liquidation and the danger that, some day, a single bank failure might exhaust the insurance fund? Although critics responded that government subsidization of inefficient banks was itself producing more, and more costly, bank failures, this is not a complete answer. Monitoring by uninsured creditors will not necessarily avert all managerial error leading to bank failure. Penn Square disasters will probably occur with or without government failure prevention. Moreover, the liquidation process may create its own costs. What if liquidation threatens other banks with large uninsured exposures to the failed bank? What if other US banks suffer a competitive disadvantage in international funding markets as investors favor non-US banks that do not pose a liquidation risk?

Although some purists may conclude that the benefits of an all-liquidation policy outweigh these costs, most US financial players probably are not so sure. This may explain why, despite immediate negative public reaction to the Continental rescue in 1984, and an immediate congressional inquiry, policymakers did not take immediate steps to curb the FDIC's discretion. It took seven years, and the threat of insolvency of the thrift insurance fund, to lead to legislative reform of bank failure policy.[20] Even then, changes were modest, and the principal weaknesses of bank failure policy were not corrected. Deposit insurance remained the sole mechanism by which bank failure policy was implemented. And cost remained the sole factor by which resolution technique was measured.

How did Congress alter bank failure policy? First, Congress tried to end the participation of the Federal Reserve in failure resolution by limiting its ability to supply financial support to ailing banks through discount window loans, a technique used in the Continental rescue (and other failures) to prevent a liquidity crisis from causing the bank to become insolvent before the FDIC arranged a resolution. These loans typically were repaid, but often out of deposit insurance funds. Congress attempted to reverse the money flow, requiring the Federal Reserve to reimburse the FDIC should Federal Reserve lending to an undercapitalized bank increase liquidation costs. The goal was twofold, to encourage prompt closing of troubled banks before insolvency (and before uninsured creditors had time to withdraw their funds) and to return the responsibility for paying for failure resolution squarely to the industry-funded deposit insurance system.

Second, Congress tried to prevent the FDIC from choosing any resolution technique that subsidized uninsured creditors (either purchase and assumption or recapitalization) unless the agency could prove real cost savings to the deposit insurance fund. The FDIC might ignore cost only if it could persuade two-thirds of the Federal Reserve Board and the Secretary of the Treasury that economic conditions or financial stability required a different disposition. Since, in any major bank failure, one or both of these agencies probably would already be involved, perhaps the more novel aspect of this new procedure was the requirement that the FDIC recoup any extra resolution costs through a special assessment levied on insured banks.

Finally, bank regulators were empowered to take prompt corrective action against troubled banks, including restrictions on asset growth, diversification and payment of interest on deposits. They were also given broader authority to close and liquidate banks for inadequate capitalization, legal violations and other unsafe and unsound practices. Again, the goal was to preserve deposit insurance monies by liquidating banks before they actually became insolvent and before their wholesale depositors had a chance to abandon ship, taking valuable assets with them.

Although congressional action apparently was designed to prevent bailouts like Continental, it is unclear what effect the changes will actually have on bank failure policy. Choice of resolution technique was always dictated by cost. Alternatives to liquidation, such as purchase and assumption and open bank assistance, were always justified as more cost efficient than liquidation. Even after the new legislation, the FDIC rescued a large New York savings bank, CrossLand, in a transaction reminiscent of the Continental recapitalization. The FDIC did not invoke the new resolution procedure, but based its decision not to liquidate CrossLand on a creative interpretation of the least cost test.[21] Predictably, the FDIC came under fire for ignoring the spirit of congressional reform, but policymakers should not have been surprised.

Moreover, since 1991, the perennial problem of the inadequacy of the insurance fund to handle bank failure has re-emerged, complicating bank failure policy. During the 1990s, rapid consolidation within the banking industry was producing a new breed of megabank. In 1999, the FDIC estimated that industry consolidation had doubled the risk that a megabank failure would cause the insolvency of the insurance fund by 2050.[22] Congressional reform may have exacerbated that risk. Prompt closings of troubled banks mean that more failed banks must be resolved with deposit insurance monies. And every megabank failure presents the question raised by the Continental bailout: is the adverse market effect of a liquidation likely to be so devastating that the government simply cannot take the risk of letting the bank fail?

Thus, although financial market players have signaled their preference to let failing banks fail, it is unclear whether the FDIC can afford, or is even expected, to adhere to a liquidation strategy in every case. Once again, Congress failed to resolve the basic conflict in US bank failure policy. Is bank failure policy a matter of public concern, designed to maintain the stability of US banking markets? Or is it simply a way to manage finite deposit insurance assets?

Long-Term Capital Management and market disruption

Although bank failure policy has attracted the most public attention and criticism in the US, other financial firms fail too. Government policy toward failing non-bank financial firms is reminiscent of bank failure policy, relying on industry-funded guarantee schemes to reimburse customers pending liquidation. These schemes, administered by the Securities Investor Protection Corporation for failed securities brokerage firms and state insurance commissioners for failed insurance companies, have been subject to complaints that they are even less adequately funded, and their coverage is even less comprehensive, than the deposit insurance scheme. As in the case of failed banks, the national government has no formal mechanism in place to address a systemic crisis in either the securities or the insurance industry.

Nevertheless, the US government does not necessarily take a hands-off approach to non-bank financial failure. Interestingly, the bank regulators have often taken the lead in responding to non-bank financial crises. For example, when Penn Central Transportation Company filed for bankruptcy in 1970 (following a failed effort to arrange a government bailout), it had $82 million in commercial paper outstanding. Its unanticipated default caused investors to panic and withdraw from the market, threatening other issuers who had expected to roll over maturing paper. Obviously, Penn Central was not a bank, nor were most other players in the commercial paper market (although many bank holding companies depended on the commercial paper market for funding). But banks were lenders to commercial paper issuers. In this case, the Federal Reserve intervened to rescue the commercial paper market by supplying liquidity to banks so that banks might lend to issuers to enable them to repay maturing paper, thereby restoring investor confidence in the creditworthiness of most borrowers.[23]

Thus, although the government declined to bail out a failing transportation company, it did act to restore order to a financial market. Two decades later, the government allowed Drexel Burnham, the large securities firm, to fail, but regulators did oversee its liquidation to ensure that the breakup of its business did not disrupt the securities markets in which it operated. So, outside of the bank area, government involvement in failure resolution does occasionally occur. Unlike in bank failure, however, intervention is motivated not by a legal injunction to minimize resolution costs but by the goal of preventing market disruption. And, usually, intervention has stopped short of actually preventing failure.

In 1998, however, in the name of preventing market disruption, the government did play a role in preventing the failure of Long-Term Capital Management (LTCM). LTCM was a hedge fund that had been established in the early 1990s by a group of former traders from Salomon Brothers, a major US securities firm now part of Citigroup; principals also included two Nobel prize winning economists and a former vice chairman of the Federal Reserve. Because LTCM limited its investors to a small group of sophisticated players, it avoided securities regulation as a mutual fund; as it was not affiliated with a bank, it also avoided bank regulation. LTCM specialized in developing complex mathematical models of interest rate spreads and price movements of financial assets that it used to identify temporary market price anomalies. The fund exploited these gaps for profit by using borrowed funds to invest heavily in securities repurchase contracts and various derivatives instruments. Although initially the fund's strategy was highly successful, in the summer of 1998, the financial crisis in Russia and resulting downward price movements in virtually every global financial market had a negative impact on the fund's positions, resulting in significant losses. Given the fund's extensive leverage, it could not absorb the losses; by September, it needed an infusion of new money in order to remain afloat.[24]

The government became involved in LTCM's rescue when officials of the Federal Reserve Bank of New York convened a meeting of LTCM's creditors to negotiate a sale or rescue of the fund. In the end, creditors agreed to contribute an additional $3.5 billion to keep the fund alive. The fund's owners saw their equity stakes diluted, but existing managers were retained to oversee the liquidation of the fund's portfolio.

The Federal Reserve contributed no money to this bailout, yet its role in brokering the private rescue package still proved very controversial, leading to public criticism and congressional hearings that were reminiscent of the aftermath of the Continental bailout. The point of contention was not whether government monies had been used to arrange the bailout, but why the government had reached the conclusion that this hedge fund could not be permitted to fail. Although there was a possibility that the failure of LTCM might have imposed serious losses on its bank lenders, and a few banks were forced to write off their investments in the fund, it was not clear in September 1998 whether the hedge fund's failure would have brought down a major US bank, or, had it done so, whether that bank's failure would have broken the deposit insurance fund. In any event, the Federal

Reserve did not cite the impact on the deposit insurance fund, or any other concern relating to bank failure policy, to justify its conclusion that LTCM had to be saved. The regulators had another motive, as Federal Reserve Chairman Alan Greenspan told Congress:

> Financial market participants were already unsettled by recent global events. Had the failure of LTCM triggered the seizing up of markets, substantial damage could have been inflicted on many market participants, including some not directly involved with the firm, and could have potentially impaired the economies of many nations, including our own.... Moreover, our sense was that the consequences of a fire sale triggered by cross-default clauses, should LTCM fail on some of its obligations, risked a severe drying up of market liquidity.... What is remarkable is not this episode, but the relative absence of such examples over the last five years. Dynamic markets periodically engender large defaults.[25]

Thus, the danger of market disruption justified government intervention to prevent failure. In effect, Chairman Greenspan had articulated a new financial failure policy: liquidation may be an unacceptable response to financial failure when the process of unwinding complex multiparty financial transactions threatens to distort the pricing of market transactions and produce cross-defaults, disrupting markets and possibly igniting panic 'runs'. Although not articulated as directly, similar concerns had influenced earlier regulatory decisions to avoid liquidation of prominent banks like Continental and CrossLand. When the bank regulators concluded in these cases that recapitalization was a less costly option than liquidation, they were taking into account the transactions costs created by the liquidation process itself, including potential losses to be suffered by counterparties (a concern in the case of Continental) and the distortive effect of a fire sale on depressed financial asset markets (a concern in the case of CrossLand).

LTCM made these concerns the primary justification for government intervention, and not just in the case of bank failure. Chairman Greenspan's warning that dynamic markets periodically engender large defaults suggests that the LTCM rescue may have to be repeated should similar risks arise in the future. Moreover, the logic of this argument suggests that, if the risk is sufficiently great, then the use of public monies is not out of the question.

But what about the salutary effect of financial failure in removing inefficient players and reallocating assets? LTCM almost failed because its principals had taken (and its lenders had let them take) too many risks. The fund's stakeholders were highly sophisticated and certainly were as undeserving of protection as any uninsured creditor in Continental. Yet, in this case, to save markets and their innocent participants, players that had gambled and lost had to be rescued. Worse, as Chairman Greenspan intimated, this choice might have to be made again and again as financial markets grow larger and more complex and more integrated. Thus, the conflict that has always plagued bank failure policy has re-emerged in the broader context of government policy toward any financial failure. When, if ever, is it proper for the government, in the name of protecting markets, to alter the results of competition on the level playing field?

The lessons

A basic theme emerges from this history. In the US, financial failure policy reflects several inconsistent goals that complicate its implementation. One contradiction is implicit in the deposit insurance guarantee. The goal of deposit insurance is to level the playing field by protecting unsophisticated small depositors who cannot efficiently bargain for their own protection against risk. Yet even this modest interference with the results of private market competition is so troubling to US financial market players that policymakers have attempted to contain the deposit insurance program as much as possible. US financial players, including regulators, want deposit insurance to operate like a private sector insurer, to serve the limited function of reimbursing insured depositors and to be self-funding.

By requiring the insurance scheme to handle all bank failure, however, policymakers ensured that the program would expand beyond its original narrow purposes. For decades, policymakers have rationalized this contradiction by citing the problem of resolution cost: so long as deposit insurance administrators can prove that preventing bank failure is cheaper than allowing banks to fail, failure prevention is tolerated. Although allowing cost to drive decision making is consistent with the conventional view of deposit insurance as a private insurance scheme, it seems an odd way to craft a public bank failure policy. This may explain why bank resolution techniques used by the FDIC, although authorized by the letter of the statute as well as by cost factors, routinely prove so controversial.

Another contradiction in financial failure policy concerns the value accorded to liquidation as a solution to failure. Liquidation is valued for its ability to rid the playing field of inefficient players and to redistribute their assets to the victors of financial competition. Thus, imposing losses on everyone connected with a failed financial firm is an affirmative goal of US failure policy; otherwise, inefficiency is rewarded, sending a dangerous message to other players who may cease protecting themselves and begin relying on government protection.

Although thousands of words have been written on the desirability of liquidation, its effectiveness ultimately depends on the quality of markets. Liquidation of failed financial firms might punish the inefficient, send a warning to the inattentive and transfer assets to their highest valued uses if financial markets were truly as integrated, transparent and liquid as many modern observers believe them to be. In this respect, however, Chairman Greenspan's observations on the markets in which LTCM operated are instructive:

> The scale and scope of LTCM's operations, which encompassed many markets, maturities, and currencies and often relied on instruments that were thinly traded and had prices that were not continuously quoted, made it exceptionally difficult to predict the broader ramifications of attempting to close out its positions precipitately. That its mistakes should be unwound and losses incurred was never open to question. How they should be unwound and when those losses incurred so as to foster the continued smooth operation of financial markets was much more difficult to assess. The price gyrations that would have evolved from a fire sale would have reflected fear-driven judgments that could only impair effective market functioning and generate losses for innocent bystanders.[26]

Thus, according to Chairman Greenspan, modern financial markets may be global in scope but they are not seamless; financial players may be highly sophisticated but they are not immune to panic; complex financial instruments may be marketable but their fire sale value cannot be guaranteed. It is instructive to contrast this assessment of modern, highly advanced financial markets with the simpler markets of 1967. Then, observers saw the growth of secondary markets for bank assets such as loans as making liquidation more efficient, reversing the illiquidity and vulnerability to panic that had prevented financial markets in the 1930s from easily absorbing failed banks.[27]

Thus, it may be that the nature of modern financial markets has reduced the efficiency of liquidation in promoting fair play on a level playing field. If the process of liquidation disrupts financial markets, then efficient players will also suffer. If markets cannot absorb the assets of failed firms, then assets will not be rapidly transferred to higher valued uses and the pricing of other transactions will be distorted. And competition will diminish if players abandon markets until the problems subside.

Another contradiction arises from the desire of US financial players to preserve the competitive position of US financial markets. US players may believe that competition is most efficient, and fairest, when the government does not alter the results of play by preventing failure. Nevertheless, what if regulators of non-US financial markets reach a different conclusion? US observers have tended to assume, correctly or incorrectly, that non-US governments will intervene actively to prevent disruption of their own national markets in the event of the failure of an important financial player. If US policy is perceived to be less interventionist, and the US government is expected to allow its major financial firms to fail, then international investors may run to safety, favoring non-US institutions. Competitive considerations may require US regulators to accord their own firms and their international investors the same protections that are available from other national regimes.

This may have been a factor in the rescue of Continental in 1984, when the regulators took the very controversial step of reassuring investors in advance that they would be protected in any future disposition of the bank. This reassurance was addressed to Continental's wholesale investors in the hope of stemming further electronic money runs, but it also may have sent a message to the markets generally that investors need not fear for the safety of other large US banks. Thus, US financial players are of two minds about preventing financial failure. They profess to disapprove of bailouts as contrary to the ideal of free competition on a level playing field. But they want the government to protect them from failure when the resulting disruption could negatively affect the position of US financial markets in global competition.

So, at times, failure prevention may be in the interest of financial market participants. In the case of LTCM, Chairman Greenspan concluded that it was 'to the advantage of all parties – including the creditors and other market participants – to engender if at all possible an orderly resolution rather than let the firm go into disorderly fire-sale liquidation following a set of cascading cross defaults'.[28] Nevertheless, this raises another question. If it was in the interest of all private market participants to prevent the failure of LTCM (and, presumably, of other financial firms whose failure threatens markets), then why was the intervention of the Federal Reserve necessary to bring the affected parties together and to persuade them to act? In financial markets in which all government interference is viewed with suspicion, why does it fall to the government to protect markets from disruption?

The failure of collective action

The apparent failure of private players to act on their own to rescue LTCM without government prodding was not unusual. Traditionally, when US financial markets have experienced crises, US players have been more likely to run than to join together to make a public demonstration of their confidence in their markets. Contrary to conventional wisdom, panic 'runs' are not restricted to small depositors who, hearing a rumor, form queues outside their banks to withdraw their money. Sophisticated investors run too, often with as little justification. For example, Penn Central's default on $82 million of outstanding commercial paper in 1970 caused the commercial paper market to contract by $3 billion in three weeks.[29] Investors refused to roll over the maturing paper of issuers that had no connection with Penn Central. Rather than reassuring themselves as to the creditworthiness of their own issuers, investors preferred to penalize all borrowers. The Federal Reserve had to act to restore market order by urging banks to take government money in order to lend to creditworthy issuers to prevent further defaults.

Commercial paper investors' reaction was not necessarily irrational. Some may have known that, for example, Issuer X was solvent, but they feared that if most of their fellow investors demanded repayment, Issuer X would quickly experience a liquidity crisis and fail. Nevertheless, if all investors in Issuer X banded together and agreed to roll over their paper, Issuer X would survive. Collective action by investors would have saved the commercial market from panic, but it did not take place, forcing the Federal Reserve to do what private participants did not.

In the huge commercial paper market, effective collective action by investors may have been impossible. Yet, within the much smaller financial industry, collective action has also failed. Financial firms traditionally have been reluctant to save one of their own even when a collective rescue effort was feasible. It is often assumed that, before deposit insurance, the private financial sector did solve its own problems, resolving the failure of financial firms without government assistance. Nevertheless, anecdotal evidence casts doubt on the effectiveness of private failure resolution even when markets were ruled by financial oligopolies. Two stories suggest the limits of collective action in US financial markets. One involves Bank of United States, one of the earliest casualties of the 1930s banking crisis. Its failure in 1930 triggered one of the first deposit runs, as customers formed huge queues outside of the bank's branches hoping, in vain, to withdraw their money. (These queues soon were to become common sights in New York and other major US cities.)

Bank of United States had grown rapidly by making New York real estate investments that declined in value after the stock market crash and resulting depression in most financial asset markets. At one point, it appeared that the bank would be merged with Manufacturers Trust and several other banks, but negotiations broke off. Bank examiners believed that Bank of United States had some value as a going concern and they feared that a liquidation would precipitate a citywide panic by depositors that would threaten other banks. The Federal Reserve Bank of New York convened a meeting of regulators and top New York City bankers to discuss a rescue plan. The meeting included representatives of the New York Clearing House Association, a private organization of the largest New York banks that had been established to clear checks for its members but that had assumed a broader self-regulatory role, assisting to maintain orderly markets during previous banking panics.

This time, however, the bankers refused to help, complaining that the failing bank's assets were so poor that they could not assume the risk of trying to sell them. They also disputed that the failure would have systemic effects on other banks. Bank of United States was closed, and in these pre-deposit insurance days, even its retail depositors were relegated to liquidation. Manufacturers Trust did experience a deposit run, although most other banks did not. Following liquidation, depositors realized 83 cents on every dollar, a very respectable recovery rate in the darkest years of the Depression, suggesting that the bankers' assessment of asset value was unnecessarily pessimistic.[30]

Perhaps the New York bankers were correct that the threat of market disruption posed by this failure was not great enough to warrant collective action.[31] Nevertheless, in 1933, after system-wide deposit runs had forced the national government to shut down all banks, they took the same position. This time, the failed bank was Harriman National Bank, which was so critically undercapitalized that its regulators refused to allow it to reopen after the national bank holiday. Again, deposit insurance was not yet in place, but the RFC, which was taking the lead in resolving troubled banks, decided that paying off the claims of this bank's depositors would be desirable. First, the amount of money required ($5–6 million) was relatively modest. Second, Harriman was the only New York City bank that had not reopened for business after the bank holiday. Finally, Harriman had been a member of the New York Clearing House, which had recently run an advertisement in the newspaper bragging that no depositor in a Clearing House bank had ever lost a dollar.

Jesse Jones, chairman of the RFC, visited J.P. Morgan and suggested that his bank, or other New York banks, should join with the government to ensure that depositors in Harriman were protected. Mr Jones noted that country bankers were looking to New York City bankers, especially Morgan, for leadership, and that a joint public/private rescue of the one New York bank that was in trouble would strengthen investor confidence in banking markets, thereby speeding recovery of the banking industry. Although his own bank was certainly not in financial difficulty, Mr Morgan refused to help, rejecting the suggestion that healthy banks had any moral obligation to act collectively to assist their fellow banks or to demonstrate their confidence in banking markets.[32]

Histoiles of the era suggest that this incident was not unusual. Throughout the banking crisis of the early 1930s, the government, and often the President personally, tried to persuade more fortunate banks to act collectively to resolve financial problems at weaker banks, with little success. President Hoover, for example, called upon the industry voluntarily to create a credit reserve for banks experiencing liquidity problems, but eventually was forced to fund a new government agency, the RFC, to perform this function.[33] When the RFC learned that many insolvent banks were reluctant to take government money because they feared that accepting public assistance would further stigmatize them in the eyes of private investors, the agency called upon solvent banks to set an example by participating in its program. Although RFC officials suspected that at least some of these solvent banks could benefit from additional capital themselves, the agency's offer met considerable resistance.[34]

Financial market participants would not help out even when the government agreed to bear most of the risk. In early 1933, Union Guardian Trust, one of the largest Michigan banks, was near insolvency. Henry Ford was a major bank customer; a member of his family served on the bank's board of directors. Yet Mr Ford refused to agree to subordinate his deposit liabilities to a government loan designed to rescue the bank. At the same time, he threatened that, should Union Guardian fail, he would withdraw $20 million from his account at another Michigan bank. When regulators warned that this would bring down Michigan's banking system and possibly affect banks in surrounding states, he reportedly replied, 'Let the crash come'.[35]

Decades later, the FDIC was still facing resistance each time that it tried to persuade private financial firms to join it in resolving bank failure. Banks did participate in FDIC-led lines of credit to several failing institutions, including Unity Bank, a minority-owned Boston firm, First Pennsylvania and Continental Illinois. In each case, however, the government bore most of the financial burden. The private sector's contribution to the First Pennsylvania loan was just $175 million, while the FDIC put in $325 million. In the case of Continental Illinois, seven major banks funded one quarter of a $2 billion temporary loan, with the FDIC providing the balance of the funds. (In addition, a consortium of twenty-eight banks provided a $5.5 billion standby line of credit.) Just two months later, however, private sector funding was replaced by a permanent capital assistance plan funded by the FDIC.

That bank rescues in the US have been principally the government's responsibility may be somewhat at odds with practices elsewhere, at least in the past. A 1991 US General Accounting Office study of bank failure policy in Europe and Japan found that financial failures that could not be handled by deposit insurance tended to be resolved through private collective action by market participants. For example, in France, the financial community apparently acted collectively to rebuild the capital base of troubled Al Saudi Banque in 1988. In 1983, Schroder, Munchmeyer, Hengst & Co. was rescued by the private German banking community. And, before the 1990s banking crisis, the Japanese government relied upon its large banks to resolve problems at smaller banks.[36]

Legal and market constraints on collective action

Why are US financial players loathe to participate in private rescues of failing financial firms? Some observers would credit the democratization of US financial markets. Markets are so highly competitive, and densely populated, that collective action is virtually impossible. There is no longer a J.P. Morgan, or other dominant banker, who has the clout to compel all firms to participate in private rescues. Even the regulators' clout is limited. Although regulators may be able to bargain with regulated firms for their cooperation, promising rewards or threatening retaliation, competition among different regulators diminishes an individual agency's bargaining power. The regulators themselves must act collectively to demand cooperation from private players. If the regulators do not agree upon the necessity of a rescue, then they cannot expect to compel private participation.

Moreover, it is possible that US financial market players do not take the threat of market disruption as a result of financial failure as seriously as the regulators do. This seemed to be the case in the early 1930s, when banks did not accept the regulators' view that helping out their less fortunate rivals was in their collective self interest, and it may still be the case today. Individual players may believe that they can take precautions to protect themselves from any disruption caused by failure, for example, by monitoring the risk levels of their counterparties and limiting their exposures to particular markets. Thus, the majority of financial firms that did not have direct exposures to Continental or LTCM may have discounted the risk to their own businesses posed by failure and liquidation of these entities. The regulators, responsible for the health of all financial institutions, may have viewed the risk differently.

Alternatively, private market participants may take the risk of market disruption seriously but may conclude that it is an inevitable hyproduct of competitive financial markets. Market volatility may be the price of better information and improved trading techniques that allow players to react quickly to real or perceived risk. If occasional disruption is part of the normal process of market evolution, then attempts to interfere with this natural process are likely to be futile. This attitude may help explain the willingness of Henry Ford and others in 1930s markets to 'let the crash come', especially when they believed that they personally were strong enough to survive.[37]

This attitude found expression in once popular economic theory: in the 1930s some economists argued that the stock market crash, banking crisis and resulting mass liquidation of assets were part of the ordinary business cycle, allowing the release of factors of production from unprofitable uses. Attempts to mitigate the disruptive effects of liquidation would be counterproductive, simply postponing the inevitable readjustment process.[38] Although this theory has little currency among modern post-Keynesian economists, US financial market participants often sound as if they still believe it when they speak of the beneficial effects of failure. The theory provides a justification for avoiding collective failure prevention even when market disruption is threatened. If disruption is inevitable, then firms strong enough to survive the storm should not waste their precious resources to delay the failure of weaker firms that sooner or later will succumb to market forces.

Perhaps US financial firms have a more practical reason to refuse to join private bailouts. After all, they already pay for failure resolution through their contributions to guarantee funds. Once a bank pays its deposit insurance premiums, for example, why should it pay again to recapitalize a failing bank? When deposit insurance assessment rates were identical for all banks, healthy banks complained that they were being forced to subsidize weaker institutions. Now, however, deposit insurance premiums are risk-based, and banks are aware that Congress is more likely to increase assessments on all banks to cover any short-falls in the fund than to appropriate public monies. Nevertheless, banks' willingness to assist the FDIC by joining in private bailouts probably has not increased as a result of these changes. Although they may disapprove of government intervention in financial markets, private financial market players may still prefer that failure resolution remains the government's responsibility.

Finally, US financial regulation may discourage private collective action to resolve financial failure. Prohibitions on ownership ties between banks and commercial firms may deprive banks of a source of strength that is present in banking systems in which cross ownership is permitted. Moreover, the absence of any procedure in banking law for the reorganization of troubled banks by their stakeholders may discourage investors and customers from taking the lead in resolving financial problems at their bank. Bank regulation allows the regulators to decide when to close a troubled bank, at which point, the interests of equity investors are destroyed and uninsured creditors and customers must await the outcome of liquidation. As a result, investors and customers who suspect trouble are more likely to sever their relationship with the bank than to offer to assist. If they contribute money yet the regulators decide to close the bank anyway, they risk the loss of their investment.

Participants in a private rescue may face even greater risks. Investors who make a significant capital contribution probably will want some say in management, at the least replacing past managers with their own nominees. If the rescue is unsuccessful, the new investors may be subject to regulatory fines and other penalties if the regulators decide that their mismanagement contributed to the failure of the rescue attempt. In contrast, the government faces no such threat if it recapitalizes the troubled firm. Therefore, private parties may have a compelling reason to let the government take the lead.

Regulation has sought to compel at least the bank's corporate owners to support their ailing bank. Holding companies have been required to serve as a source of strength to their subsidiary banks, and, in the event of failure, the FDIC has the power to reach the assets of healthy affiliated banks. Yet the need to compel contribution from unwilling corporate owners simply highlights the inability of the regulators to count on voluntary collective action. If its own stakeholders are reluctant to rescue a bank from financial difficulty, then its competitors certainly will be unlikely to do so.

The globalization of failure policy

The conflicts that beset financial failure policy in the US are not likely to be resolved so long as financial market players remain convinced that failure prevention is inconsistent with fair play on the level playing field. Many players apparently believe that, unless failure is punished by immediate liquidation, the winners of the competition are harmed. Although players may be coming to believe that liquidation, if it disrupts financial market play, is equally harmful, this does not make the decision to prevent failure any easier. Since both choices are undesirable, private players leave it to the regulators to choose and then criticize the decision.

A resolution of this conflict may be forced by the continued globalization of financial markets. In the past, the reaction of global financial investors probably played a part in persuading US regulators to opt for failure prevention in order to keep US firms competitive with their non-US rivals in wholesale funding markets. Recently, however, the globalization of financial markets has put new pressures on US failure policy. Financial markets and financial transactions have become so intertwined that a financial crisis in one national market is likely to have ripple effects throughout international markets. For example, one sobering aspect of the LTCM story is how it began: LTCM's problems could be traced to a financial crisis in Russia that led to a surprise announcement by the Russian government of a debt moratorium that, in turn, produced a worldwide decline in investor confidence.[39] LTCM suffered the most, but most financial players felt some effect from this series of events. Likewise, how LTCM's difficulties were ultimately resolved was expected to have its own repercussions in both US and global financial markets.

Thus, in global financial markets, domestic financial crises cannot necessarily be contained, and how a government responds to crisis has its own global ramifications. This may force national regulators to consider developing a uniform collective response to financial crisis and failure. Internationalization of failure resolution may not please US financial market players, since it may produce results that are at odds with US notions of fairness on the level playing field. For example, different national governments may have different views as to when the risk of global financial disruption, in Chairman Greenspan's words, 'rises to a level of seriousness warranting central bank involvement'.[40] Certainly, many of the considerations that drive US financial failure policy, such as the desire to impose losses on uninsured investors, may not necessarily influence international failure policy.

Moreover, internationalization may result in a return to a form of the 'too big to fail' policy if multinational financial firms are treated differently from smaller firms. For example, it is possible that, in the future, the failure of a multinational megabank may pose such a risk to global financial markets that national regulators may be forced to agree on failure prevention. In contrast, smaller firms whose failure poses no risk to global markets may be handled exclusively by domestic deposit insurance schemes, resulting in most cases in their liquidation. In fact, if the US deposit insurance scheme were freed from the responsibility of resolving the failure of international mega-banks, then the FDIC could liquidate all other failed banks without endangering the deposit insurance fund. Small financial firms once again would have reason to complain of competitive unfairness.

How then may the demands of failure resolution in global financial markets be reconciled with the norms that animate US bank failure policy? It may be that US financial players will prove successful in exporting their approach to failure resolution to the international arena. The recent trend toward the creation of some form of deposit guarantee program in most banking systems suggests that, in the future, most ordinary bank failures will be handled by payoff and liquidation outside of the US. Moreover, US regulators' recent reliance on more aggressive supervision and enforcement, including insistence on prompt corrective action as soon as problems emerge at financial firms and the prompt closing of firms that do not solve their problems, is likely to appeal to other national regulators as a way to contain a local financial crisis before it can spread to other markets, requiring an international response. Finally, as global financial firms become larger and transnational, bailouts, even of megabanks, may become less common because they are simply too costly to arrange. If US policy toward financial failure, particularly its antipathy to bailouts, does become the global standard, then perhaps even US regulators may be willing in practice to let financial firms fail.

Alternatively, US financial players may be able to avoid internationalization of failure policy by resorting more frequently to private collective action to resolve financial failure before government involvement becomes necessary. At the least, greater voluntary industry participation in government-led efforts to negotiate a solution will give private players a greater say in the choice of resolution technique. Ideally, in return for greater voluntary participation, the US government may even be willing to remove some of the regulatory disincentives that still discourage private investment in troubled financial firms. Yet this may require a sea change in traditional public attitude toward failure that does not seem likely to occur. In fact, as the next chapter describes, the desire of US players to let the market pick the winners and losers appears to be becoming stronger as financial markets become increasingly integrated and competitive.

8
Let the Market Pick the Winners

In October 1997, Citibank and Chase Manhattan Bank, New York City's two largest banks, working with Visa and Mastercard, the world's two largest credit card companies, launched a joint trial to test the viability of 'smart cards' in US retail consumer markets. The two banks issued reloadable stored value cards to approximately 100 000 people living on Manhattan's Upper West Side. The cards functioned as electronic purses: customers could transfer up to $100 to the cards from their bank accounts using automated teller machines and could use the cards to make purchases from 600 participating local merchants. The banks hoped that customers eventually would be willing to pay $1.00–$1.50 monthly to use the cards and that merchants would be willing to pay fees to accept them, just as they already paid fees to accept traditional magnetic strip credit cards.

The experiment, the largest to date in the US, was watched with great interest by both US financial market participants and by representatives of the smart card industry. Although the cards issued by Citibank and Chase were relatively simple stored value cards, smart card technology, which permits a computer chip embedded in a small plastic card to contain significant amounts of information that can be accessed and verified easily at point of sale, offers the promise of multiple applications, not all necessarily financially related. For example, the same smart card that is used by a bank customer in lieu of cash to buy groceries might also function as a 'health passport',[1] containing the holder's complete medical history.

In the US in 1997, however, the smart card's potential was far from being realized. Even simple stored value cards were not yet in widespread use. The New York pilot program, its sponsors hoped, would help to change that. Key players in the US banking and credit card industries were on board, and the test market was large, diverse and financially sophisticated, composed of customers who seemed likely to embrace new technology.

By late 1998, however, the banks had terminated their program. During the trial period, less than $2 million had been spent by consumers using smart cards. Many who had tried their cards never reloaded them. Two-thirds of participating merchants had dropped out. Mondex USA, the MasterCard controlled US venture that had supplied the smart cards used by Chase in the test program, cut back its US operations in January 1999, citing the demise of the New York program as evidence that it may have been ahead of the market.[2]

It may seem somewhat ironic that US financial markets that traditionally have prided themselves on their commitment to innovation have lagged behind other national markets, particularly European markets, in embracing smart card technology. In early 1997, as Citibank and Chase prepared to test 100 000 cards in New York City, observers were predicting that by the end of the year more than 100 million smart cards would already be in use worldwide, with 95 percent in Europe.[3] (The number of active cards was expected to grow to 3.1 billion by 2000.[4]) In France, for example, where embedded chip technology had been pioneered in the early 1990s, smart cards were everywhere. Even in the UK, where retail consumers, like their US counterparts, were wedded to the competing magnetic strip technology traditionally used for credit cards, introduction of the smart card appeared to be proceeding more rapidly, and in a more organized fashion, than in the US. In July 1998, for example, following several years of study and a successful trial run that had resulted in acceptance of the smart card at more than 200 000 point of sale terminals and cash machines, the UK's Association for Payment Clearing Services announced its decision to begin a nationwide transition to the new technology by putting computer chips in all newly issued plastic cards.[5]

Despite the relatively disappointing results of the New York experiment, proponents of smart card technology were still confidently predicting that it would be just a matter of time before US markets caught up to European markets. After all, in the past, US consumers had been slow to accept other new financial technologies, such as automated teller machines. Nevertheless, although observers may have been correct that, sooner or later, smart cards would become as commonplace as automated teller machines in the US, the comparison simply underscores the anomaly that US financial markets are highly competitive and innovative yet also occasionally resistant to change.

Why then in the 1990s were US financial markets reluctant to embrace the smart card, and why were US financial firms reluctant to introduce it? The second question may be the more interesting of the two because its answer reveals much about US financial players' commitment to the ideal of competitive fairness on a level playing field. Although in many instances this commitment has fostered a competitive process that has promoted financial innovation, at least in this instance it may have had the unintended effect of delaying the successful introduction of a new technology.

The easy answer to the question why the US lagged behind other markets in promoting the smart card was that, at least in the 1990s, the smart card industry was far more enthusiastic about the technology than was the average bank, or the average bank customer. From the US retail consumer's point of view, there were several reasons to be cautious about the usefulness of smart card technology, particularly as applied to standard retail financial transactions. Nevertheless, it is unlikely that consumer resistance was unique to the US. Retail consumers everywhere tend to be skeptical, at least initially, about the benefits and costs of an unfamiliar new technology.

But what may have set US financial markets apart from some other national markets was that, through much of the 1990s, US financial institutions and their regulators apparently were willing to accept the customer's initial negative verdict on smart cards. Given lack of customer enthusiasm, financial firms may not have invested heavily in ensuring the success of the new technology. Moreover, the US government did not attempt to promote the technology either by subsidizing research and development or even by creating uniform national operating and regulatory standards that might have encouraged private investment. As a result, introduction of the smart card in US proceeded slowly, with little industry, and even less government, coordination. Magnetic strip technology, although branded as obsolete by many experts, remained dominant.

That consumer preference should drive product introduction in US financial markets is not in itself surprising. On the level playing field, the market, not the pundits and certainly not the government, should pick the winners and losers. Thus, no matter how many experts argued that smart cards with their embedded computer chips promised tremendous gains in efficiency over outmoded magnetic strip technology, so long as US retail customers did not agree, US financial firms listened to the market, not to the experts.

Nevertheless, consumer preference does not provide a complete explanation of the slow progress of smart card technology in the US in the 1990s. In competitive financial markets, firms may prosper by taking the lead in creating and promoting innovative new products. The resulting gains in efficiency, once demonstrated to the market, tend to overcome any initial consumer resistance to change. In the US, novel products have caught the fancy of retail as well as wholesale financial markets, suggesting that retail customers are as quick as their more sophisticated counterparts to appreciate the virtues of financial innovation. For example, in the 1970s, small bank depositors, usually considered the most risk averse of all financial product consumers, were willing to abandon the safety of their banks for the relatively higher returns offered by an innovative and unfamiliar securities product called the money market mutual fund.

Thus, if smart card technology was more efficient than magnetic strip technology, then one would have expected enterprising financial firms to be able to capitalize on that advantage to sell the product to US consumers. Certainly, proponents of smart cards were making the argument that the technology had limitless applications, and some major financial players were conducting ambitious pilot programs in some key markets. And most had allocated at least some resources to continued research and development.[6] Nevertheless, the same financial industry that had successfully introduced the money market mutual fund in the 1970s was forced to admit in the late 1990s that it had not yet been able to convince the public of the benefits of smart cards.[7] As one expert put it, the elusive 'killer application' that would propel smart cards into every home in America had not yet been discovered.[8]

So why was the introduction of smart cards in the US so much less successful than the introduction of other retail innovations such as the money market mutual fund? The answer may be found in the definition of success. By all accounts, money market mutual funds were successful, but success did not require the replacement of all traditional bank deposits with money market mutual funds. Bank deposits did not disappear; to the contrary, the challenge posed by the money market mutual fund caused banks, threatened with the loss of their customer base, to fight back, overcoming both regulatory and business hurdles to make the traditional bank deposit more attractive to savers. The result of this competitive process, for retail investors, was greater product choice.

In contrast, in order to succeed, smart card technology may have to do more than merely provide another choice to consumers. Unlike money market mutual funds, smart cards require a huge initial investment in infrastructure. Cards with embedded chips must be manufactured and distributed to customers. Point of sale terminals at stores and banks must be built or upgraded in order to accept the new cards. In the UK, for example, the switch to smart cards promised in 1998 was expected to require the replacement of 104 million existing cards and the upgrade of 530 000 existing terminals.[9]

Such an investment cannot be justified unless financial firms believe that the smart card eventually will capture a significant share of the retail payments market. In other words, banks must be able to persuade large numbers of customers to use smart cards regularly and large numbers of merchants to accept smart cards for payment. Moreover, joint customer and retailer commitment to the product is a predicate to smart card success. If few customers are willing to use smart cards, then most merchants will not be interested in accepting them. At the same time, if few merchants are interested in accepting smart cards, than most customers will see little advantage in using them. So success requires the cooperation and active participation of three groups, financial institutions, merchants and retail customers.

This commitment was missing from the New York pilot program, where customers and merchants each cited the other group's failure to participate as an explanation of their own lack of enthusiasm. In this case, the banks were even willing to offer rebates to customers and merchants to encourage them to cooperate.[10] Yet smart cards still failed to capture a sufficient share of the market to justify continuation of the pilot program. To potential investors in smart card technology that anticipated recouping their investments by charging fees to loyal smart card customers, the New York experiment was not very reassuring.

Of course, the problem of high start-up costs is likely to affect the introduction of any expensive new technology. In the US, however, the problem may have been exacerbated by the structure and regulation of financial markets. As previous chapters described, US regulation has discouraged financial oligopoly and encouraged consumer choice, particularly in retail markets where customers may not have sufficient bargaining power to protect themselves from unfair sales pressure. For example, antitying regulation prevents banks from limiting consumer choice by requiring borrowers to purchase related financial products, such as credit insurance, from the bank. Likewise, an agreement among competing financial firms to offer just one product, at one price, would surely be condemned as anticompetitive. As a result, financial product markets tend to be fractionalized. Financial firms compete by offering a variety of specialized products that appeal to customers' different preferences and needs.

Yet, in order to succeed, smart card technology requires standardization, not specialization. This suggests that successful introduction of the smart card must proceed in a different fashion from the competitive process that produced successful financial innovations such as the money market mutual fund. Rather than competing, US firms must act collectively to develop a uniform strategy for mass marketing the smart card and to share the cost of converting the existing financial infrastructure to one that is more smart card friendly.

This is not impossible in US markets. After all, the introduction of credit cards required the same standardization and cooperation among financial firms, retailers and consumers. It is not an accident that the credit card business is controlled by a few large firms that have ownership or other links to issuing banks. In fact, because of their organizational structure and dominant market position, these credit card companies were considered to be the logical pioneers of smart card technology in the US.

Nevertheless, introduction of smart cards faced the additional problem that embedded chip cards were intended to compete with and eventually replace the traditional magnetic strip credit cards that these very companies had promoted so successfully in the US. Financial market players had to be persuaded that the new technology offered something that the old technology did not. Given their relatively recent investment in credit card technology, many players were initially reluctant to make the change, particularly when they could not be sure that enough of their fellow players would switch to make the smart card option viable.

The solution to this collective action problem was, of course, more collective action. The selling of smart cards to US markets would require a carefully planned and coordinated effort by all financial players to solve technological problems and overcome consumer reluctance. Nevertheless, as noted in Chapter 7, voluntary collective action by US financial firms is difficult to achieve under any circumstances and may run afoul of regulation designed to ensure the competitiveness of financial product markets. Therefore, it was unlikely that the US financial industry as a whole could or would agree on a sweeping plan to replace magnetic strip technology with embedded chip technology on a nationwide basis. As a result, in the 1990s, introduction of smart cards was occurring through the old fashioned competitive process. Despite some coordination between the major credit card companies to attempt to rationalize technical standards, different players were entering the field at their own paces and in their own ways. And some continued to ignore the new technology altogether.

Further, the government was doing little to encourage the introduction and use of smart cards. Direct government subsidization would have been greeted with suspicion, if not outright resistance, by US financial market players as an unwarranted intrusion into competitive financial markets. The government also did not seem to be in a rush to regulate smart cards. Regulation may have actually encouraged technological innovation by resolving uncertainties about the legal status of smart cards and removing legal impediments to joint development and marketing. Nevertheless, policymakers were unwilling to use the regulatory process to favor one technology over another, preferring to let the market decide when and how smart card technology would be introduced, what form it would take and who would offer it.

Let the consumer decide

In the 1990s, observers should not have been surprised by the rather disappointing results of the New York smart card test. Earlier experiments with stored value cards had suggested the dearth of any real consumer excitement about the new technology. For example, in 1996, Visa had tested its stored value card at the Summer Olympics in Atlanta, hoping that acquainting consumers with the technology in this closed setting would make them eager to use smart cards at home. Nevertheless, once the games were over, Visa was not able to expand its program. Citing lack of a market, most participating banks withdrew.[11]

Why, at least in the past, have US retail consumers been reluctant to use smart cards? According to some, the problem was not the technology but the application. US bank customers were so accustomed to deferring payment, either charging purchases on their credit cards or paying by checks that took several days to clear, that they saw no advantage in using a stored value card. Stored value cards were not even an improvement over debit cards or cash, which at least permitted customers to keep control of their funds until they made a purchase. Smart cards had to be loaded in advance; once a customer loaded her card with funds from her bank deposit account, her money, although not yet exchanged for goods, no longer accumulated interest. At the same time, however, her money remained in the bank to be used for its own business purposes.

Thus, each time that a customer loaded her smart card, she saw herself as making an interest-free loan to her bank.[12]

Of course, the amount of lost interest was likely to be negligible, far less than the interest and late fees that many US consumers paid on their credit card balances each month. Nevertheless, even for these customers, smart cards were not an efficient alternative. These customers ran up balances on their credit cards because they did not have the funds on hand to pay for their purchases. If they had no money in their bank accounts, they could not load their smart cards either.

Of course, the early stored value cards used in trials like the New York pilot program were not designed for expensive items, such as airplane tickets, that many consumers bought on credit, but for small purchases made at a select group of participating stores. Yet this also discouraged smart card use, because customers were denied choice and mobility. During the New York experiment, which was limited to the Upper West Side of Manhattan, customers complained that, because only 600 merchants were participating, they could not use their cards all over the city.[13] Participating merchants had a similar complaint: only a small percentage of their customers were using the cards.

The New York experience suggested that customers would be more willing to use smart cards if the cards were welcomed virtually everywhere that they shopped, but this was not likely to occur until more customers had smart cards. This may explain why pilot programs in the US have proved most successful when they have been confined to closed markets, such as military bases or universities, where the number of merchants is limited and the number of repeat customers is large.[14] In more open markets, smart card pioneers had to find a way to make sure that everyone wanted and needed smart cards in order to persuade merchants that it was worth their while to accept them.

This is not impossible in US markets, as the successful introduction of nationwide credit cards has proved. Nevertheless, as mentioned, the 'killer application' that will make smart cards indispensable has not yet been found in the US. In Europe, fear of credit card fraud probably enhanced the appeal of smart cards to consumers and banks alike,[15] but this fear is not as widespread in the US. And, as the New York test demonstrated, the electronic purse capabilities of smart cards do not excite consumers who are comfortable using cash for small purchases.

In the 1990s, some experts were predicting that the US retail market might eventually be won over by the multifunctional capacity of the smart card, which promised efficiencies for consumers.[16] For example, a single card could encode the financial, medical and personal biography of the holder, allowing him to use his card to qualify for a loan, to buy groceries and to receive medical treatment anywhere in the world. Nevertheless, although US consumers are not particularly worried about credit card fraud, they are concerned about privacy. Multifunctional smart cards may not appeal to US customers if they suspect that their personal information may be easily accessed not just by their bank and hospital but also by employers and marketing firms and even the government.

Obviously, without comprehensive surveys, it is impossible to estimate the depth of early US consumer resistance to smart cards. Nevertheless, in the 1990s, the perception that consumers were indifferent or openly hostile to smart cards was probably widespread enough to discourage many US financial firms from making large, long-term commitments of resources to the technology. In competitive US financial markets, unless individual firms can expect to recoup their investment in new technology, they may be reluctant to get too far ahead of the market. As one industry executive put it, the problem in the 1990s was that no one could predict whether the smart card would turn out to be a Ford Edsel or a Ford Explorer (two automobiles with two very different records of success in US consumer markets).[17]

Moreover, even if smart cards eventually did gain popularity, US firms still had reason to wonder whether the promised efficiencies would ever materialize. Although replacing magnetic strip cards with embedded chip cards might allow banks to economize on the cost of retail payments in the long run, savings would only be realized if most customers were persuaded to switch to the new technology. If some switched, but a significant number remained wedded to their old cards, the financial industry would be forced to maintain two separate infrastructures to support two incompatible technologies.

The banking industry had experienced a similar problem when it had attempted to shift retail deposit transactions away from costly bank branches to less expensive automated teller machines. Originally, pundits had predicted the demise of the brick and mortar bank branch, anticipating that depositors would be willing to conduct all of their routine deposit and withdrawal transactions by machine. Nevertheless, although many bank customers welcomed electronic banking (and vowed never to re-enter a bank branch), many others insisted on dealing with a live human teller. Subtle and not so subtle attempts to alter these customers' preference (for example, by charging high fees for teller transactions) led to protests from the public and the threat of regulatory action. As a result, most banks were forced to maintain two product delivery systems for identical retail banking transactions. This experience may have suggested to many banks that they could not count on being able to replace magnetic strip technology with smart card technology. To keep customers happy, both systems would have to be maintained, adding complexity and cost to the retail payments business.

In the case of automated teller machines, banks at least had a good reason to believe that customer preferences could be changed. Automated teller machines were far faster than human tellers, allowing busy bank customers to avoid the dreaded lunchtime bank queues. Most customers were happy with magnetic strip credit cards that they could already use at virtually every grocery store, gas station and doctors' office. Convincing even a portion of these customers of the superiority of smart cards would be a difficult task. Making the case for smart cards was easier in national markets such as Japan's in which magnetic strip card usage was low.[18]

Introduction of smart cards in UK financial markets, where credit cards were popular, was likely to face the same problem of consumer acceptance that plagued US markets. As a result, despite its strategic decision in 1998 to rely more heavily on embedded chip technology, the UK financial Industry planned, at least initially, to support both technologies.[19] Nevertheless, US markets presented another challenge to smart card pioneers. In the US, it was difficult to imagine the financial industry acting collectively to make a uniform strategic decision about anything.

Failure of collective action

One solution to the problems involved in introducing a costly new technology like the smart card is risk sharing. If US financial firms agreed to work together to promote smart cards, they could share the cost of research and development. Moreover, joint introduction of the technology by multiple financial firms might help to overcome consumer concerns that hindered market acceptance, such as the fear that smart cards could not be used widely. In the UK, acting through a nationwide payments systems policy body, banks and multinational card associations agreed jointly to put chips in all newly issued cards, to adhere to uniform technical operating standards and to assist in the process of upgrading of all point of sale terminals to read the new cards.[20]

Why was there no similar industry-wide strategic planning in the US? Fragmentation of the US financial industry, coupled with lack of a tradition of collective action, may have discouraged cooperation. For example, successful introduction of smart card technology on a nationwide basis requires some agreement as to the technical standards that will govern the product. In the US, however, during much of the 1990s, the two major credit card companies, Visa and Mastercard, were promoting different and potentially incompatible operating systems for smart cards.[21]

Moreover, large-scale introduction of the smart card would have required cooperation between the financial industry and non-financial firms, particularly the merchants who ultimately had to agree to accept smart cards for payment. Yet, if cooperation within the financial industry was elusive, agreements across industry lines were even harder to achieve. Many merchants tended to be suspicious of large financial firms, particularly the credit card companies that already dominated the magnetic strip card market, accusing these firms of extracting monopoly rents from retailers that were required to accept their cards. To the extent that the same companies were likely to play a leadership role in introducing smart card technology, they could expect to face some skepticism, and perhaps hostility, from merchants.

Despite these impediments to collective action, there was at least some evidence in the 1990s that industry cooperation was possible. The New York smart card trial, although disappointing from a marketing point of view, did involve a cooperative effort between rivals Visa and MasterCard that used the experiment to test the convergence between their two separate operating systems. Further, the competitive threat posed by non-financial firms such as Microsoft to enter the electronic money market created powerful incentives for the US financial industry to develop a uniform smart card strategy before Microsoft found ways to allow consumers to bypass the traditional payments system entirely.

Nevertheless, as US financial players have been quick to point out, even when private financial firms believe that it is in their interest to act cooperatively to introduce and market a standardized new technology, regulation may discourage collective action. In the US, the notion of a banking 'consortium' has negative connotations, suggesting oligopolistic behavior by market participants that is considered both anticompetitive and potentially illegal. The US antitrust laws prohibit agreements among suppliers that suppress competition by eliminating consumer choice, which is exactly how some experts explain the successful introduction of smart cards in parts of Europe and Asia. Outside of the US, 'large institutions ... can adopt new programs easily by foreclosing consumer choices. This has made it relatively easy to form large consortia of banks, merchants, telecommunications companies and governments to launch smart card programs.'[22]

Regulators may protest that they would be unlikely to take legal action against financial firms for developing coordinated technical standards or marketing plans for smart cards. Nevertheless, to the extent that financial firms are unsure about legal limits, regulatory uncertainty may discourage substantial investment in new technology. Moreover, in the US, firms must be concerned about the appearance as well as the reality of anticompetitive market behavior. Any perception by consumers and merchants that large financial and industrial firms were attempting to dictate market choice by foisting smart cards on an unwilling public could cause joint marketing efforts to backfire, strengthening rather than weakening public distrust of the product.

Failure of government strategic planning

If US financial market players were concerned in the 1990s that their markets were lagging behind other national markets in adopting the smart card, they might have lobbied the government to play a role. The government might have encouraged smart card technology in a variety of ways. Direct government subsidization of research and development could have overcome the unwillingness or inability of private firms to invest in costly new technology. Alternatively, the government might have facilitated private introduction of the technology by establishing uniform operating standards to prevent the proliferation of potentially incompatible technologies, by creating a friendly regulatory framework to encourage entry into the smart card market and by educating the public as to the virtues of smart cards. At the very least, the government might have used its market power as a major consumer of financial services to favor smart card technology over its alternatives.

Although the US public generally prefers its government to stay out of private markets, from time to time, US business scholars have suggested that some degree of government strategic planning may be necessary and advisable to ensure that US markets and firms remain on the cutting edge of new technologies. For example, in the early 1990s, some scholars were warning that without coordinated long-term strategic planning by industry and government, the US (and Europe) could lose control of the emerging information technology industry.[23] Presumably, the same point might be made with respect to financial technologies such as the smart card. Given the huge start-up costs, as well as the need for uniformity of operating standards and for nation-wide consumer education in order for smart cards to gain acceptance, some strategic planning might be useful. If industry groups could not or would not take the lead, the government might play this role.

Moreover, the national interest might warrant government involvement in order to keep US financial markets competitive. Should the US eventually become the sole nation to continue to rely on outmoded magnetic strip technology, US financial firms would be disadvantaged in global competition and cross-border retail financial transactions would become difficult if not impossible. These possibilities might justify government efforts to help US markets to switch from magnetic strip to computer chip in order to stay current with the rest of the financial world.

Nevertheless, this kind of government interference with market choice, whether in the financial or the non-financial sector, tends to be viewed more favorably in academia than in Washington. The reluctance of the government to interfere with the results of the competitive process has discouraged government action that may have the effect of favoring one technology over another, particularly direct government subsidization of technologies intended for purely private application. Of course, indirect subsidization does occur. For example, government-funded military research and development has yielded successful commercial applications, and government funding supports university research that also may lead to the creation of commercial products. Nevertheless, by the late 1990s, military downsizing and government budget cutting were putting an end even to this indirect funding of technological research. Without an apparent military or government application, smart card technology was unlikely to receive direct public support.

Why is government subsidization of private financial innovation frowned upon? In most cases, it violates several principles of competitive fairness on the level playing field. First, some private financial player, whether bank or credit card company, would be receiving the subsidy and would thereby enjoy an instant and unfair starting advantage over its unsubsidized competitors. Second, since government subsidization would be likely to ensure the success of the subsidized technology (in fact, this would be the intended goal of the subsidy), the government, not the market, would be determining the results of competition, picking the winners and losers. Finally, since the success of the subsidized product, and producer, presumably would come at the expense of its rivals, who would either disappear or fail, government subsidization would allow the subsidized producer to monopolize the market, limiting consumer choice and permitting the extraction of monopoly rents from helpless retail customers.

Of course, the government might have facilitated the introduction of smart cards in more subtle ways that did not involve direct subsidization of a particular producer. For example, as previously suggested, the government, working with private market players, might have brokered uniform operating standards for future smart card development, thereby short circuiting lengthy and costly competition among different operating systems for acceptance. In the absence of some standardization, the nationwide introduction of smart cards had to wait for one operating system to emerge as superior to its competitors, or for manufacturers of different systems to develop ways to improve interoperability.

In addition, the government might have created a uniform and comprehensible regulatory framework to guide future development and introduction of smart card technology. In the US in the 1990s, many regulatory questions concerning smart cards remained unresolved, not the least of which was which regulatory agency ultimately would become responsible for regulating the new technology. For example, would electronic money be issued exclusively through banks that were already subject to extensive consumer protection and soundness regulation, as European banking authorities were suggesting in the 1990s,[24] or would anyone, including non-financial firms, be allowed to participate in the retail payments business? Would the rules of fair play developed to govern credit card transactions be extended to smart cards, or would new, more stringent regulation be put in place to address problems of consumer protection and insolvency risks in smart card transactions?

These unresolved regulatory issues added an element of uncertainty to the emerging smart card market, preventing firms from calculating the costs associated with long-term investment in the technology. Moreover, failure to resolve these questions caused banks to complain of an unlevel playing field, since their operations were already subject to federal oversight yet rival non-financial firms were not. Finally, to the extent that regulation cast doubts on the ability of industry participants to reach agreements to act collectively, regulatory clarification might have encouraged more joint industry action.

Nevertheless, through much of the 1990s, the government declined to act either to regulate or to deregulate smart card technology.

Policymakers voiced concern that any premature regulation might actually impede innovation. On the other hand, they seemed equally reluctant to use regulation to encourage smart card innovation. Regulatory inaction avoided the danger that the government, through regulatory subsidy or burden, would be favoring one technology over another, thereby distorting the competitive process and allowing the government to pick the winners and losers.

Finally, the government might have played some role in facilitating greater market acceptance of smart card technology. As a major consumer of financial products, the government might have used its substantial market power both to ensure the viability of smart cards and to make smart card use more acceptable among consumers. To some extent, this did occur: by encouraging smart card test programs on military bases, the government was promoting smart card technology, albeit in a limited fashion.

Nevertheless, these programs were limited to the kind of closed markets in which private financial firms had been able to introduce the technology even without government assistance. Where the financial industry needed help was in marketing smart cards to the vast national retail consumer market that was wedded to its credit cards. Here, however, government intervention to speed acceptance of smart cards, or of electronic commerce generally, has been limited. Moreover, occasionally, the government has acted at cross purposes, at once encouraging and discouraging the same financial technology.

For example, in the 1990s, proponents of electronic commerce welcomed the decision of Congress to require the national government to make all payments except tax refunds electronically.[25] Direct deposit of government benefits was expected to result in large costs savings to the US Treasury. It also was expected to have the beneficial side effect of making consumers more aware of and more comfortable with electronic banking. Once consumers were convinced of the virtues of a paperless banking system, the private sector, especially employers who had resisted direct deposit, might be more willing to switch to electronic payments without fear of employee complaints.

Nevertheless, the government's plan to switch from paper checks to direct deposit elicited the same negative reaction that had followed the banking industry's earlier attempt to force depositors to use machines instead of live tellers. Consumer advocates complained that many recipients of government assistance, especially the elderly, needy and veterans, did not even have bank accounts. Forcing these customers to establish banking relationships in order to receive their government benefits would subject them to bank fees, such as minimum balance charges, check cashing charges and charges for use of automated teller machines, that they could not afford. Thus, the government's change of policy would deny freedom of choice to the most vulnerable consumers who did not have sufficient bargaining power to negotiate for a better deal from their bank.

Further, the government's decision to encourage direct deposit was depicted as subsidizing the banking industry by expanding its customer base, thereby providing banks with a competitive advantage over other financial firms, such as check cashing firms, that had previously provided services to recipients of government assistance. Finally, by favoring one payment method (electronic deposit) over another (checks), the government was interfering with competitive outcomes. In sum, the government's mandate to use electronic money, although perhaps motivated by considerations of efficiency, violated several principles of competitive fairness.

Eventually, the government was forced, at least temporarily, to rethink its resolve to do away with old fashioned checks.[26] In doing so, the government defeated its own attempt to use its market power to encourage a particular technology. This suggests that the government, as well as private market participants, must bow to market preferences.

Regulatory competition may also frustrate the government's efforts to develop a coordinated strategic plan to further the acceptance of new financial technologies such as the smart card. Had US policymakers determined early on that electronic money would be issued solely through the regulated banking system, then the bank regulators would have had the authority to use regulation to encourage or discourage the development of particular electronic commerce technologies. Yet, in the late 1990s, it appeared likely that, at least initially, the US government would permit relatively free entry into the nascent electronic commerce market, imposing regulation only after products had been perfected and successfully introduced. This choice responded to market demands for competitive freedom and flexibility, but it also promoted regulatory competition. Once non-banks entered the electronic commerce market, their non-bank regulators would follow, giving them a place at the table when any future regulatory decisions had to be made.

As previous chapters described, different financial regulators traditionally have different and occasionally competing priorities and supervisory styles. They also tend to be very jealous of their regulatory authority. Added to the mix is the presence in the electronic commerce market of non-financial firms that are not supervised by any financial regulator. Competition for regulatory jurisdiction over previously unregulated firms and transactions may hinder efforts to achieve uniform comprehensive regulation of the electronic commerce market. Successful introduction of the smart card may require the cooperation not just of competing players but also of competing regulatory agencies.

Lessons from the level playing field

Most observers still anticipate that smart cards will gain widespread acceptance in the US. Nevertheless, the willingness of US financial market players to tolerate the rather slow and haphazard process by which this particular financial innovation has been introduced in US markets is a tribute to their faith in the ideal of the level playing field. Reaping the benefits of the rapid introduction of a standardized and efficient new technology is less important than honoring the norms of competitive fairness and consumer choice. Financial innovation by government decree is undesirable even when government intervention facilitates the adoption of uniform standards and promotes public acceptance of smart cards as alternatives to credit cards.

Instead, US financial market participants prefer to let smart cards succeed or fail the old fashioned way. Competing versions of the technology will be developed and marketed by different firms. If and when public acceptance grows, the most efficient product will emerge as market leader. Government regulation, if necessary, will be used to ensure that all players seeking to participate in the electronic commerce market enjoy equal starts on a level playing field and that vulnerable retail consumers are protected by rules of fair play. Multiple regulators may eventually become involved in regulating different aspects of smart card transactions. The resulting electronic commerce market may be almost as diverse and as fragmented as other financial product markets.

Of course, an alternative scenario is possible. Fearful of competition from non-US firms (or from non-financial firms) with the capacity and willingness to invest heavily in introducing smart cards to the US, US financial firms may be compelled to act collectively to control market developments. This raises the broader question of whether the changed nature of global financial competition, which is likely to pit US firms against new rivals, including non-financial firms, in increasingly integrated international financial markets, may eventually force

US financial players to abandon their commitment to maintaining a level playing field. Other firms, and other markets, may not be wedded to the particular norms of fairness that animate play in US financial markets. Faced with new challenges, US financial firms may demand changes in their own rules of play that make it easier to compete with their new challengers on their own terms. Although US firms will cite the need for regulatory change in order to level the playing field, the resulting playing field may be quite different from the fragmented, highly competitive markets with which US players are familiar.

So will US financial players be able to maintain their ideal of a level playing field? The evidence, at the beginning of the new century, is mixed. US experience with smart card technology raises doubts about US players' continued ability to favor competition and fragmentation over cooperation and consolidation at either an industry or a regulatory level. Successful introduction of the smart card seems to require more coordinated effort than has been possible in US financial markets, at least in the past. Competitive pressure from other markets that are ahead of the US in developing new technologies may overcome resistance to collective action on the part of both financial firms and the government.

More generally, the rapid consolidation of the US financial industry in the 1990s is making financial oligopoly more acceptable in US financial markets than at any time since before the 1920s. Industry consolidation is producing the de facto centralization of financial regulatory power as well as the end of traditional powers-based regulatory competition. Financial modernization legislation adopted in 1999 did preserve, for the time being, financial firms' discretion to opt among competing regulatory regimes by choosing among several different organizational structures for diversification. Nevertheless, the legislation designated the Federal Reserve as principal umbrella regulator of the largest diversified financial firms. Moreover, by requiring greater coordination among different agencies on regulatory issues such as future expansions of bank powers and classification of innovative financial products, the legislation continued the trend, begun in the rules of fair play, toward greater uniformity of regulation. Thus, the US appears to be moving away, at least slightly, from the classic decentralized model that traditionally characterized both financial market and regulatory structure. This may require some revision to the ideal of a playing field composed of many equally handicapped and fiercely competitive players supervised by many equally handicapped and fiercely competitive regulators.

Nevertheless, some principles of competitive fairness on the level playing field remain as important as ever to US financial players and are influencing the development of global regulatory standards, proving that the notion of a level playing field may be exportable. The US emphasis on procedural rules of fairness, such as retail consumer protection rules, that ensure equality of bargaining power seems to be resonating outside of US markets as financial regulators everywhere take a more aggressive approach to the problems of maintaining confidence in financial markets and preventing fraud and other unfair practices. Globalization may actually be enhancing the significance of rules of fair play. As market mobility continues to improve for retail as well as wholesale financial customers, the ability of a national market to offer guarantees of fair play to all participants may be essential to its success.

Further, the principle of regulatory handicapping, which ensures that competing financial firms enjoy equal starts on a level playing field, appears to be influencing the development of international supervisory standards for financial firms. International standards are emerging from a bargaining process among interested industry players and their regulators designed to ensure some degree of competitive equality among diverse financial firms. Likewise, the global movement toward deregulation of the conduct of financial market transactions appears to reflect general acceptance of the notion, firmly held by US financial market players, that, so long as competitors enjoy equal starts on a level playing field, competition should proceed without government interference.

Finally, the US preference for letting the market pick the winners and losers may influence how financial failure is handled globally. In the future, government bailouts of financial firms seem less likely to occur, particularly as more national firms become part of transnational financial conglomerates that are simply too big for individual governments to save. The US approach, that at least in theory attempts to minimize market disruption resulting from failure rather than preventing failure itself, may be emerging as the global standard.

Of course, the globalization of financial markets is too new to permit a final assessment of the future of the level playing field. Nevertheless, history suggests a reason why the notions of fairness that drive US financial regulation may endure. US financial players' commitment to a level playing field has survived many challenges in the past, from the delegitimization of markets in the 1930s to delegitimization of regulation in the 1990s. Regulation and market structure have changed, but the basic underlying principles of fairness have not. To the extent that US markets owe much of their strength and vitality to these norms of fairness, US financial players may have good reason to resist any alterations to their level playing field.

Notes and References

Introduction: Regulation and the Level Playing Field

1. In 1998, this legislation passed the US House of Representatives but died in the Senate. In 1999, it was resurrected and eventually enacted as the Gramm-Leach-Bliley Act.
2. Dean Anason, 'Citicorp Decides to Back House Reform Bill', *American Banker*, 16 April 1998, p. 4.
3. Travelers Group Inc. (1998), *Federal Reserve Bulletin*, vol. 84, p. 985.
4. This principle was endorsed by the US Supreme Court in *Chevron U.S.A. Inc. v. National Resources Defense Council*, 467 U.S. 837 (1984).
5. Glass-Steagall was the familiar name for a group of national laws enacted by Congress in 1933 to bar banks from the securities business and securities firms from the banking business. In 1999, Congress repealed two key provisions of Glass-Steagall (Sections 20 and 32) to permit affiliations and management interlocks between banks and securities firms.
6. Originally, Section 20 securities affiliates could earn up to 5 percent of their total revenues from 'ineligible' securities activities, such as corporate securities underwriting and dealing, without being considered by the Federal Reserve Board to be 'engaged principally' in impermissible securities activities. (The other 95 percent of their revenues came from 'eligible' securities activities, such as dealing in US Treasury securities, that were not expressly forbidden to banks by Glass-Steagall.) The Federal Reserve soon increased the revenue limitation to 10 percent and later to 25 percent, where it remained until Section 20 was repealed in 1999.
7. *Securities Industry Association* v. *Board of Governors of the Federal Reserve System*, 839 F.2d 47 (2d Cir.), *cert. denied*, 486 U.S. 1059 (1988).
8. David Harrison, 'Banks See a 16,000 Branch Rival as State Farm Gets Thrift Charter', *American Banker*, 13 November 1998, p. 1.
9. Thomas K. McCraw (1984), *Prophets of Regulation* (Cambridge: Harvard University Press), p. 305.
10. Brian P. Volkman (1998), 'The Global Convergence of Bank Regulation and Standards for Compliance', *The Banking Law Journal*, vol. 115, pp. 550–76.
11. George L. Priest (1993), 'The Origins of Utility Regulation and the "Theories of Regulation" Debate', *Journal of Law and Economics*, vol. 36, p. 290.
12. E.g., Alfred E. Kahn (1990), 'Deregulation: Looking Backward and Looking Forward', *Yale Journal on Regulation*, vol. 7, pp. 349–50.
13. These market developments are described from the banking industry's perspective by Helen A. Garten (1991), *Why Bank Regulation Failed: Designing a Bank Regulatory Strategy for the 1990s* (Westport, CT: Quorum Books), pp. 1–20, and from the securities industry's perspective by Joseph Auerbach and Samuel L. Hayes, III (1986), *Investment Banking and Diligence: What Price Deregulation?* (Boston: Harvard Business School Press), pp. 86–94.

14. This legislation was the Federal Deposit Insurance Corporation Improvement Act of 1991, especially Subtitle E.

1. How to Think About Financial Regulation

1. E.g., Ellis W. Hawley (1966), *The New Deal and the Problem of Monopoly* (Princeton: Princeton University Press), pp. 304–9 (tracing 1930s-era US banking legislation to the uniquely American fear of concentration of financial power).
2. E.g., Edwin J. Perkins (1971), 'The Divorce of Commercial and Investment Banking: A History', *Banking Law Journal*, vol. 88, p. 485 (tracing 1930s-era US banking legislation to English precedent).
3. E.g., Ferdinand Pecora (1939), *Wall Street Under Oath: The Story of Our Modern Money Changers* (New York: Simon and Schuster), pp. 283–92, especially p. 283 (arguing that legislators adopted Depression-era financial regulation after congressional hearings revealed 'a shocking corruption in our banking system').
4. E.g., George J. Benston (1996), 'The Origins of and Justification for the Glass-Steagall Act', in Anthony Saunders and Ingo Walker (eds), *Universal Banking: Financial System Design Reconsidered* (Chicago: Irwin), pp. 59–65 (arguing that legislators adopted Depression-era financial regulation to further their constituents' private political and commercial interests).
5. For example, economists have credited federal insurance of bank deposits, created by Congress in 1933, with 'achieving what had been a major objective of banking reform for at least a century, namely, the prevention of banking panics'. Milton Friedman and Anna Jacobson Schwartz (1963), *A Monetary History of the United States, 1867–1960* (Princeton: Princeton University Press), p. 440.
6. This phrase was used to characterize the attitude of today's economists toward now-discredited 'business cycle' theories that influenced US monetary policy in the early 1930s. J. Bradford DeLong (December 1990), '"Liquidation" Cycles: Old-Fashioned Real Business Cycle Theory and the Great Depression' (Washington: National Bureau of Economic Research), Working Paper No. 3546. Similarly, today's financial scholars fault drafters of Depression-era financial legislation for relying on now-discredited banking theories such as the 'real bills' doctrine, which posited that 'excessive' money creation might be avoided by limiting bank credit to short-term self-liquidating loans, e.g., Walter M. Cadette (1996), 'Universal Banking: A U.S. Perspective', in Anthony Saunders and Ingo Walter (eds), *Universal Banking: Financial System Design Reconsidered* (Chicago: Irwin), pp. 711–12.
7. For the origins of public choice theory, see Richard A. Posner (1974), 'Theories of Economic Regulation', *The Bell Journal of Economic and Management Science*, vol. 5, p. 335.
8. *Camp v. Pitts*, 411 U.S. 138 (1973).
9. The power to set interest rate ceilings on retail time deposits, provided to government regulators by 1933 legislation, was gradually eliminated in the 1980s, beginning with the Depository Institutions Deregulation and Monetary Control Act of 1980.

10. *Investment Company Institute v. Camp*, 401 U.S. 617 (1971).
11. E.g., Gregory A. Mark (1995), 'Some Observations on Writing the Legal History of the Corporation in the Age of Theory', in L.E. Mitchell (ed.), *Progressive Corporate Law* (Boulder: Westview Press), p. 80.
12. 401 U.S. at 631–4, especially 634.
13. Representative Luce noted that, since most banks had already abandoned the securities business voluntarily by 1933, the abuses described by Senator Bulkley were not likely to reoccur. 77 *Congressional Record* H.3917 (22 May 1933).
14. For an example of this approach, see Benston, *op. cit.*, note 4, pp. 31–65.
15. *Camp* involved a challenge to a regulation of the Comptroller of the Currency allowing national banks to operate investment funds; the Supreme Court read the purposes of the Glass-Steagall Act broadly to invalidate the Comptroller's action. 401 U.S. 636.
16. E.g., *Securities Industry Association v. Board of Governors of the Federal Reserve System*, 839 F.2d 47 (2nd Cir.), *cert. denied*, 486 U.S. 1059 (1988).
17. E.g., Benston, *op. cit.*, note 4, pp. 49–59.
18. For descriptions of the operations of J.P. Morgan and other 'private' banks in the pre-Glass-Steagall era, see Pecora, *op. cit.*, note 3, pp. 4–19; Ron Chernow (1990), *The House of Morgan: An American Banking Dynasty and the Rise of Modern Finance* (New York: Atlantic Monthly Press), pp. 205–377.
19. Perkins, *op. cit.*, note 2, pp. 496, 506 ; Benston, *op. cit.*, note 4, p. 62. Many scholars have relied upon Perkins' 1971 account of the origins of Glass-Steagall for the proposition that the legislation was adopted at the behest of established investment banking firms (such as Morgan and Kuhn Loeb) that had been losing the competitive battle with the bank securities affiliates. See Benston, *op. cit.*, note 4, p. 62, quoting Perkins, *op. cit.*, note 2, p. 516. Perkins' study however focused exclusively on the provision of Glass-Steagall that forced banks to divest their securities affiliates (Section 20) and not on the equally important provisions that forced private investment banks like Morgan and Kuhn Loeb to give up their power to take deposits. Moreover, Perkins actually concluded his study by suggesting that both industries – banking and securities – may have welcomed the relief from competitive pressure that the separation of commercial and investment banking promised. Perkins, *op. cit.*, note 2, pp. 524–5. In any event, Perkins' suggestion that established investment banks like Morgan and Kuhn Loeb tacitly approved of Glass-Steagall is contradicted by more recent studies, such as Chernow, *op. cit.*, note 18, pp. 374–84, that find evidence that Morgan strongly opposed the legislation and argued unsuccessfully against its passage.
20. According to a 1932 account, five major banks had terminated or limited their securities operations by the end of 1931, Steven L. Osterweis (October 1932), 'Security Affiliates and Security Operations of Commercial Banks', *Harvard Business Review*, p. 125 n.11. This was before the introduction in Congress of the first version of the Glass-Steagall Act (which occurred in 1932) and before the commencement of congressional hearings on the alleged abuses of bank securities operations (which began in 1933). Perkins, *op. cit.*, note 2, p. 515; Pecora, *op. cit.*, note 3.
21. Arthur N. Johnson (1968), *Winthrop W. Aldrich: Lawyer, Banker, Diplomat*

(Boston: Harvard Graduate School of Business Administration Division of Research), pp. 149–53.

22. Chernow, *op. cit.*, note 18, pp. 374–91; Pecora, *op. cit.*, note 3, p. 54; Johnson, *op. cit.*, note 21, pp.151–2 (quoting New York *World Telegram* banner); Arthur M. Schlesinger, Jr. (1958), *The Coming of the New Deal*, vol. 2 of *The Age of Roosevelt* (Boston: Houghton Mifflin Company), p. 443.

23. Chernow, *op. cit.*, note 18, p. 374.

24. E.g., Joseph P. Kalt and Mark A. Zupan (1990), 'The Apparent Ideological Behavior of Legislators: Testing for Principal-Agent Slack in Political Institutions', *Journal of Law and Economics*, vol. 33, pp. 103–31.

25. Louis D. Brandeis (1914), *Other People's Money and How the Bankers Use It* (New York: Frederick A. Stokes).

26. Hawley, *op. cit.*, note 1, p. viii.

27. E.g., Mark D. Flood (July/August 1992), 'The Great Deposit Insurance Debate', Federal Reserve Bank of St. Louis *Review*, vol. 74, pp. 53–6.

28. Flood, *op. cit.*, note 27, p. 55 (quoting Roosevelt).

29. Joseph Auerbach and Samuel L. Hayes, III (1986), *Investment Banking and Diligence: What Price Deregulation?* (Boston: Harvard Business School Press), pp. 17–21.

30. Hawley, *op. cit.*, note 1, p. 305; Pecora, *op. cit.*, note 3, at 283–85; Raymond Moley (1966), *The First New Deal* (New York: Harcourt, Brace & World), p. 317.

31. For examples, see Flood, *op. cit.*, note 27.

32. 76 *Congressional Record* S.2508 (25 January 1933) (Senator Long); 75 *Congressional Record* S.2987 (1 February 1932) (reprinting Lippmann column).

33. 77 *Congressional Record* H.3955–6 (22 May 1933) (summarizing US Chamber of Commerce arguments in opposition to legislation).

34. 76 *Congressional Record* S.1405 (9 January 1933).

35. Arthur M. Schlesinger, Jr. (1960), *The Politics of Upheaval*, vol. 3 of *The Age of Roosevelt* (Boston: Houghton Mifflin Company), p. 301.

36. David T. Llewellyn (1996), 'Universal Banking and the Public Interest: A British Perspective', in Anthony Saunders and Ingo Walter (eds), *Universal Banking: Financial System Design Reconsidered* (Chicago: Irwin), p. 177.

37. Rankings are from *Euromoney*, June 1984, p. 80; *American Banker*, 27 July 1992, p. 16A; *American Banker*, 2 July 1998, p. 11.

38. For a similar argument that government regulation encourages industry innovation, see Edward J. Kane (1980), 'Accelerating Inflation, Regulation and Banking Innovation', *Issues in Bank Regulation*, vol. 4, p. 7.

39. Chernow, *op. cit.*, note 18, pp. 302–8; Auerbach and Hayes, *op. cit.*, note 29, pp. 10–21.

40. Perkins, *op. cit.*, note 2, pp. 491–5.

41. Auerbach and Hayes, *op. cit.*, note 29, pp. 12–22.

42. Stephen Prouse (1996), 'Comments', in Anthony Saunders and Ingo Walter (eds), *Universal Banking: Financial System Designed Reconsidered* (Chicago: Irwin), p. 551.

43. Compare the Federal Deposit Insurance Corporation Improvement Act of 1991, section 301 (imposing interest rate caps on brokered deposits) with the Depository Institutions Deregulation and Monetary Control Act of 1980 (removing interest rate ceilings).

44. Senate Report 101–19 (13 April 1989), p. 40 (quoting Federal Reserve Chairman Alan Greenspan).

2. Is Regulation Beneficial?

1. E.g., Jeffrey Kutler, 'U.S. Firms Seen Best-Placed On World Financial Speedway', *American Banker*, 4 June 1998, p. 1; James R. Kraus, 'U.S. Banks Look Like Leaders in the Euro Race', *American Banker*, 16 July 1998, p. 1.
2. *The Economist*, 'Survey: International Banking', 30 April 1994, p. 40.
3. Suggested revisions included a proposal to allow nationally chartered banks to underwrite securities subject to the approval of the Comptroller of the Currency (which passed the Senate but was eliminated in conference with the House of Representatives), and a proposal to repeal the requirement that private banks that continued to accept deposits would henceforth be subject to federal bank regulation (which passed the House of Representatives but was eliminated from the final legislation). See 79 *Congressional Record* S.11 827 (25 July 1935); 79 *Congressional Record* H.13 703 (19 August 1935).
4. Securities and Exchange Commission (1963), *Report of Special Study of Securities Markets*, Part I, Chap. 3, p. 395.
5. Joseph Auerbach and Samuel L. Hayes, III (1986), *Investment Banking and Diligence: What Price Deregulation?* (Boston: Harvard Business School Press), p. 94.
6. Some of these market and regulatory changes were discussed in the Introduction and also in Auerbach and Hayes, *op. cit.*, note 5, pp. 85–105.
7. This changed in 1998 with the combination of Citicorp and Travelers and the merger of BankAmerica and NationsBank. James R. Kraus, '2 Merging U.S. Banks to Crack Top 10 in Assets', *American Banker*, 2 July 1998, p. 11.
8. Citicorp's change of heart is noted in Dean Anason, 'Little Change in House as Reform Bill Faces Second Date for Vote', *American Banker*, 11 May 1998, p. 4. Despite the strength of a powerful pro-reform coalition, however, Glass-Steagall reform failed in 1998.
9. For example, see James R. Kraus, 'Europe's Universal Banks: Flawed Models', *American Banker*, 8 June 1998, p. 10A.
10. Gordon Matthews, 'Global Titans' Market Cap Sinks; U.S. Share Steady', *American Banker*, 12 November 1998, p. 1.
11. Statistics are reprinted in Kutler, *op. cit.*, note 1, p. 1.
12. Kraus, *op. cit.*, note 9, p. 10A.
13. Adolf A. Berle, Jr. (1926), 'Non-Voting Stock and "Bankers' Control"', *Harvard Law Review*, vol. 39, p. 676.
14. Adolf A. Berle, Jr. and Gardiner C. Means (1932; rev. ed. 1948), *The Modern Corporation and Private Property* (New York: Macmillan). As this author has pointed out, Berle and Means' data, which documented the dispersal of equity ownership in the largest US corporations, was collected in 1930 and reflected market changes that had occurred in the 1920s, including (1) the growth of public securities markets as the favored avenue for corporate financing; (2) a significant increase in individual ownership of corporate stock, both directly and through collective investment vehicles such as mutual funds; (3) the development of active secondary trading markets,

which facilitated the dispersal of equity ownership; and (4) enhanced competition and innovation in the market for financial services. All of this occurred, and was documented by Berle and Means, *before* regulation such as Glass-Steagall took aim at the traditional structure of the financial industry. See Helen A. Garten (1992), 'Institutional Investors and the New Financial Order', *Rutgers Law Review*, vol. 44, pp. 585–603.

15. As described in Chapter 1, as a result of Glass-Steagall, private banks like Morgan were forced to opt between deposit banking and investment banking. Morgan chose deposit banking, spinning off its securities business to the new firm of Morgan Stanley. For more on this decision and its competitive implications, see Ron Chernow (1990), *The House of Morgan: An American Banking Dynasty and the Rise of Modern Finance* (New York: Atlantic Monthly Press), pp. 378–91.

16. Arnoud W.A. Boot and Anjan V. Thakor (1996), 'Banking Structure and Financial Innovation', in Anthony Saunders and Ingo Walter (eds), *Universal Banking: Financial System Design Reconsidered* (Chicago: Irwin), pp. 420–9.

17. E.g., George W. Mitchell (1967), 'Exogenous Forces in the Development of Our Banking System', *Law and Contemporary Problems*, vol. 1997, p. 3 (accusing the banking industry of 'a pattern of traditional services, an imposed molecular structure, and a pedestrian operating technology').

18. Helen A. Garten (1991), *Why Bank Regulation Failed: Designing a Bank Regulatory Strategy for the 1990s* (Westport, CT: Quorum Books), pp. 81–8.

19. Carter H. Golembe, 'Commentary: A Little Moral Hazard', *Bank Expansion Reporter*, vol. 8, 20 November 1989, p. 5; Helen A. Garten (1994), 'A Political Analysis of Bank Failure Resolution', *Boston University Law Review*, vol. 74, pp. 447–9.

20. For an historical treatment of US regulators' reliance on market discipline, see Helen A. Garten (1991), 'Whatever Happened to Market Discipline of Banks?' *Annual Survey of American Law*, vol. 1991, pp. 749–800.

21. For a colorful description of the thrift industry and regulation in the 1980s, see Martin Mayer (1990), *The Greatest Ever Bank Robbery: The Collapse of the Savings and Loan Industry* (New York: Charles Scribner's Sons), especially pp. 63–4.

22. These points have been made by, among many others, Kraus, *op. cit.*, note 9, at 10A; Peter Martin, 'Ghosts of Business Future', *Financial Times (London)*, 11 December 1997, p. 20.

23. For example, when the Citicorp/Travelers merger was announced, not all experts were predicting that megabanks were the wave of the future of banking in the US. See, e.g., Edward Kulkosky, 'Citi-Travelers Deal Magnifies Risks', *American Banker*, 8 June 1998, p. 4A.

24. In 1999, an example of the former was J.P. Morgan; an example of the latter was NationsBank.

25. In the 1990s, the US financial press made these points, see sources cited in note 1. So did some non-US observers. E.g., 'Being All You Want to Be', *The Economist*, 30 April 1994, pp. 30–43.

26. Statistics come from US General Accounting Office (1996), *Foreign Banks: Assessing Their Role in the US Banking System* (GAO/GGD-96–26).

27. US General Accounting Office, *op. cit.*, note 26.

28. US General Accounting Office, *op. cit.*, note 26.
29. Louis Whiteman, 'Some Banks Find Good Cause to Form Holding Companies', *American Banker*, 9 February, p. 6.
30. Rob Garver, 'Foreign Banks Say US Reforms Leave Them at a Disadvantage', *American Banker*, 16 March 2000, p. 1.

3. Deposit Insurance and the Politics of Regulatory Subsidy

1. In another context, I have characterized traditional US bank regulatory strategy as reflecting the viewpoint of the typical private debtholder, who uses contract to restrict the borrower's discretion to alter its risk posture in the future. In US bank regulation, these regulatory 'covenants' have included laws restricting bank investments, diversification and payment of excessive dividends to shareholders. Helen A. Garten (1990), *Why Bank Regulation Failed: Designing a Bank Regulatory Strategy for the 1990s* (Westport, CT: Quorum Books), pp. 23–59.
2. This special responsibility occasionally has been mandated by law, such as the Community Reinvestment Act of 1977, a national statute that compels banks (but not non-banks) to meet the credit needs of the local communities in which they are chartered.
3. Carter H. Golembe (1960), 'The Deposit Insurance Legislation of 1933: An Examination of Its Antecedents and Its Purposes', *Political Science Quarterly*, vol. 76, p. 188; Jesse H. Jones (with Edward Angly) (1951), *Fifty Billion Dollars: My Thirteen Years with the RFC (1932–1945)*, (New York: Macmillan), pp. 45–6; Arthur M. Schlesinger, Jr. (1958), *The Coming of the New Deal*, vol. 2 of *The Age of Roosevelt* (Boston: Houghton Mifflin Company), p. 443.
4. Milton Friedman and Anna Jacobson Schwartz (1963), *A Monetary History of the United States, 1867–1960* (Princeton: Princeton University Press), pp. 421–42, especially p. 427.
5. Federal Deposit Insurance Corporation (1934) *Annual Report*, p. 47.
6. Friedman and Schwartz, *op. cit*, note 4, p. 434; also Golembe, *op. cit.*, note 3, p. 194 ('the primary function of deposit insurance is, and has always been, protection of the circulating medium from the consequences of bank failures').
7. The alternative solution, once popular among banking scholars but unacceptable politically, was to restrict banks to making only short-term, self-liquidating loans, a theory of banking known as the 'real bills' doctrine. This solution, however, would have been virtually impossible to legislate and would not have addressed the urgent demand for long-term capital that, after the stock market crash, was not forthcoming from moribund securities markets.
8. (1939) 'Behavior of Deposits Prior to Suspension in a Selected Group of Banks–Analysis By Size of Account', *Federal Reserve Bulletin*, vol. 25, p. 178.
9. Jones, *op. cit.*, note 3, pp. 61–6; Arthur M. Schlesinger, Jr. (1957), *The Crisis of the Old Order 1919–33*, vol. 1 of *The Age of Roosevelt* (Boston: Houghton Mifflin Company), pp. 475–6.
10. Golembe, *op. cit.*, note 3, p. 193; Federal Deposit Insurance Corporation (1934) *Annual Report*, p. 61.

11. Jones, *op. cit.*, note 3, pp. 28–9; Helen A. Garten (1994), 'A Political Analysis of Bank Failure Resolution', *Boston University Law Review*, vol. 74, pp. 460–1.
12. Jones, *op. cit.*, note 3, pp. 25, 30–2.
13. Garten, *op. cit.*, note 11, pp. 461–4.
14. Golembe, *op. cit.*, note 3, pp. 195–9.
15. This legislation was the Riegle-Neal Interstate Banking and Branching Efficiency Act of 1994.
16. For discussion, see Garten, *op. cit.*, note 11, pp. 453–4.
17. Compare *Weir v. United States*, 92 F.2d 634 (7th Cir. 1937) (upholding FDIC's authority to enforce substantive banking laws against state-chartered insured banks).
18. The political organization and status of each of these three bank regulatory agencies is somewhat complicated. The Federal Deposit Insurance Corporation (FDIC), like the Federal Reserve Board, is an independent agency whose staff is theoretically insulated from political influence. (The Federal Reserve may be more independent than the FDIC because it is self-funding and therefore does not have to rely on appropriations by Congress to meet its budget.) The Comptroller of the Currency is an official of the Department of the Treasury, which is part of the executive branch of government; in addition, the Comptroller automatically serves as one of the FDIC's five directors. Complicating matters further, within the Federal Reserve, much supervisory responsibility over banks is exercised by the 12 Federal Reserve banks, which themselves are independent entities. Each of these agencies is responsible for applying many of the same federal banking laws to its own stable of banks as well as for formulating its own regulation. The result is occasional regulatory conflict but, as Chapter 4 explains, on balance this conflict is welcomed as promoting efficient regulatory competition and innovation.
19. Stephen K. Halpert (1988), 'The Separation of Banking and Commerce Reconsidered', *Journal of Corporation Law*, vol. 13, pp. 497–8; Helen A. Garten (1990), 'Subtle Hazards, Financial Risks, and Diversified Banks: An Essay on the Perils of Regulatory Reform', *Maryland Law Review*, vol. 49, p. 344.
20. An example of the former approach was Glass-Steagall, which barred deposit-taking banks from entering most securities businesses (and securities firms from accepting deposits). An example of the latter approach was the Bank Holding Company Act, which allowed banks to enter certain financial businesses through separately incorporated and separately capitalized non-bank affiliates that could not accept insured deposits.
21. This policy is discussed in greater detail in Chapter 7.
22. The best known example, described in Chapter 7, was the 1984 rescue of Continental Illinois, which protected the investments of all creditors of both the bank and the bank's holding company.
23. When Penn Central filed for bankruptcy, it had $82 million of commercial paper (short-term unsecured debt) outstanding. Wary investors withdrew from the market, and other issuers were unable to roll over their maturing paper. In three weeks, outstanding commercial paper contracted by $3 billion. For details, see William C. Melton (1985), *Inside the Fed: Making Monetary Policy* (Homewood, Illinois: Dow Jones-Irwin), pp. 157–8.
24. Statistics are from US General Accounting Office (1991), *Deposit Insurance: A Strategy for Reform* (GAO/GGD-91-26), pp. 156–8.

25. Robert Oshinsky (1999), *Effects of Bank Consolidation on the Bank Insurance Fund* (Federal Deposit Insurance Corporation), p. 5.
26. US General Accounting Office, *op. cit.*, note 24, pp. 152–3.
27. This change in regulatory direction is described in Helen A. Garten (1993), 'United States Bank Failure Policy', *The International Journal of Regulatory Law & Practice*, vol. 1, pp. 239–44, and is explored in greater detail in Chapter 7.
28. Gregory Elliehausen (1998), 'The Cost of Banking Regulation: A Review of the Evidence', *Federal Reserve Staff Study* No. 171, pp. 30–1.
29. Elliehausen, *op. cit.*, note 28, p. 29.
30. As I have suggested elsewhere, after the Continental Illinois rescue, in wholesale deposit markets, investors probably used size as a proxy for risk. Helen A. Garten (1986), 'Banking on the Market: Relying on Depositors to Control Bank Risks', *Yale Journal on Regulation,* vol. 4, pp. 145–8.
31. The procedure that regulators must now follow to complete a bailout, however, is complex, possibly discouraging its use. For details, see Garten, *op. cit.*, note 27, p. 242, as well as Chapter 7.
32. E. Gerald Corrigan (1982), 'Are Banks Special?' *Federal Reserve Bank of Minneapolis Annual Report.*
33. Melton, *op. cit*, note 23, pp. 157–8.
34. Remarks Prepared for Delivery by Federal Reserve Board Chairman Alan Greenspan Before the House Committee on Banking and Financial Services Re: 'Private-Sector Refinancing of the Large Hedge Fund, Long-Term Capital Management', *Federal News Service,* 1 October 1998 (available in LEXIS, News Library, FEDNEW file).
35. *National Credit Union Administration* v. *First National Bank & Trust Company,* 118 S. Ct. 927 (1998).
36. Dean Anason, 'Senate Passes Credit Union Bill; Big Loss For Banks', *American Banker,* 29 July 1998, pp. 1–2. In 1999, small banks again tried to obtain relief from the Community Reinvestment Act. Again, Congress refused to exempt them, but did ease their examination burden somewhat.

4. Results Matter

1 Business and financial data come from the Federal Reserve's decision approving Travelers' application to become a bank holding company by acquiring Citicorp. Travelers Group Inc. (1998), *Federal Reserve Bulletin*, vol. 84, p. 985.
2. According to the Federal Reserve, these non-conforming activities accounted for 'less than 40 percent' of Travelers' total revenues, although how much less is unclear.
3. The combined entity proposed to do business under the name of Citigroup.
4. The statute required the Federal Reserve to consider the financial and managerial resources and future prospects of the companies and banks involved in the transaction, the convenience and needs of the communities to be served (for example, the applicants' record of compliance with the lending obligations of the Community Reinvestment Act) and antitrust and other competitive factors – and, of course, the legality of the transaction under existing banking laws.

5. Up to and even after the announcement on 6 April 1998 of its proposed merger with Travelers, Citicorp had lobbied against the Leach bill. Finally, on 14 April, Citicorp's chairman John Reed announced a change of heart, promising to support the legislation. Travelers' chairman Sanford Weill already favored the bill. Dean Anason, 'Citicorp Decides to Back House Reform Bill', *American Banker*, 16 April 1998, p. 4.

6. The McCarran-Ferguson Act, adopted in 1945, was an anti-preemption statute; in other words, Congress gave state statutes regulating the business of insurance priority over any potentially conflicting federal statute unless that federal statute specifically related to the business of insurance.

7. As will be discussed, state authority to block affiliations between insurance firms and nationally chartered banks was challenged in the 1990s by several decisions of the Comptroller of the Currency, chief regulator of national banks, and of the Supreme Court. In 1995, congressional supporters of states' rights responded by attaching a provision that would have barred future entry by national banks into the insurance business over the objections of the states to pending national legislation to repeal Glass-Steagall. Since any limitations on national bank powers were unacceptable to the banking industry and to the US Treasury Department (and their supporters in Congress), the addition of this provision effectively killed Glass-Steagall reform, at least in 1995. For background on this political stalemate, see Helen A. Garten (1996), 'Devolution and Deregulation: The Paradox of Financial Reform', *Yale Law and Policy Review*, vol. 14, pp. 60–75. After 1995, however, it became apparent that there was insufficient support in Congress for passage of new restrictions on national bank insurance powers. Many states, recognizing that they could no longer bar national banks from conducting an insurance business within their jurisdictions, began to capitulate, dismantling their anti-affiliation laws so that their own state-chartered banks would have equal opportunities to diversify. For a description of state law as of 1998, see Michael D. White (1998), *A Comprehensive Guide to Bank Insurance* (Cincinnati, Ohio: The National Underwriter Company), pp. 80–95.

8. This amendment was added to the Bank Holding Company Act by the Garn-St Germain Depository Institutions Act of 1982.

9. *Board of Governors of the Federal Reserve System* v. *Dimension Financial Corporation*, 474 U.S. 361 (1986).

10. This revision was contained in the appropriately named Competitive Equality Banking Act of 1987, which provides a good illustration of the handicapping process. In this case, regulation expanding the definition of bank was designed to restore a level playing field by ensuring that non-banks could not obtain the benefits of the deposit insurance subsidy without bearing the same regulatory burden as real banks (including the barriers to diversification contained in the Bank Holding Company Act).

11. Interestingly, banks traditionally were the exception: state-chartered banks were required to locate their deposit-taking offices within their state of incorporation and, at least until recently, were not permitted to establish branches across state lines. But, as will be described, banks had a national chartering option that could be exercised at any time without having to relocate their deposit-taking branches.

12. Examples of the corporate literature on charter competition that raise these and other issues include William L. Cary (1974), 'Federalism and Corporate Law: Reflections upon Delaware', *Yale Law Journal*, vol. 83, p. 663 (citing dominance of Delaware in corporate charter competition as evidence of a race to the bottom); Ralph K. Winter, Jr. (1977), 'State Law, Shareholder Protection, and the Theory of the Corporation', *Journal of Legal Studies*, vol. 6, p. 251 (citing equilibrium in corporate charter competition as evidence of a race to the top); Lucian A. Bebchuk (1992), 'Federalism and the Corporation: The Desirable Limits on State Competition in Corporate Law', *Harvard Law Review*, vol. 105, p. 1435 (citing agency problems that affect the decision to incorporate).

13. For application of charter competition theory to banking, see Kenneth E. Scott (1977), 'The Dual Banking System: A Model of Competition in Regulation', *Stanford Law Review*, vol. 30, p. 1.

14. For more of this argument, see Garten, *op. cit.*, note 7, pp. 65–97.

15. Federal Reserve membership historically provided some benefits to banks, such as access to the Federal Reserve's payment system and discount window borrowing. Although these privileges are less exclusive than they once were, membership still conveys some prestige, and most large state-chartered banks remain members.

16. This argument, as well as other objections to interagency competition, have been made by, among others, John C. Coffee, Jr. (1995), 'Competition Versus Consolidation: The Significance of Organizational Structure in Financial and Securities Regulation', *The Business Lawyer*, vol. 50, pp. 447–84.

17. Merchants National Corporation (1987), *Federal Reserve Bulletin*, vol. 73, p. 878.

18. Before passage of the International Banking Act of 1978, non-US banks were not subject to the branching restrictions applicable to US banks. Subsequent to that Act, however, non-US banks, like their US counterparts, had to choose a home state and were not permitted to establish branches outside of that state. As a result, for non-US banks as well as for US banks, the holding company structure became the favored option for expansion across state lines.

19. Coffee, *op. cit.*, note 16, p. 447.

20. Some notable examples from the 1990s are cited in note 24. One exception, described in Chapter 3, was the Supreme Court's decision invalidating the National Credit Union Administration's expansive reading of the common bond requirement that had allowed credit unions to broaden their membership. *National Credit Union Administration* v. *First National Bank & Trust Company*, 118 Sup. Ct. 927 (1998).

21. *Barnett Bank of Marion County, N.A.* v. *Nelson*, 517 U.S. 25 (1996).

22. Citicorp, Order Denying the Acquisition of a Bank (1985), *Federal Reserve Bulletin*, vol. 71, p. 789.

23. This provision appeared in the Federal Deposit Insurance Corporation Improvement Act of 1991, which was enacted in response to the thrift crisis and resulting public concern over the solvency of the banking industry and bank insurance fund; as might be expected, it reflected strong, although perhaps short-lived, political preference for reregulation of the banking industry.

24. *NationsBank of North Carolina* v. *Variable Annuity Life Insurance Company*, 513 U.S. 251 (1995) (upholding Comptroller's annuity ruling); *Independent Insurance Agents of America* v. *Ludwig*, 997 F.2d 958 (D.C. Cir. 1993) (upholding Comptroller's insurance agency interpretation).
25. *Barnett Bank of Marion Country, N.A.* v. *Nelson*, 517 U.S. 25 (1996).
26. White, *op. cit.*, note 7, pp. 80–95.
27. White, *op. cit.*, note 7, pp. 37–8.
28. White, *op. cit.*, note 7, pp. 38–9.
29. For the text of the Federal Reserve's interpretations, commonly referred to as the Section 20 decisions, see Citicorp, J.P. Morgan & Co. Incorporated and Bankers Trust New York Corporation (1987), *Federal Reserve Bulletin*, vol. 73, pp. 473–509 and J.P. Morgan & Co. Incorporated, The Chase Manhattan Corporation, Bankers Trust New York Corporation, Citicorp and Security Pacific Corporation (1989), *Federal Reserve Bulletin*, vol. 75, pp. 192–217.
30. Citicorp, J.P. Morgan & Co. Incorporated and Bankers Trust New York Corporation, *op. cit.*, note 29, pp. 505–6.
31. *Securities Industry Association* v. *Board of Governors of the Federal Reserve System*, 839 F.2d 47 (2d Cir.), *cert. denied*, 486 U.S. 1059 (1988).
32. 'OCC Approves Zions Application to Underwrite Municipal Revenue Bonds', Office of the Comptroller of the Currency News Release 97–110, 11 December 1987.
33. The full decision is printed in *Federal Reserve Bulletin*, vol. 84, p. 985 et seq.
34. Congress also required that real estate and, temporarily, merchant banking be conducted only by financial holding company affiliates. Non-US banks need not form US financial holding companies to own financial affiliates in the US, but they are subject to the same regulation (by the Federal Reserve) that governs US financial holding companies.

5. Regulatory Conflict and Competitive Equality

1. Testimony of Eugene A. Ludwig, Comptroller of the Currency, Before the Subcommittee on Telecommunications and Finance of the House Committee on Energy and Commerce, Office of the Comptroller of the Currency News Release 94–40, 14 April 1994.
2. David W. Roderer, quoted in Jaret Seiberg, 'Regulatory Conflicts Seen Better for Banking Than a Superagency', *American Banker*, 30 November 1998, p. 2.
3. US General Accounting Office (1996), *Bank Oversight Structure* (GAO/GGD-97–23).
4. *Investment Company Institute* v. *Federal Deposit Insurance Corporation*, 815 F.2d 1540 (D.C. Cir. 1987) (upholding this reading of sections 16 and 20 of Glass-Steagall).
5. At the time, many federal judges and constitutional scholars believed that congressional authority under the US Constitution to regulate interstate commerce did not extend to corporate firms, such as state-chartered banks, that operated solely in local markets. Questions as to the reach of national congressional authority over financial firms were repeatedly raised in the 1930s by critics of both the new federal banking legislation and the new federal laws regulating the securities markets. These questions

subsequently were resolved in the favor of the national government, and today's judges and scholars take a far more generous view of the scope of congressional power to regulate financial markets and firms.

6. Sections 3(a)(4) and (5) of the original Securities Exchange Act of 1934 excluded banks from the statutory definition of 'broker' and 'dealer'. In 1999, Congress amended this blanket exemption to require banks engaged in most securities activities to register as broker-dealers.

7. For examples, see John C. Coffee, Jr. (1995), 'Competition versus Consolidation: The Significance of Organizational Structure in Financial and Securities Regulation', *The Business Lawyer*, vol. 50, pp. 458–9.

8. The details of the transaction whereby Travelers, an insurance company, became a bank holding company by acquiring Citicorp were described in Chapter 4.

9. Ferdinand Pecora, general counsel to the committee, later wrote that all three statutes (and the Public Utility Holding Company Act of 1935) were enacted in direct response to his hearings. Ferdinand Pecora (1939), *Wall Street Under Oath: The Story of Our Modern Money Changers* (New York: Simon and Schuster), pp. 284–92.

10. The exchange took place between Thomas Corcoran, an administration official intimately involved in drafting the Exchange Act, and a member of the House Interstate and Foreign Commerce Committee that was considering the legislation. When Mr Corcoran noted that 'banks cannot normally go into the business, like a broker, of dealing in securities', the congressman objected, 'But they do.' Mr Corcoran responded that banks 'are not allowed to do those things any longer, under the Glass-Steagall bill. They cannot go into a business of dealing in securities'. When the congressman then asked Mr Corcoran to clarify what businesses were forbidden to banks after Glass-Steagall, Mr Corcoran replied, 'You may be able to answer that better than I can.' At that point, discussion of Glass-Steagall ended. 'Stock Exchange Regulation', Hearing Before the House Interstate and Foreign Commerce Committee, 73rd Congress, 16 February 1934, p. 86.

11. In the colloquy described in note 10, a source of confusion is whether the parties were referring to securities dealing (trading as principal) or securities brokerage (executing trades as agent for customers). The relevant section of Glass-Steagall provided that the 'business of dealing in investment securities by [banks] shall be limited to purchasing and selling such securities without recourse, solely upon the order, and for the account of, customers, and in no case for its own account'. Thus, after Glass-Steagall, banks could no longer act as securities dealers (principals). Nevertheless, Glass-Steagall's language did leave some room for banks to act as securities brokers (agents), and the particular provision of the Securities Exchange Act under discussion would have affected securities brokers as well as securities dealers.

12. This story is told in James Landis (1938), 'The Legislative History of the Securities Act of 1933', *George Washington Law Review*, vol. 28, pp. 44–5.

13. This exemption appeared in section 3 of the Securities Act of 1933.

14. This exemption derived from sections 3(a)(4) and (5) of the Securities Exchange Act of 1934; it was greatly narrowed in 1999.

15. The original version of the Securities Exchange Act of 1934 did not exempt banks from the periodic disclosure requirements applicable to all firms

with public shareholders, but the Securities and Exchange Commission quickly exempted banks by rule. Later, Congress amended the Exchange Act to provide that banks were subject to the law's periodic disclosure requirements, but that they would be administered and enforced against banks by their own bank regulators.

16. These provisions originally appeared in sections 7 and 8(a) of the Securities Exchange Act of 1934. In 1996, section 7 was substantially amended and section 8(a), which had required broker-dealers to borrow against securities only from banks approved by the Federal Reserve, was repealed.

17. 'Stock Exchange Practices' (1934), Hearings Before the Senate Committee on Banking and Currency, 73rd Cong., 2d Sess., vol. 16, p. 7555.

18. Congress eventually made this explicit in an amendment to the Securities Exchange Act, *op. cit.*, note 15.

19. It is possible that Congress hoped to 'soften' disclosure regulation as applied to banks by delegating enforcement authority to friendly bank regulators who might be more sympathetic than securities regulators to pleas by banks to delay or omit negative disclosures. Yet such a policy surely would have proved counterproductive, since knowledgeable investors, fearing that some banks' disclosure was not as timely or trust-worthy as disclosure by other firms, would avoid all banks' securities. In any event, the evidence supporting this explanation of the bank exemption is scanty at best, and it certainly does not reflect modern attitudes of US bank regulators toward disclosure. See Helen A. Garten (1986), 'Banking on the Market: Relying on Depositors to Control Bank Risks', *Yale Journal on Regulation*, vol. 4, pp. 139–43.

20. The statutory language that admitted of these two very different readings was quoted in note 11.

21. *American Bankers Association v. Securities and Exchange Commission*, 804 F.2d 739 (D.C. Cir. 1986).

22. *Barnett Bank of Marion County, N.A. v. Nelson*, 517 U.S. 25 (1996), is discussed in Chapter 4.

23. Seiberg, *op. cit.*, note 2, p. 2 (quoting banking industry representatives).

24. Some securities industry representatives say yes. Yvette D. Kantrow, 'Umbrella Regulator Would Stifle Creativity', *American Banker*, 24 March 1998, p. 15 (quoting securities trade group official).

25. *Barnett Bank of Marion County v. Nelson*, 517 U.S. 25. In 1999, Congress reaffirmed state authority to license and regulate insurance firms.

26. Prepared Statement of Arthur Levitt, Chairman, Securities and Exchange Commission, Before the Senate Committee on Banking, Housing and Urban Affairs, Federal News Service, 25 June 1998 (available in LEXIS, News Library, FEDNEW file).

27. It is suggested in Chapter 6 that bank regulators as well as securities regulators are taking an aggressive approach to policing the marketing practices of banks that sell retail securities products.

28. Securitization comes to mind. In the securitization process, a bank product (loans) is marketed as a securities product (undivided interests in a pool of similar loans) and secured by an insurance product (financial guarantees). Even under a regime of functional regulation, the hybrid product may be subject to three different regulatory schemes.

29. For descriptions of these efforts, see Geoffrey R.D. Underhill (1997), 'Private Markets and Public Responsibility in a Global System: Conflict and Co-operation in Transnational Banking and Securities Regulation', in Geoffrey R.D. Underhill (ed.), *The New World Order in International Finance* (London: Macmillan), pp. 17–44; Brian P. Volkman (1998), 'The Global Convergence of Bank Regulation and Standards for Compliance', *Banking Law Journal*, vol. 115, pp. 550–96.
30. Underhill, *op. cit.*, note 29, p. 29; Volkman, *op. cit.*, note 29, pp. 558–9.
31. E.g., Underhill, *op. cit.*, note 29, p. 36.
32. For description of these organizations and their members, see Underhill, *op. cit.*, note 29, pp. 23–38.
33. Underhill, *op. cit.*, note 29, pp. 38–43; Volkman, *op. cit.*, note 29, p. 561.
34. Underhill, *op. cit.*, note 29, pp 43–4

6. The Level Playing Field and Rules of Fair Play

1. This story is recounted in Ferdinand Pecora (1939), *Wall Street Under Oath: The Story of Our Modern Money Changers* (New York: Simon and Schuster), pp. 84–8.
2. The Term Trusts are described in the order issued by the Securities and Exchange Commission *In the Matter of NationsSecurities and NationsBank, N.A.*, 4 May 1998, available at 1998 SEC LEXIS 833.
3. Pecora, *op. cit.*, note 1, p. 89.
4. Elsewhere I have called this change in regulatory orientation the 'consumerization' of financial regulation. Helen A. Garten (1999), 'The Consumerization of Financial Regulation', *Washington University Law Quarterly*, vol. 77, pp. 287–318. This chapter expands upon some of the ideas developed in that paper.
5. 401 U.S. 617, 633 (1971).
6. *Jefferson Parish Hospital District No. 2* v. *Hyde*, 466 U.S. 2 (1980).
7. *Alabama Association of Insurance Agents* v. *Board of Governors of the Federal Reserve System*, 533 F.2d 224, 250 (5th Cir. 1976).
8. Garten, *op. cit.*, note 4, p. 304.
9. For citations to populist opponents of Glass-Steagall, see notes 32 and 33 to Chapter 1.
10. For example, see George J. Benston (1996), 'The Origins of and Justification for the Glass-Steagall Act', in Anthony Saunders and Ingo Walker (eds), *Universal Banking: Financial System Design Reconsidered* (Chicago: Irwin), pp. 47–59 (noting that modern researchers have found little evidence to support allegations of retail customer abuses in 1920s securities markets).
11. Garten, *op. cit.*, note 4.
12. For further discussion of this point, see Garten, *op. cit.*, note 4.
13. *In the Matter of NationsSecurities and NationsBank, N.A.*, *op. cit.*, note 2.
14. Benston, *op. cit.*, note 10, pp. 47–59, especially p. 53.
15. National Westminster Bank, PLC (1986), *Federal Reserve Bulletin*, vol. 72, p. 584.
16. Bank of New England Corporation (1988), *Federal Reserve Bulletin*, vol. 74, p. 700.
17. 'Retail Sales of Nondeposit Investment Products: Interagency Statement',

Federal Reserve Regulatory Service 3–1579.51 (November 1995).

18. NASD Rule 2350, 'Broker/Dealer Conduct on the Premises of Financial Institutions', 1997 NASD Notice to Members 89.

19. *In the Matter of NationsSecurities and NationsBank, N.A., op. cit.*, note 2.

20. *Federal Register*, vol. 63, p. 14 803 (27 March 1998).

21. For example, in its 1998 decision approving the Citicorp/Travelers combination, the Federal Reserve cited the public benefits of cross-marketing, such as increased customer convenience, as a reason to permit the combined Citigroup to cross-market retail bank and insurance products. See Travelers Group Inc. (1998), *Federal Reserve Bulletin*, vol. 84, p. 985.

22. Bank antitying law, created by section 106(b) of the Bank Holding Company Act Amendments of 1970, treated as a coercive tying arrangement any promise by a bank to vary the consideration for one product conditioned on the purchase of a second product. In the 1990s, however, the Federal Reserve created exceptions to this rule permitting banks to offer certain discounts for joint purchases of bank and securities products, e.g., Federal Reserve System, 'Revisions Regarding Tying Restrictions', *Federal Register*, vol. 60, p. 20 186 (25 April 1995).

23. *Alabama Association of Insurance Agents* v. *Board of Governors of the Federal Reserve System*, 533 F.2d 224, 250 (6th Cir. 1976) (considering evidence of a bank lender's 'penetration rate' – the percentage of borrowers who actually purchased insurance from the bank – as well as the competitiveness of the relevant lending market as indicators of voluntary tying).

24. Bernard Schull (1993), 'Tying and Other Conditional Agreements Under Section 106 of the Bank Holding Company Act: A Reconsideration', NERA Working Paper #19.

25. Kelley Holland, 'Fed Probing Alleged Ties Of Loans to Underwriting', *American Banker*, 13 October 1992, at 1.

26. 'New Derivatives Safeguards Imposed As Bankers Trust, Fed Reach Agreement', *BNA's Bank Report*, vol. 63, p. 895 (12 December 1994).

27. For example, see Geoffrey R.D. Underhill (1997), 'Private Markets and Public Responsibility in a Global System: Conflict and Cooperation in Transnational Banking and Securities Regulation', in Geoffrey R.D. Underhill (ed.), *The New World Order in International Finance* (London: Macmillan), pp. 36–8, for a description of how international regulatory organizations have accepted private industry risk measurement models in arriving at international capital standards for financial institutions with substantial derivatives portfolios.

28. For example, the US securities laws treat high net worth individuals as accredited investors who may freely purchase unregistered securities in private offerings. In the past, at least the Federal Reserve has also treated these individuals as wholesale customers, excluding them from the category of retail bank customers who must receive special disclosures when buying nondeposit investment products from their bank. Garten, *op. cit.*, note 4, p. 109.

29. Individuals are not included as 'qualified institutional buyers' who may participate in the Rule 144A market, an institution-only private trading market for unregistered securities.

7. Failure on a Level Playing Field

1. A. Dale Tussing (1967), 'The Case for Bank Failure', *The Journal of Law and Economics*, vol. 10, pp. 129–47, especially p. 136 ('Banks which mismanage their own assets are poor managers of the nation's financial processes and should be replaced. Low profits, losses, and at the extreme failure are appropriate devices for accomplishing this replacement, either through changes in management or closure of the bank.').

2. There is a distinction: technically, deposit insurance is self-funding, with monies coming solely from premiums paid by the banking industry.

3. The story of Long-Term Capital Management is told later in this chapter.

4. For discussion of the liquidation function of federal deposit insurance, see Helen A. Garten (1994), 'A Political Analysis of Bank Failure Policy', *Boston University Law* Review, vol. 74, pp. 443–5.

5. John Hanna (1936), 'The Banking Act of 1935', *Virginia Law Review*, vol. 22, pp. 638–9.

6. For background on the RFC and its relation to the federal deposit scheme in the 1930s, see Garten, *op. cit.*, note 4, pp. 429–79. Among today's generation of US banking scholars, the history of the RFC is little known. The best contemporaneous account of its operations, written by its long-time chairman, is Jesse H. Jones (with Edward Angly) (1951), *Fifty Billion Dollars: My Thirteen Years with the RFC (1932–45)* (New York: Macmillan).

7. Garten, *op. cit.*, note 4, pp. 462–3.

8. E.g., Hanna, *op. cit.*, note 5, pp. 638–9.

9. Tussing, *op. cit.*, note 1, p. 136.

10. Tussing, *op. cit.*, note 1, p. 140.

11. Between 1930 and 1933, demand deposits of $100 000 and up were withdrawn at a faster rate than deposits of $200 and under. See (1939) 'Behavior of Deposits Prior to Suspension in a Selected Group of Banks – Analysis by Size of Account', *Federal Reserve Bulletin*, vol. 25, p. 178.

12. For background on changes in bank liability structure during the 1980s, see Helen A. Garten (1991), 'Whatever Happened to Market Discipline of Banks?' *Annual Survey of American Law*, vol. 1991, pp. 761–2. As Chapter 3 noted, these trends have continued into the 1990s, with all domestic deposits continuing to decline as a funding source especially for large banks. Robert Oshinsky (1999), 'Effects of Bank Consolidation on the Bank Insurance Fund' (Federal Deposit Insurance Corporation), p. 5.

13. In a traditional purchase and assumption transaction, the financial assistance provided by the deposit insurance fund equaled (1) the value of the failed bank's liabilities less (2) the value of the failed bank's performing assets less (3) the franchise premium. The FDIC typically retained and liquidated assets, usually non-performing, that the acquiring bank refused to take. Joseph F. Sinkey, Jr. (1979), *Problem and Failed Institutions in the Commercial Banking Industry* (Greenwich, CT: JAI Press), pp. 34–9.

14. In fact, although perhaps the largest, Penn Square was certainly not the first bank to be liquidated; between 1934 and 1983, the FDIC liquidated 328 banks and merged 340. Federal Deposit Insurance Corporation (1983), *Annual Report*, p. 14.

15. Helen A. Garten (1986), 'Banking on the Market: Relying on Depositors to

Control Bank Risks', *Yale Journal on Regulation*, vol. 4, p. 146 n.99.

16. For background on Continental's financial position and the regulators' decision to intervene to prevent failure, see 'Inquiry into Continental Illinois Corp. and Continental Illinois National Bank' (1984), Hearings Before the Subcommittee on Financial Institutions Supervision, Regulation and Insurance of the House Committee on Banking Finance and Urban Affairs, 98th Cong., 2d Sess., especially pp. 457–69.

17. To non-US observers, the distinction between bank and holding company creditors may not seem important, but it was to US observers, since the holding company was a legal entity distinct from the bank. According to the FDIC, the decision to protect holding company creditors was necessary to avoid violation of several outstanding indentures and irrelevant, since the holding company had sufficient assets to cover its liabilities and its creditors would not have suffered losses even had it been liquidated. 'Inquiry into Continental Illinois Corp. and Continental Illinois National Bank', *op. cit.*, note 16, p. 465. Nevertheless, critics complained that the decision to protect holding company creditors sent a dangerous message to wholesale markets that henceforth the government would subsidize uninsured investors not just in large banks but also in all bank affiliated entities.

18. Garten, *op. cit.*, note 15, p. 148 n.111.

19. Alternatively, the regulators could use an 'insured deposit transfer', a modified version of the purchase and assumption, whereby the acquiring bank assumed only insured deposits (and sufficient assets to cover them), leaving uninsured creditors to recover their investments from the proceeds of the FDIC's liquidation of the bank's remaining assets.

20. The legislation was the Federal Deposit Insurance Corporation Improvement Act of 1991. Its provisions are summarized in Helen A. Garten (1993), 'United States Bank Failure Policy', *The International Journal of Regulatory Law and Practice*, vol. 1, pp. 239–44.

21. Interestingly, the FDIC cited the transactions costs of liquidation as a reason to choose an alternative resolution. Recent thrift failures had glutted the secondary loan market, and a fire sale of CrossLand's assets would probably have yielded very little, certainly not enough to cover the cost of paying off insured depositors. For the same reason, private bids for part or all of CrossLand's assets had been disappointingly low. The FDIC calculated that CrossLand was worth more than could be realized by selling its assets immediately in depressed markets. By delaying liquidation or sale, the agency believed that it would eventually recoup its investment in CrossLand. Garten, *op. cit.*, note 4, p. 474.

22. Oshinsky, *op. cit.*, note 12.

23. William C. Melton (1985), *Inside the Fed: Making Monetary Policy* (Homewood, Illinois: Dow Jones-Irwin), pp. 157–8.

24. For background on LTCM, see Remarks Prepared for Delivery by William J. McDonough, President, Federal Reserve Bank of New York, Before the House Committee on Banking and Financial Services, Federal News Service, 1 October 1998 (available in LEXIS, News Library, FEDNEW file); Walter F. Todd, 'Financial Problems of a Large Hedge Fund', *FOMC Alert*, 22 December 1998, pp. 6–8.

25. Remarks Prepared for Delivery by Federal Reserve Chairman Alan

Greenspan Before the House Committee on Banking and Financial Services Re: 'Private-Sector Refinancing of the Large Hedge Fund, Long-Term Capital Management', Federal News Service, 1 October 1998 (available in LEXIS, News Library, FEDNEW file).

26. Greenspan, *op. cit.*, note 25.
27. Tussing, *op. cit.*, note 1, p. 140.
28. Greenspan, *op. cit.*, note 25.
29. Melton, *op. cit.*, note 23, pp. 157–8.
30. This story is told in James Grant (1992), *Money of the Mind: Borrowing and Lending in America from the Civil War to Michael Milken* (New York: Farrar Straus Giroux), pp. 202–11.
31. Some people believe that other factors were at play: Bank of United States, with its Jewish managers and its substantial involvement in the 'unsavory' (to banks at the time) world of real estate, was simply not part of the bankers' club.
32. Jones, *op. cit.*, note 6, pp. 23–5.
33. Arthur M. Schlesinger, Jr. (1956), *The Crisis of the Old Order 1919–33*, vol. 1 of *The Age of Roosevelt* (Boston: Houghlin Mifflin Company), p. 236.
34. Jones, *op. cit.*, note 6, pp. 26–34.
35. Jones, *op. cit.*, note 6, p. 62.
36. US General Accounting Office (1991), *Deposit Insurance: Overview of Six Foreign Systems* (GAO/NSIAD-91–104).
37. Jesse Jones wrote that Henry Ford felt sure that he was young enough to rebuild if the crash came. Jones, *op. cit.*, note 6, p. 62.
38. For background on this business cycle theory, popularized by economists like Hayek and Schumpeter, see J. Bradford De Long (December 1990), '"Liquidation" Cycles: Old-Fashioned Real Business Cycle Theory and the Great Depression' (Washington: National Bureau of Economic Research), Working Paper No. 3546.
39. McDonough, *op. cit.*, note 24.
40. Greenspan, *op. cit.*, note 25.

8. Let the Market Pick the Winners

1. The term comes from Alistair Duncan, 'Smart Cards in the United States: Swan-in-Waiting or Just an Ugly Duck?', *FutureBanker*, December 1998, p. 125.
2. Information about the New York pilot program comes from news reports, including 'Smart Card Test Is News To New York City Merchants', *Debit Card News*, 30 August 1997; Saul Hansell, 'Got a Dime? Citibank and Chase End Test of Electronic Run', *New York Times*, 4 November 1998, p. C2; Jeffrey Kutler, 'Mondex USA Pulls Back as Smart Cards Lag Forecasts', *American Banker*, 11 January 1999, p. 1.
3. 'The U.S. Smart Card Debate Rages On', *American Banker*, 17 March 1997, p. 10A.
4. 'Bankers Are Cool To Smart Cards, But Other Chip Markets Heat Up', *Debit Card News*, 17 February 1998.
5. Jeffrey Kutler, 'U.K. Adoption of Chip Cards May Affect U.S.', *American Banker*, 15 July 1998, pp. 1, 12.

6. Duncan, *op. cit.*, note 1, p. 125 (citing survey results from 1998).
7. Jeffrey Kutler and Antoinette Coulton, 'Smart Card: Industry Inertia Subdues Conference Mood', *American Banker*, 6 May 1998 (citing industry experts).
8. Duncan, *op. cit.*, note 1, p. 125.
9. Kutler, *op. cit.*, note 5, p. 12.
10. Hansell, *op. cit.*, note 2, p. C1.
11. Saul Hansell, '"Smart" Cards Flunk Manhattan Test', *International Herald Tribune*, 5 November 1998, p. 16.
12. 'The U.S. Smart Card Debate Rages On', *op. cit.*, note 3, p. 10A.
13. Hansell, *op. cit.*, note 2, p. C1.
14. E.g., Antoinette Coulton, 'NationsBank Testing Visa Cash at Air Force Base', *American Banker*, 15 July 1998, p. 13.
15. Kutler, *op. cit.*, note 5, p. 12.
16. Kutler, *op. cit.*, note 2, p. 12 (quoting Mondex officials).
17. Quote from Daniel R. Fitingon, president of global support services, Visa International, cited in Kutler and Coulton, *op. cit.*, note 7.
18. Antoinette Coulton, 'Smart Cards: Visa Using Tokyo as Proving Ground', *American Banker*, 22 July 1998, p. 14.
19. Kutler, *op. cit.*, note 5, p. 12.
20. Kutler, *op. cit.*, note 5, p. 1.
21. Antoinette Coulton, 'Smart Cards: Visa Acting as Smart Technology Guide', *American Banker*, 18 March 1998, p. 19.
22. Quote from 'The U.S. Smart Card Debate Rages On', *op. cit.*, note 3, p. 10A.
23. Charles H. Ferguson, 'Computers and the Coming of the U.S. Keiretsu', *Harvard Business Review*, July-August 1990, pp. 55–70.
24. Jeffrey Kutler, 'Europe Report Gives a Boost to Banks in E-Money Future', *American Banker*, 30 September 1998, p. 11.
25. Debt Collection Improvement Act of 1996, Pub. L. No. 104–134.
26. Dean Anason, 'Electronic Benefits Mandate Gets Caught in Crosswinds', *American Banker*, 23 November 1998, p. 4.

Index

Aldrich, Winthrop, 25
antitying laws, 11, 144, 156–7, 161, 198

Bank Holding Company Act of 1956, 76, 85, 91–4, 102, 105, 106, 107, 109, 111, 113–15, 125
Bank of United States, 186
Banking Act of 1933, *see* Glass-Steagall
Berle, Adolph, 55–56
Brandeis, Louis, 28, 29, 34, 37

capital markets (US)
in the 1920s, 24–5, 29–30, 34–5, 37–8, 55–6
in the 1990s, 33, 46, 50–3, 54–63
capital regulation, 58–9, 138–9
Chase, 23, 25, 26, 29, 49, 194, 195
Citibank, 91, 102, 194, 195
Citicorp, 91, 102, 103, 107
merger with Travelers, 1–2, 10, 91–2, 112–5
opposition to Glass-Steagall reform, 2, 51, 92, 111
Citigroup, 1, 51, 60, 113, 117, 121, 143, 180
commercial paper, 50, 79, 81, 83–4, 179, 185
Community Reinvestment Act of 1977, 76, 77, 87, 88, 89, 90
Comptroller of the Currency, 19, 75, 86–7, 93, 98, 100, 129

rivalry with the Federal Reserve, 101–4, 107–18
consumer regulation, *see* rules of fair play
Continental Illinois, 12, 80, 82, 159, 163–4, 167, 170, 173–8, 180–2, 184, 188, 189
Corrigan, E. Gerald, 83
credit unions, 10, 69, 88–9
CrossLand 178, 181
cross-funding (of non-bank affiliates by banks), 76, 86–7, 112
cross-marketing of financial products, 114–15, 155–7

deposit brokerage, 42–3, 169
deposit insurance, 9, 32–3, 57–8, 69–88
and failure resolution, 77, 80–1, 82, 163–93
regulatory subsidy provided by, 9, 43, 48, 69–85
deregulation (in US), 1, 14, 46, 52, 67–8, 116–18
derivatives, 160
diversification, 54–5, 65, 75–6

entity regulation, 10, 122–32

failure resolution, 163–93
see also deposit insurance
Federal Deposit Insurance Corporation (FDIC), 74–5, 80, 99, 100, 166–8, 171–4, 176–8, 188, 192
see also deposit insurance

Federal Reserve Board, 2–3, 22, 50, 61, 65, 751, 86–7, 92–3, 99, 100, 101, 128, 134, 137, 181
  rivalry with the Comptroller of the Currency, 101–4, 107–18
Federal Reserve system, 74, 99, 100, 123, 137, 168, 177
financial modernization legislation (1999), *see* Gramm- Leach-Bliley Act
Ford, Henry, 72, 187–8, 189
Foreign Bank Supervision Enhancement Act, 63–4
functional regulation, 10, 132–5

General Accounting Office, US (GAO), 64, 65, 80, 121, 188
Glass, Carter (Senator), 25, 31, 32–3, 71, 127–8
Glass-Steagall Act, 7–8, 19–27, 28–33, 35–6, 48–50, 56, 91, 123–4, 125, 126, 150
  impact on non-US banks, 9, 63, 65–8
  reform of, 8–9, 40–1, 65–8, 86–7, 111–12, 115–16, 150–1
  Section 20 of, 2–3, 8, 9, 22, 24, 50, 61, 65, 86–7, 109–10, 113, 129
Gramm-Leach-Bliley Act (1999), 2, 68, 75, 87, 116, 133, 134–5, 211
Greenspan, Alan
  and Long-Term Capital Management, 84–5, 181–4, 192
  views on brokered deposits, 43

Harriman National Bank, 186–7
holding companies, 66, 86–7, 93, 99, 102–3, 110–11, 115, 124–5, 133, 191
insurance
  bank entry into, 106–9, 114–15, 116, 130
  state regulation of, 108, 111–12, 122, 131, 137
interest rate ceilings, 18, 38, 43, 50, 57–8, 63, 65
International Banking Act of 1978, 63
international financial supervision, 5, 11, 138–41, 160–2, 191–3, 212
interstate banking, 33, 63, 65, 74, 102–3, 110
Investment Company Institute v. *Camp*, 20–1, 22, 23, 143–4, 150, 151

judicial deference to regulatory agencies, 2, 89, 105–6

Kuhn Loeb, 23

Leach, Jim (Congressman), 92, 93, 94, 111, 114, 115, 116
Long-Term Capital Management (LTCM), 12, 84–5, 163, 164, 182–5, 189, 191

market discipline, 58, 59, 145
Mondex USA, 195
  see also smart cards
money market mutual funds, 8, 24, 38, 43, 50, 58, 62, 75, 83, 131, 152, 197, 199
moral hazard, 73, 75, 159
Morgan, J.P., 23, 25, 29, 31, 35, 49, 55, 56, 187, 188

National Bank Act, 17, 106, 108

NationsSecurities, 142, 147, 149,
154, 155
New York Clearing House
Association, 186, 187
non-bank banks, 93–94, 105–6
non-US banks in US markets,
62–8, 79, 147–8
and Glass-Steagall, 9, 63, 65–8

Pecora, Ferdinand, hearings on
1920s stock market practices,
29, 126, 143
Penn Central Transportation
Company, 79, 84, 179, 185
Penn Square Bank, 163, 171–3,
174
populism as regulatory theory, 4,
27–33
public choice theory of
regulation, 18–27

Reconstruction Finance
Corporation (RFC), 167, 168,
173, 186–7
regulatory competition, 3, 10–11,
95–141, 211
Riegle-Neal Interstate Banking
and Branching Efficiency Act
of 1994, 103
rules of fair play, 11, 142–62,
212

Section 20 of the Glass-Steagall
Act, 2–3, 8, 9, 22, 24, 50, 61,
65, 86–7, 109–10, 113, 129
see also Glass-Steagall Act
Sections 23A and 23B of the
Federal Reserve Act, 86

Securities Act of 1933, 20, 24, 28,
126, 127
securities affiliates of banks
in the 1920s, 20, 22, 23, 31,
35, 125, 143, 151
in the 1990s, 2, 24, 43, 65–6,
86–7, 109–10, 113, 129
see also Glass-Steagall Act
Securities and Exchange
Commission, 99, 100–1, 122,
128, 129–30, 131–2, 134
securities brokerage
bank entry into, 109, 126,
129–30, 150–1
regulation of in retail markets,
152–9
Securities Exchange Act of 1934,
24, 124, 125, 126–30
bank exemption from, 124,
127, 129–30
smart cards, 12, 194–210, 211
state chartering and regulation of
banks, 23, 71, 98, 100,
106–8, 136–7
State Farm Mutual Automobile
Insurance Company, 3

thrifts, 3, 12, 59, 69, 76, 79, 80,
88, 104, 164, 170
Travelers, 1–2, 10, 91–2, 94,
112–15, 125–6

umbrella regulator, 134, 211
universal banking, 9, 23, 45, 50,
51, 54, 55, 56, 57, 60, 61–2,
63, 66

Volcker, Paul, 110, 111